THE
WILLIAM O. DOUGLAS INQUIRY INTO THE STATE OF INDIVIDUAL FREEDOM

THE
WILLIAM O. DOUGLAS INQUIRY
INTO THE STATE
OF INDIVIDUAL FREEDOM

edited by Harry S. Ashmore
with an Introduction by Vern Countryman

Contributors

William H. Alsup   Thomas I. Emerson
Leonard B. Boudin   Jerome B. Falk
William Cohen   Peter M. Kreindler
Vern Countryman   Robert B. McKay
Steven B. Duke   L. A. Scot Powe, Jr.
William Reppy, Jr.

Westview Press
Boulder, Colorado

Copyright © 1979 by The Center for the Study of Democratic Institutions

Published in 1979 in the United States of America by
  Westview Press, Inc.
  5500 Central Avenue
  Boulder, Colorado 80301
  Frederick A. Praeger, Publisher

Library of Congress Catalog Card Number: 78-21438
ISBN: 0-89158-371-8 (hardcover)
      0-89158-493-5 (paperback)

Printed and bound in the United States of America

Justice William O. Douglas

CONTENTS

PART 4
FREEDOM AND THE DUTY OF THE GOVERNMENT
TO CONTROL PRIVATE POWER

PREFACE

Harry S. Ashmore

A lifetime of experience and reflection has supplied me with reasons for defending the faith in which I was brought up. That faith, I say again, was faith in the independent mind. Its educational consequences were belief in free inquiry and discussion. Its political consequences were belief in democracy, but only in a democracy in which the minority, even a minority of one, could continue to differ and be heard. Those who desire to conform, but are prohibited from doing so by intolerance and prejudice must be aided; the non-conformist conscience must not be stifled.

—*Robert M. Hutchins*

Early in their careers, this deeply ingrained faith brought Robert Hutchins together with another remarkable son of the Calvinist parsonage. As dean of the Yale Law School, Hutchins made room at New Haven for a fledgling professor of business law named William Douglas, who had resigned from Columbia in protest against what he considered improper intervention into faculty prerogatives by the nation's most celebrated educator, Nicholas Murray Butler. When Hutchins moved on to become president of the University of Chicago he sent shock waves through his new constituency by offering Douglas an unprecedentedly high professorial salary. That reunion was canceled by a call from the new Securities and Exchange Commission which introduced Professor Douglas to the public service that would engage him for more than four decades.

The two came together again when Hutchins left Chicago to help organize the Ford Foundation. As president of the Fund for the Republic, the Ford subsidiary chartered to "defend and advance the principles of the Bill of Rights," Hutchins in 1959 established the Center for the Study of Democratic Institutions at Santa Barbara. Justice Douglas helped design the Center's "Basic Issues" program, joined its Board of Directors, and for many years served as chairman.

When declining health forced Douglas to leave the bench after a record tenure of more than thirty-six years, Hutchins concluded that the center ought to provide an appropriate memorial to his notable career. The old friends shared an indifference to bricks and mortar; Douglas spent as much time as possible out of doors, and Hutchins once suggested that the physical facilities of a university ought to be razed every thirty years. A proper memorial would have to be living, and, if it were to be true to the spirit of both men, functional. Hutchins found the answer in a "continuing program of inquiry and public education dealing with fundamental trends in contemporary society that affect the status of the individual citizen." In his invitation to a group of distinguished Americans to serve as the organizing committee for the William O. Douglas Inquiry into the State of Individual Freedom he wrote:

> During his tenure on the Supreme Court Justice Douglas was preoccupied with the age-old relationship between the individual and the state. His years of study of the Constitution and its first ten amendments led him to conclude that the "essential scheme of our Constitution and the Bill of Rights was to take government off the backs of the people." As he interprets them, the provisions of the Constitution dealing with the powers of government are properly entitled to a generous construction to achieve objectives beyond those specified in terms of Eighteenth Century experience; so too the entire Bill of Rights is entitled to a generous construction to achieve its broad objectives within a changing society.
>
> Thus Douglas took a leading role in the constitutional revolution by which virtually the whole Bill of Rights has been made applicable to the states. His hundreds of opinions delineated appropriate boundaries of individual freedom in American society. The positions he took on religion, speech, the press, assembly, searches and seizures, double jeopardy, self-incrimination, a fair trial, and cruel and unusual punishment have for many years been central in the argument on these issues.
>
> Although Douglas' voice is now missing, the argument has continued since his retirement. The results reached, the reasoning processes used, the opinions written suggest that his departure deprives the Court of an approach to protection of the individual that may weaken the Bill of Rights in important particulars. Since the Bill of Rights is at the core of the Constitution, expressing the essential characteristic of American democracy, any significant retreat from its application is of great concern to all Americans. If changes are impending it is essential that the American people be reminded of the importance of the initial amendments to the Constitution, of the contribution Justice Douglas made to advancing the proposition that liberty is indivisible, and of the great debt all of us owe him.

The project Hutchins initiated came into being after his death in May 1977. The steering committee he had assembled elected to carry on, and, with the strong endorsement of Hutchins' successor, Maurice Mitchell, the Board of the Center incorporated the undertaking into its program.

Four persons close to Justice Douglas agreed to share the chairmanship:
his wife, Cathleen, a practicing attorney and advocate of public causes;
Clark Clifford, whose career in public service coincided with Douglas'
Washington years; Abe Fortas, who served with him on the Yale faculty,
the SEC, and the Supreme Court; and David Ginsburg, the first law clerk
named by Douglas when he took his seat on the Court in April 1939.

* * *

Although he never practiced law, and never taught it after he
departed the Yale Law School, Hutchins continued to read the
legal journals and court reports until the end of his life. At the
Center for the Study of Democratic Institutions he regularly reported to
his colleagues on jurisprudential trends, and frequently published his
findings in the *Center Magazine*. His method was to select landmark
cases, ignore the narrow legalism imposed by court procedure, and deal
with the central issues raised in terms of what he called "practical
philosophy." He consistently forecast the direction in which the courts
were likely to move—which often ran counter to his own philosophical
predilection. His legal studies became a key part of the center's "early
warning" function.

Hutchins had intended personally to supervise the Douglas
Inquiry's monitoring activity, designed to inventory shifts in the
status of individual rights, liberties, and immunities. He recognized that
this would involve the whole range of executive, legislative, and popular
actions and attitudes, as well as the findings of the courts. The end
product would be a set of papers basic to an exercise in public education
intended to reach far beyond the audience addressed by law journals and
professional reports.

"It is never easy to convey the concepts and content of law to numbers
of people," Hutchins wrote. "Yet in a democracy as large and diverse as
ours it is essential that there be an informed public, comprehending the
nature of the issues and choices facing it. The William O. Douglas
Inquiry will attempt to fulfill this function with respect to fundamental
issues of individual liberty."

The steering committee has assigned responsibility for this monitoring function to Vern Countryman, the distinguished Harvard Law
School professor who edited the widely acclaimed *Douglas Opinions*.
Countryman had been a law clerk to Justice Douglas, and it followed
that others of like interest could be found among the more than forty
lawyers and legal scholars who had served in similar capacity. They
might be conditioned, too, by Douglas' insistence on laying bare the
issues in language Countryman described as "frequently blunt and

bold," prompting another of his clerks to say of his opinions: "He doesn't write for the law professors." The Board of Review Countryman agreed to chair was drawn primarily from those who had served with Douglas in the inner reaches of the high court.

In his letter convening the initial meeting of the board at Santa Barbara, Countryman wrote: "While the status of the individual is broadly conceived to reach from legal rights to the physical environment (just as Justice Douglas conceives it) the topics selected for treatment in any periodic review will necessarily be more specifically focussed."

The Board of Review began by considering two areas suggested by its chairman—"The Individual and Governmental Inquiry" and "Aspects of Privacy." Two days of spirited exchange pushed these guidelines in new directions; four major areas, with a dozen subtopics, were identified. As refined, these are reflected in the titles of the papers assembled in this volume.

Beyond the monitoring of trends in the field of civil rights lay the need for public education. The center had enjoyed considerable success with its series of *Pacem in Terris* convocations on foreign affairs and world order. These brought together experts in an atmosphere of free give-and-take not usually available to them or to the large audiences they attracted. In addition to spot coverage in the mass media, large segments of the *Pacem in Terris* convocations have been televised, and the proceedings have been reproduced in part of the center's periodicals and audiotape programs, and in full in published volumes.

Adapting these procedures to the Douglas Inquiry, a testimonial convocation was scheduled for December 1978 in Washington. Due note was taken of the broad sweep of Justice Douglas' concerns—which are by no means bounded by the more than 1,200 written opinions he delivered during his tenure on the Supreme Court. In that connection his colleague, Abe Fortas, wrote an instructive memorandum:

> Mr. Justice Douglas is first thought of as a stalwart champion of civil rights and a conservationist. But these are not the total measure of the man. He is, in its broadest sense, a humanist—a man whose life and works are dedicated to the interests and values of the individual, of all individuals.
>
> The issues to which he addressed himself were myriad; they encompassed all of life. He dealt with them as teacher, lawyer, world-traveler, writer, environmentalist, government official and Associate Justice of the Supreme Court. But in all of these activities, Douglas' point of reference—his touchstone—was always the individual—the living, breathing person.
>
> He believes that laws, whether they relate to complex questions of finance or to criminal justice, should always be judged in terms of their

impact upon the individual; that governments and governmental policies should be critically appraised by the single standard of their effect upon individuals; that man's custodianship of nature should be guided by the fundamental fact that it is a trust for individuals living and generations to come.

It is in that spirit that the convocation and testimonial to Justice Douglas was designed.

* * *

Scott Buchanan, the philosopher who joined Hutchins and Douglas in the formulation of the original program for the Center for the Study of Democratic Institutions, always insisted that the law is a great teacher. The rulings of the Supreme Court and the opinions that accompany them are not addressed merely to the parties in litigation. They also serve to instruct all of us in the deepest meaning of our national charter as it applies to a society vastly different from that which produced it.

The founding fathers intended to place the Supreme Court above the partisan political battle, and in fact it usually does so rise—despite the durable suspicion that the Justices, as Mr. Dooley suggested long ago, follow the election returns as well as the legal precedents. In a backhanded way, Douglas, who never avoided a public controversy and precipitated quite a few, proved the point. An abortive impeachment move by the Republican leader of the House of Representatives foundered on the absurdity of the effort to impute un-American tendencies to perhaps the most conspicuous living exemplar of the American tradition of rugged individualism.

The Supreme Court, however, is the natural center of the continuing ideological conflict inherent in what Thomas Jefferson called the free marketplace of ideas. In spirited exchanges with his brethren on the bench, Douglas emerged as one of the great dissenting Justices. On occasion he identified himself as a strict constructionist of the Constitution, a position usually thought to be on the conservative side. "The First Amendment says 'Congress shall pass no law abridging freedom of speech or press'," he wrote. "I take it to mean what it says. That's strict construction." But on another occasion he dismissed legal precedent by saying, "It is better that we make our own history than be governed by the dead."

These seeming contradictions arise, as Fortas suggests, from Douglas' use of the individual as his touchstone. As the source of legitimacy for maximum personal liberty, he read the Bill of Rights to mean what it said; when it did not reach far enough, as in the case of the enslaved black minority unmentioned in the

Constitution, Douglas found that the Bill of Rights also meant what it did not say. Moving forward from the historic *Brown* decision that banned segregation in the public schools, he pushed that constitutional reading to its ultimate interpretation: "I believe that discrimination based on race, creed or color has become by reason of the Thirteenth, Fourteenth and Fifteenth Amendments one of the 'enumerated rights' under the Ninth Amendment that may not be voted up or down."

The Supreme Court majority has not yet followed Douglas all the way to the position on minority rights he offered in dissent in 1971. "Certainly we cannot expect the Douglas views to advance very far under the Court as presently constituted," Vern Countryman observed. Yet he also noted that in the span of his service on the Court more of Douglas' dissents have become the law than have the dissents of his great, trail-blazing predecessors, Holmes and Brandeis. Acceptance of the Douglas position by the Court majority has created landmarks in the areas of speech and belief, privacy, equal treatment, and fair governmental procedure. And, as Countryman concluded, the Court as presently constituted also will pass: "If we remain a society of decent aspiration we may expect more of the Douglas dissents to become the law of the land."

The law, as William O. Douglas interpreted it, has taught us many lessons—including some we were reluctant to learn. It is the ambition of the inquiry mounted in his name to see that the tutelage continues.

INTRODUCTION
Vern Countryman

As Harry Ashmore has indicated, Justice Douglas' concern for individual freedom is not narrowly confined, but ranges over broad ground to reach any instance where governmental or private power imposes restraints upon individual fulfillment. The topics selected for treatment in this book do not by far exhaust, but are only illustrative of, the range of his concerns.

The treatment follows a plan which is, we hope, comprehensible. Each of the separate papers deals with one aspect of a more general theme. Of the latter, there are four.

The first theme embraces the proposition that there are some freedoms—certain areas of human behavior and personality—so fundamental that, in a society committed to individual freedom, they should be immune from governmental control. William Alsup perceptively probes one aspect of this matter: the tension between the concept of the people's "right to know" in order that they may hold their government to account, and the concept of a "right of privacy" in order to maximize individual freedom, including but not limited to freedom from governmental surveillance. His paper will also be informative to lay readers in demonstrating how the courts act to resolve this tension by constitutional decisions, based on their interpretation of a document written in 1787; by statutory decisions, based on their interpretation of legislative enactments; and by common law decisions, based on their interpretation or rejection of previous judge-made law. William Cohen explores another aspect of the same theme in his paper on efforts by the government to protect the individual against himself—a paper which well describes the difficulties of fixing the limits of the basic theme. The final aspect of that theme dealt with here is Leonard Boudin's essay on freedom of scientific inquiry. He fairly presents the arguments for and against controls on such inquiry so that the reader may reach his or her own conclusion whether to agree with Boudin that there should be more freedom and fewer controls.

Our second basic inquiry, the reconciliation of individual freedom with law enforcement, begins with Thomas Emerson's typically scholarly and thorough paper on the control of intelligence agencies. Readers of this paper should join the ranks of the (so far) too few who appreciate the enormity of the danger resulting from the fact that we have to date exercised far too little control. Next, Peter Kreindler's paper explores problems of preserving individual freedoms in the midst of governmental investigations, whether conducted by legislative committees, administrative agencies, or grand juries. Our examination of aspects of law enforcement concludes with Jerome Falk's article on governmental inspections in the interest of security. As that article demonstrates, the arcane body of law that is the product of judicial interpretation of the Fourth Amendment traditionally was invoked when a person subjected to search was clearly or at least quite probably guilty of crime (the innocent rarely sue to challenge the legality of a search). Now it offers only a thin shield of protection in the government's attempts to protect the innocent against terrorists, airplane hijackers, or a single criminal who has terrorized a local community.

Our third theme addresses some threats to freedom involved in governmental expenditures designed generally to advance the common good. One aspect of this matter is addressed by William Reppy's paper on control of the academic community through governmental grants. Another is treated in Stephen Duke's article on the rights of government employees.

Our final theme stems from the assumption that government has a duty to protect our freedom from abridgments imposed by private power. My own long-winded contribution on private discrimination against racial minorities, women, the aged, and the disabled indicates both that governmental action is usually taken only in response to pressure from the victimized groups and that, as the Constitution is currently interpreted, there are some limits on the power of government to act. Next, Robert McKay explores an area where traditionally government control has been most limited—that of the self-regulated professions. As his thoughtful paper illustrates, there is reason to ask whether such governmental restraint has been justified and whether it should continue. Finally, Scot Powe analyzes the thorny problems involving access to the media, an access which is essential in today's society if the people's First Amendment freedoms are to be exercised, but an access which, if government-compelled, may be viewed as abridging the First Amendment's protection of the media itself.

While many problems are left untouched in this initial survey, the coverage is broad enough to indicate both how difficult the problem of preserving individual freedom can be and how frequently inadequate are the tools with which we must work.

No contributor to this volume undertook merely to present Justice Douglas' views on the matters discussed, which is the way Justice Douglas wanted them to proceed. Probably the views of no contributor coincide with the views of Justice Douglas in all respects. But it is apparent from these pages that they all share his fundamental view that the primary function of a democratic society should be to maximize the individual freedom of its citizens.

PART ONE

FUNDAMENTAL FREEDOMS:
AREAS OF HUMAN BEHAVIOR
AND PERSONALITY
IMMUNE FROM GOVERNMENTAL CONTROL

ONE

FREEDOM OF INFORMATION
AND PRIVACY

William H. Alsup

The concepts of the "right to know" and the "right to privacy," each with its many facets, have developed separately in the law, largely without any common anchor in the Constitution. The right to know derives, as Justice Douglas has said, from "the right of the people, the true sovereign under our constitutional scheme, to govern in an informed manner."[1] This broad precept comprehends several distinct concepts, not all of which have been recognized by the Supreme Court: the right to speak, the right to publish, the right to confidentiality of journalists' sources, and the right of access to government information. The right to privacy derives from many constitutional sources—the express provisions and the penumbras of the First, Fourth, Fifth, and Ninth amendments and liberty itself, ensured by the Constitution. The right to privacy also embraces many different concepts: the right to make fundamental decisions (e.g., abortion), freedom from intrusion or observation in one's private affairs (e.g., wiretapping), and the right to maintain personal control over certain information about oneself.[2]

In their respective roles in suppressing tyranny and promoting democracy, however, the right to know and the right to privacy, despite their separate origins, work hand-in-glove and, it might even be said, in their combined and complementary operation they better serve democracy than almost any other concept guaranteed by the Constitution. Tyranny thrives on government secrecy and surveillance of the people, whereas democracy thrives upon open government, within certain limits, and maximum privacy of its citizens. Thus, "secrecy in government is fundamentally antidemocratic," Justice Douglas wrote in the *Pentagon Papers* case. And, regarding privacy, he once said in dissent: "[Our] system cannot flourish if regimentation takes hold. The right of privacy . . . is a powerful deterrent to anyone who would control men's minds."[3]

William H. Alsup is a partner in Morrison & Foersler, San Francisco, and has recently been appointed assistant solicitor general of the United States.

There is both a negative role and a positive role in this combined function. In the negative sense, these rights "keep the government off the backs of the people." In the positive sense, the right to know and the right to privacy cause democracy to "flourish" by affirmatively enriching the quality and justice of collective decisions made through representative government. Thus, the right to know not only guarantees that incipient oppression will be promptly exposed but affirmatively advances the quality of the products in the marketplace of ideas and ensures that every approach to every possible problem will receive the consideration it merits. The right to privacy likewise prevents tyrannical surveillance and intrusion into our lives. In the positive sense, privacy provides fertile fields for innovation and diversity in the development of our minds and values; privacy allows us naturally and at our own pace to march to different drumbeats; and freedom from fear of surveillance encourages frank discussion and exchange of ideas in our private worlds before, if at all, they are offered in the marketplace of ideas.[4]

Complementary as the right to know and the right to privacy are, there is an inherent conflict between them. To know what the government has done or should be doing to us or for us necessarily means that our private affairs will be exposed to the government, the press, and the public. It is this conflict which is the principal subject of this chapter. Specifically, putting aside all other aspects of the right to know and the right to privacy, this chapter addresses the present status of the right of access to information from the government and the conflicting right of citizens to control private information about themselves.

I

The right to know embraces many interests—from the interest in protecting journalists' confidential sources to the right to publish. In recent years, as mentioned, Justice Douglas and others have also argued for a constitutional right of *access* to government information based upon the need to inform the people about what their representative government has done or proposes to do.[5]

In fact, however, an affirmative constitutional right of access to information in the government's hands has now been rejected by the Supreme Court. In June of this year, the Supreme Court concluded, in *Houchins v. KQED, Inc.*,[6] that neither the First Amendment nor the Fourteenth Amendment mandates a right of access to government information or sources of information within the government's control. Specifically, the Court held that KQED, a San Francisco television station, had no greater or special right of access to the Alameda County Jail in order to expose its inhuman conditions than the public generally.

In fact, the broad language of the opinion clearly states that the prison could constitutionally deny investigative access to the prison altogether to the public and the press. The degree of such access, reasoned the Court, was best left to legislatures and the political process.

Prior opinions of the Court had suggested without deciding that there might be some First Amendment right in gathering news to obtain access to government information.[7] Even the Warren Court, however, had written, in sustaining a prohibition against travel to Cuba, "The right to speak and publish does not carry with it the *unrestrained* right to gather information."[8] The Burger Court in the *KQED* case essentially dropped the possible qualification of "unrestrained" and said flatly there was no constitutional right of access.

Despite the existence of the Freedom of Information Act (FOIA), this decision has enormous practical consequences because its broad language eliminates any constitutional right of Americans to inspect any records of Congress, of state and local governments, or to interview or speak with bureaucrats, including federal agency employees, none of which is guaranteed by the Freedom of Information Act. For example, assume that instead of seeking interviews, KQED or the League of Women Voters had sought access from Governor Brown to a confidential internal government factual study on the effectiveness of a controversial project, and that Governor Brown had refused to disclose the study without any substantial ground. Under the *KQED* decision, access to the report could constitutionally be denied to the press and the public. This result is fundamentally antidemocratic.

The right of access to government information, however, still survives in four important respects:

1. *Right-of-access statutes.* Without question the single most important advance in the public right of access is the Freedom of Information Act, passed in 1966. This law allows any person to demand access, without regard to any "need" to have access, to any record or document in the hands of any executive agency (other than the Office of the President), subject only to nine exemptions (national defense, trade secrets, executive privilege, certain investigative files, etc.). The present administration's policy is to allow access even to exempt material when it is in the public interest to do so. In 1974, the act was strengthened to impose short time limits for agency compliance and to require courts to judge for themselves whether withheld materials are properly exempt.

The existence of the Freedom of Information Act and its state counterparts has probably retarded the course of constitutional adjudication toward the right of access to government information because it shows that the problems of access can be solved through legislation and accordingly reduces the need to create a constitutional right of access. Since even the proponents of the constitutional right of access would recognize exemptions from access similar to those in the act, there is little need to expand the limits of the constitutional right. If the day ever comes, however, when Congress repeals or severely narrows the act, a long tradition of disclosure under the act may persuade some judges that there is a workable and traditional and fundamental right of access of constitutional dimensions.

We will not explore the scope of the nine FOIA exemptions; it is enough for our purposes to understand that, despite the lack of any constitutional right of access, the FOIA is a major milestone in advancing the right to access and the right to know. One very recent breakthrough expanding the right of access under the FOIA, however, deserves special mention.

One major restraint on the right of access has been the government's refusal to produce classified materials for inspection, a refusal that is permitted under Exemption One of the FOIA.[9] No real problem would arise if the classification stamp were not so widely used to conceal important material whose disclosure would not be injurious to the national security. Justice Douglas described the practice in these terms:

> Anyone who has ever been in the executive branch knows how convenient the "Top Secret" or "Secret" stamp is, how easy it is to use, and how it covers perhaps for decades the footprints of a nervous bureaucrat or a wary executive.[10]

In the *Mink* decision, Justice Douglas protested the Court's holding that under Exemption One the federal courts could in no way second-guess the agency's decisions to classify documents requested under the act. Since then, there have been two major developments expanding FOIA rights to classified materials. First, Congress overruled *Mink* (as well as a presidential veto) with the 1974 amendments and instructed courts to determine for themselves, *in camera* if need be, whether withheld documents were properly classified according to the executive order on classification. Second, President Carter recently issued Executive Order 12065, creating a new classification system to go into effect on December 1, 1978. Significantly, it will require declassification of any material requested under the FOIA when the "public interest in disclosure outweighs the damage to national security that might reasonably be expected from disclosure."[11] Previously, the agency was not required to weigh the public interest in disclosure as a factor in deciding whether to release. This change in the standard, plus the "de novo" review provisions of the 1974 amendments, suggests that after December 1, 1978, a federal court may substitute its judgment for that of the agency as to whether the public interest in disclosure outweighs the expected injury to national defense or foreign relations from disclosure.

2. *Common-law right to access.* Another means of access to government information which survives the *KQED* decision is the applicability of a "common law" right of access to records of public agencies. In *Nixon v. Warner Communications*,[12] the Supreme Court assumed, for purposes of argument, that such a right to inspect judicial or public records existed, although the Court concluded that access by the press to the White House tapes used as exhibits in the Watergate trial had been properly denied by Judge Sirica because of the need to protect the defendants from distorted publicity, at least pending appeal. Interestingly, the Court cited, as examples of the common law right of access, a state decision in which a publisher sought "to publish information concerning the operation of government," and another state case in which "the interest necessary to support the issuance of a writ compelling access [was] found . . . in the citizen's desire to keep a watchful eye on the workings of public agencies."[13] This common law right might well supply a remedy, at least against local and state governments, for access to government information. (It would not supersede any exemption under the FOIA since Congress may override any common law rule with impunity.)

3. *Whistle blowing.* With the exception of 18 U.S.C. sec. 798, which prohibits willful disclosure of classified information concerning secret codes, there is still in this country no prohibition against disclosing, receiving, or publishing secret or classified information for the purpose of exposing unacceptable government action and not for the purpose of injuring the national defense. In the United Kingdom, in contrast, section 2 of the Official Secrets Act has been construed to prohibit even mere receipt of state secrets and was used in 1970-71 to prosecute four journalists and the Sunday *Telegraph* for publishing a confidential but leaked assessment of the situation in Nigeria by the defense advisor at the British High Commissions in Lagos.[14] Unlike the Official Secrets Act and unlike President Nixon's sweeping criminal law proposal, which in part would have outlawed such receipt, there is no prohibition in the United States against merely *receiving* classified or other information so long as the recipient's specific intent is not to injure the United States.[15]

Having obtained the information, moreover, a newspaper may not be enjoined in advance from publishing it except in extraordinary cases. Even so sensitive a document as the Pentagon Papers may not be enjoined from publication, although publication of the location of troops or sailing times of combat ships may be.[16] Although the *Pentagon Papers* decision left open the risk of postpublication sanctions, federal statutes do not authorize prosecution except where the specific intent is to injure the United States' security or foreign policy.

Laws have been proposed to punish the leaking or publishing of any classified information for any purposes, such as those proposed by the Wright Commission in 1957, but they have never been enacted because such laws would, due to the overuse of the classification stamp, result in prosecutions of newspapers like the *St. Louis Post-Dispatch,* for example, for having published secret documents in the exposé of the Teapot Dome scandal. A recent First Amendment decision of the Supreme Court even suggests, at least by analogy, that such a law would be unconstitutional.[17] The Nixon administration tried to circumvent the specific intent requirement of the espionage laws by prosecuting "whistle-blowers" such as Daniel Ellsberg and Anthony Russo under criminal statutes prohibiting theft of government property.[18] Because this smacked of an Official Secrets Act, the present administration (in a Justice Department directive dated September 6, 1978) has specifically instructed United States attorneys that prosecutions under such statutes are inappropriate for whistle-blowers who release classified government documents to the press. (At the same time, the administration continues to successfully enforce CIA Confidentiality Agreements signed by CIA employees as a condition of employment; these contracts require CIA censorship of all manuscripts to be published by employees, a practice that some believe constitutes an Official Secrets Act by contract.)

To be sure, a right to receive and to publish the confessions of a whistle-blower, done in the public interest, is not really the same as a right of access to the records ourselves. Still, such an official, because of his or her proximity to the center of the problem, is an invaluable contributor to the right to know. Our tradition of protecting such disclosures done in furtherance of the public interest and the absence of an Official Secrets Act in this country are valuable components of our right of access.

4. *Congressional access.* Finally, we should not forget that even if the people and the press, as a "fourth branch," were totally denied direct access to government files, the right to know, in at least a representative sense, would still be served through congressional inquiry and publication. After all, one of the reasons we elect representatives and senators is so they may inquire into and expose governmental operations in a more systematic way than virtually anyone else is able to do. At least since 1885, when Woodrow Wilson wrote *Congressional Government,* the "informing function" of Congress has been one of its

preferred functions. If, therefore, the constitutional right of access by the people themselves now lies in shambles, the constitutional right of Congress to demand information from the executive branch remains and is "subject only to whatever limitations the executive privilege may be held to impose. . . ."[19]

The Supreme Court itself has never had to determine the extent to which the executive privilege may defeat a congressional demand for information. In *United States v. Nixon*,[20] the Court held that the executive privilege had a constitutional basis derived from the separation of powers doctrine, among others, but ruled that the privilege was not absolute and had to yield to a specific need for subpoenaed tapes in a pending criminal trial in order, among other things, to insure that the defendants' Fifth and Sixth amendment rights were honored. The Court reserved the question of the extent to which a claim of executive privilege must yield to a congressional demand for information.[21] The only judicial decision on point is *Senate Select Committee v. Nixon*,[22] decided two months before *United States v. Nixon* was rendered by the Supreme Court. The Court of Appeals held that the Senate Select Committee's showing of need for presidential tapes was insufficient to overcome the presumptive claim of executive privilege, especially in view of the fact that copies of all of the subpoenaed tapes were already in the custody of the House Impeachment Committee.

However the contours of executive privilege are ultimately drawn in the congressional arena, the fact is that Congress' power to demand information from the executive branch is secured by Article I of the Constitution and that power, representative though it may be, is an invaluable component of the right to know. It is, moreover, a constitutional power that is largely self-executing through the political process. When necessary, the implicit or explicit threat of an exercise of the congressional power of the purse, or a refusal by Congress to confirm nominees absent satisfactory information, or to take other actions requested by the executive branch are usually sufficient to disgorge withheld secrets. There are some who believe that, if anything, the congressional right of access is so powerful that the danger is in its abuse to expose private matters for little or no public purpose, as was the case when Senator McCarthy insisted that the executive produce personnel files on suspected communists.

Before turning to the subject of the right to privacy and its conflict with the right to access, it is worth pausing to consider another fundamental conflict—the conflict between the right to access and the competing need, for the sake of effective government, for the confidentiality of some governmental actions. Confidentiality encourages innovative, candid, and considered thinking before final decisions are made in the halls of government. Several of the nine exemptions in the FOIA, in fact, represent congressional determinations that democracy is better served by maintaining secrecy about certain governmental actions than by disclosing them. The extent to which official actions, recommendations, investigations, advice, defense planning, and the like should be open to the public or the Congress is a question whose importance is not intended to be minimized by its omission from this chapter.

II

Congress determined in the Privacy Act of 1974 that "the right to privacy is a personal and fundamental right protected by the Constitution of the United States."[23] The extent to which a majority of the Supreme Court today would agree with Congress is unsettled. Justice Stewart went out of his way in a recent concurring opinion in *Whalen v. Roe*[24] to state that "there is no general constitutional right to privacy," citing the majority's statement in *Katz v. United States*.[25]

While this observation is correct in the sense that the Constitution nowhere mentions privacy and in the sense that there is no implied "general" constitutional right to privacy, there have been recent Supreme Court decisions recognizing a more general privacy interest than those narrower privacy interests protected by the First, Fourth, and Fifth amendments. Professor Kurland has identified three broad but distinct rights of privacy that have gained some constitutional protection: freedom from intrusion or observation in one's private affairs (e.g., wiretapping), the freedom to act without outside interference (e.g., abortion), and the right to maintain personal control over certain information about oneself (e.g., data banks).[26]

Here we are concerned with the last of these meanings of privacy and, specifically, the conflict between the individual's right to informational privacy and the public's right to know. As Professor Emerson has observed, there really is no issue whether press or the public may demand information from private individuals or companies. Reporters cannot wiretap or burglarize homes or offices or compel information from such sources in the name of the public's right to know. We all accept that.

The real issue is the conflict between the right of informational privacy, on the one hand, and (1) the right of the government to collect information in the first place, and (2) the right of access of Congress, the press, and the public to that information once collected, on the other hand.

Over the last century, two approaches have been used, on occasion, by the Supreme Court to protect individuals and businesses from compulsory disclosure of personal or propriety information. The first is simply to construe the scope of the "authorized" inquiry so as not to reach compulsory disclosure of private materials. This approach does not derive from any constitutional right or expectation of privacy in the individual but from the restricted scope of the authorized inquiry, although many of the decisions were obviously influenced by the spectre of unwarranted invasions of privacy. The second approach has actually found a right of privacy residing in the individual, a right which overrides even an otherwise authorized inquiry. Although the Supreme Court has not unequivocally established such a right, some of the recent opinions of the Court do, in fact, state that there is a right to refuse to disclose personal information to the government, except when there is an overriding need of the government for the information *and* when governmental safeguards will insure the confidentiality of the information.

The first of these two approaches originated at least as early as 1880 as *Kilbourn v. Thompson*,[27] which held that the legislative function of a committee of Congress was not broad enough to investigate into the private affairs of individuals who hold no office in the government. Thus the House erroneously held Kilbourn in contempt for refusing to answer questions regarding his private business affairs. The Court reasoned that since the purpose of the committee was to determine the property rights of the government in pending litigation with Kilbourn, and not to frame legislation, the inquiry into Kilbourn's private affairs was a judicial, not legislative, function. A few weeks later, Justice Miller, who wrote the Court's opinion in *Kilbourn*, expressed the view in correspondence that Congress was running roughshod over the privacy rights of individuals:

> I think the public has been much abused, the time of legislative bodies uselessly consumed and the rights of citizens ruthlessly invaded under the now familiar pretext of legislative investigation and that it is time that it was understood that courts and grand juries are the only inquisitions into crime in this country. I do not recognize the doctrine that Congress is the grand inquisitor of the nation. . . .[28]

Justice Miller's philosophy gradually receded but, with the advent of federal agencies and their own attempts to investigate private affairs, the same approach was turned against them, as shown in Justice Holmes' famous remark for the Court in *Federal Trade Commission v. American Tobacco Company*, 1924, wherein the Court invalidated an FTC subpoena seeking all of the correspondence received by a company during a seven-year period:

> Anyone who respects the spirit as well as the letter of the Fourth

Amendment would be loathe to believe that Congress intended to authorize one of its subordinate agencies to sweep all of our traditions into the fire, and to direct fishing expeditions into private papers on the possibility that they may disclose evidence of crime. . . . The interruption of business, the possible revelation of trade secrets, and the expense that compliance with the Commission's wholesale demand would cause, are the least considerations. It is contrary to the first principles of justice to allow a search through all respondent's records, relevant or irrelevant, in the hope that something will turn up. . . . The right of access given by statute is to documentary evidence—not to all documents, but to such documents as are evidence.[29]

Likewise, in *Jones v. Securities and Exchange Commission*, 1936, the Supreme Court refused to enforce an overly broad subpoena against an individual under SEC investigation:

A general, roving, offensive, inquisitorial, compulsory investigation, conducted by a commission without any allegations, upon no fixed principles, and governed by no rules of law, or of evidence, and no restrictions except its own will, or caprice, is unknown to our constitution and laws; and such an inquisition would be destructive of the rights of the citizen, and an intolerable tyranny.[30]

By 1950, however, the Supreme Court reversed this trend too and permitted fishing expeditions—at least when the agency was acting as an "investigating body," as opposed to a judiciary body, and was acting within the scope of its mission. The Court in *United States v. Morton Salt*[31] stated "Even if one were to regard the request for information . . . as caused by nothing more than official curiosity, nevertheless law enforcing agencies have a legitimate right to satisfy themselves that corporate behavior is consistent with the law."

As far as the right of business to resist disclosures is concerned, the law stands today as stated in *Morton Salt*, although it might be said that some courts are increasingly interpreting statutory authorizations to conduct investigations as narrowly as the language permits. For example, in 1977 Judge Merhige in *United States v. Richards*[32] refused to enforce an IRS summons requiring a taxpayer to answer the "eleven questions," on the ground that all the questions were not relevant to the tax liability of the taxpayer's corporation. Instead, the judge fashioned four questions which were confined to tax liability–related issues.

The scope-of-authority approach today is more frequently used to restrict dissemination of the information once obtained than to prevent its collection. In *Doe v. McMillan*,[33] the Supreme Court held that a citizen could sue the public printer to prevent dissemination to the public of a House report that was "actionable under local law" as an invasion of privacy (and that there was no immunity for such dissemination), even though dissemination of the report had been specifically approved by the House and its distribution was authorized by 44 U.S.C. secs. 501 and 701. The report (on public schools in the District of Columbia) disclosed very personal details of named children's school records.

Although not addressing the issue of any affirmative right to privacy, the majority defined the legislative function not to comprehend intrusions upon privacy without reason, at least with respect to issuing reports to the public. After referring to "gratuitous injury to citizens for little if any public purpose," the majority stated: "We are unwilling to sanction such a result, at least absent more substantial evidence that, in order to perform its legislative function, Congress must not only inform the public about the fundamental of its business but also must distribute to the public generally materials otherwise actionable under local law."[34] Unwarranted dissemination of personal information is thus *outside* the constitutional scope of the legislative function and presumably the executive function as well.

In *McMillan* the objectionable material was assumed to be truthful, simply embarrassing. The scope-of-authority approach has, not surprisingly, also been used when the information to be disseminated was inaccurate. In 1974 Judge Bazelon wrote for the Court of Appeals in *Tarlton v. Saxbe*[35] that, absent a clear congressional directive to the contrary, the FBI should not be presumed to have the authority to disseminate inaccurate criminal information in derogation of common law principles of privacy without taking reasonable precautions to prevent inaccuracy. Likewise, in *G.T.E. Sylvania Inc. v. Consumer Product Safety Commission*,[36] the Court enjoined publication of a CPSC report on the safety of various manufacturers' television sets because it was inaccurate and misleading. The Court held that the commission had abused its discretion under the Administrative Procedures Act.

In short, the courts today will still define the function of an agency or Congress in such a way as to prohibit, in severe cases, at least, the dissemination of private, even truthful information and will narrowly construe statutory grants of investigative authority to prevent abusive inquiries into private matters.

Assuming, however, that the inquiring body is authorized to compel the private information, is there any overriding constitutional privilege to withhold the information? This brings us to the second approach used by the Supreme Court to protect the privacy of information about individuals' politics, beliefs, family, health, employment, and financial affairs.

In applying certain guarantees of the Bill of Rights the Court has explained their purposes sufficiently broadly in terms of privacy that an independent concept of privacy, greater than the sum of its parts, has taken root. In 1886, in *Boyd v. United States*,[37] the Court held that the Fourth Amendment proscription against unreasonable and warrantless searches as well as the Fifth Amendment privilege to withhold materials from the government that might be self-incriminating seeks to preserve "the sanctity of a man's home and the privacies of life." Eventually, the Court abandoned property tests to determine whose Fourth Amendment rights were violated and focused instead on whether the complaining party had a "reasonable expectation of privacy" in the place searched. Likewise, the First Amendment was held implicitly to protect a citizen from having to disclose his political beliefs to a legislature or agency, to protect the NAACP from having to turn over its membership lists to the State of Alabama, or to protect a schoolteacher from disclosing, as a condition of employment, all of the organizations to which the teacher belonged. Without such privacy, the Court held that fundamental principles of the First Amendment rights of association and belief would be defeated. By the time *Griswold v. Connecticut*[38] reached it in 1965 the Supreme Court had already established privacy zones protected by the First, Fourth, and Fifth amendments. None of these specific zones, however, was really present in *Griswold*, which nonetheless held unconstitutional a Connecticut law prohibiting the use of contraceptives, even by married couples. Justice Douglas wrote for the Court that the statute concerned a relationship (marriage) lying within the combined zones of privacy created by the penumbras of several guarantees—not only the above three but also the Third and Ninth amendments. The statute was held defective because it swept too broadly into this integrated zone of marital privacy and was not limited to regulating whatever specific evil the state had in mind.

For our purpose it is unnecessary to consider the controversial question whether there is or should be a general right to privacy under the Constitution. We need only be concerned with whether there is a right to informational privacy that is greater than the sum of the limited privileges from disclosure established by the First, Fourth, and Fifth amendments. There is room to argue that there *is* such a broader right to informational privacy, but the decisions of the Supreme Court to date are inconclusive. Four decisions merit discussion.

In *Watkins v. United States*, 1957,[39] the Supreme Court reversed a conviction for contempt of Congress for Watkins' refusal to answer HUAC questions about whether certain persons had once been members of the Communist Party. A strict reading of the holding is merely that the questioning was outside the scope of any defined subject the committee was created to study. The majority opinion by Chief Justice Warren, however, stated:

> *We cannot simply assume . . . that every congressional investigation is justified by a public need that overbalances any private rights affected.* To do so would be to abdicate the responsibility placed by the Constitution upon the judiciary to insure that the Congress does not *unjustifiably encroach upon an individual's right to privacy nor abridge his liberty of speech, press, religion, or assembly.*
> . . . We have no doubt that there is no congressional power to expose for the sake of exposure. The public is, of course, entitled to be informed concerning the workings of its government. That cannot be inflated into a general power to expose where the predominant result can only be an *invasion of the private rights of individuals.* (Emphasis added.)[40]

Thus, *Watkins* suggests that the need for gathering such political information might not outweigh the need to preserve its confidentiality. To be sure, the Court referred to "an individual's right to privacy." Whether this was intended as support for a more general right to privacy is unclear in view of the Court's stressing of the First Amendment interests.

In *Whalen v. Roe*[41] the Supreme Court in 1977 sustained a New York statute that established a comprehensive data collection and storage scheme for the use of certain prescribed drugs. A form for each prescription, identifying the doctor, the drug, the pharmacy, the dosage, and the patient's name and address had to be filed with the state health department, which then stored and collated the data on a computer. The Court rejected the argument that the scheme violated the constitutional right of privacy, but did so in a way that offers hope for continued recognition of the right. The Court observed that the "privacy" cases have involved two kinds of interests—avoidance of disclosure of personal matters and freedom to make certain kinds of important decisions. Neither interest, however, was sufficiently threatened to render the statute unconstitutional. The statute strictly regulated (and mostly prohibited) governmental disclosure of the data; thus no substantial threat of dissemination of personal facts was presented. Nor was there any restriction on the choice of dosage or drugs, which was left entirely to the doctor and patient. The Court's closing words suggest a sensitivity to the threat of centralized data on our personal lives:

> We are not unaware of the threat to privacy implicit in the accumulation

of vast amounts of personal information in computerized data banks or other massive government files. The collection of taxes, the distribution of welfare and social security benefits, the supervision of public health, the direction of our Armed Forces and the enforcement of the criminal laws all require the orderly preservation of great quantities of information, much of which is personal in character and potentially embarrassing or harmful if disclosed. *The right to collect and use such data for public purposes is typically accompanied by a concomitant statutory or regulatory duty to avoid unwarranted disclosures.* Recognizing that in some circumstances that duty arguably has its roots in the Constitution, nevertheless New York's statutory scheme, and its implementing administrative procedures, evidence a proper concern with, and protection of, the individual's interest in privacy. (Emphasis added.)[42]

In short, since the invasion of privacy was slight, in view of the safeguards, the invasion was permissible and necessary to regulate the use of dangerous drugs. The Court, however, warned that in other cases the balance might be struck differently. Significantly, the types of information referred to in this passage are not usually thought to be protected by the limited privileges from disclosure under the First, Fourth, or Fifth amendments. Such information could be protected only by a more general right to informational privacy.

It is perhaps ironic that the most ringing Supreme Court pronouncement in support of a constitutional freedom from disclosure in recent years was achieved at former President Nixon's urging. In *Nixon v. Administrator of General Services*[43] the Court in 1977 sustained the Presidential Recordings and Materials Preservation Act, which directed the administrator to take custody of the presidential papers and tape recordings of the former president and to promulgate regulations for the orderly preservation and review of them by executive branch archivists for the purpose of returning to Mr. Nixon those that were personal and private in nature and to determine the conditions for public access to the rest.

One of five constitutional challenges by the former president was that the statute impermissibly invaded his privacy. It will surprise some that the Chief Justice was, among all the Justices, the most ardent supporter of the privacy claim. The Chief Justice would have found the act unconstitutional on the privacy ground alone. He was most concerned over the invasion of privacy resulting from access to the tapes and papers not relevant to the duties of the president. He saw two intrusions: intrusion into the papers relating to Mr. Nixon's decisions as a leader of the Republican Party and intrusion into family and personal matters. "Both interests," he wrote, "are of the highest order, with perhaps some primacy for family papers." Both interests "are of the most private nature, enjoying the highest status under our law."[44] Indeed, "there are certain documents," he said, "no person ought to be compelled to produce at the government's request," citing an earlier opinion of Justice Marshall. The papers "involve," he said, the "most fundamental First and Fourth amendment interests." The Chief Justice failed to see how any paramount need existed to invade the privacy of these papers and, in any event, felt that the statute was not the "least drastic" means for invading such privacy in that it failed to specify enough procedural safeguards and substantive standards of what should be thrown open to the public, such details being left to the administrator and his staff.[45]

The majority agreed that "one element of privacy" is "the individual interest in avoiding disclosure of personal matters."[46] The Court agreed that "when government intervention is at stake, public officials, including the president, are not wholly without constitutionally protected privacy rights in matters of personal life unrelated to any acts done by them in their public capacity." (The majority even suggested that the ordinary private individual would have even greater expectation of privacy, observing that, to some extent, Mr. Nixon voluntarily surrendered some privacy when he entered the public spotlight.)[47] Even so, the majority balanced Mr. Nixon's privacy claim against the need to provide the public with the full truth about Watergate, to preserve evidence for trials, and to provide public access to materials of important public interest. The Court conceded that the administrator's staff would have to examine some ultraprivate materials in order to screen them, but no less restrictive alternative could be imagined, analogizing the problem to the screening of telephone conversations pursuant to a wiretap, wherein the relevant and the irrelevant all must be heard. The Court emphasized the act's sensitivity to Mr. Nixon's privacy interests and the procedural safeguards (mandated by the act) for minimizing the intrusion. These, taken with the great public need to preserve the materials, most of which were clearly public in nature, sustained the statute. The majority opinion and Justice Powell's concurring opinion emphasized that the holding was that the act was not facially unconstitutional and that the question of whether the specific procedures adopted pursuant to the statute would sufficiently protect the privacy interest had been reserved.[48]

To summarize, *Watkins* holds that the government may not force an individual to disclose private political information when it is not directly related to his governmental function and suggests that, even when it is related, data may be withheld on privacy grounds to avoid unwarranted disclosures. *Whalen* suggests (without so holding) that governmental collection of private personal information from the individual or his doctor may be unconstitutional unless strict controls are imposed to prevent unwarranted dissemination of the information. The *Nixon* case comes very close to holding, if it does not so hold, that there is an affirmative constitutional right to privacy "in avoiding disclosure of personal matters"; that the need by the government for information must outweigh the individual's need for privacy, and that if disclosure is to be made, it must be made in a way least destructive of the privacy interest, which means, for all practical purposes, strict limits on dissemination of the information. If this assessment sounds more tentative than the words of the Court in *Nixon,* it is because the dicta in all three decisions might later be explained away by the Court as going no further than to recognize that the First and Fourth amendments create limited privacy rights within their spheres but that there is no broader right to privacy in the Bill of Rights, as Justice Stewart has written in every case of this sort since and including *Griswold.*

It is difficult to reconcile fully these propositions with *Paul v. Davis*[49] wherein the Supreme Court held that it was constitutionally permissible for local police to circulate a flyer to business shops advising them to be watching for a man who had only been arrested of suspected shoplifting and not convicted at the time of the circulation (and whose charges were in fact subsequently dismissed) because he was an "active shoplifter." No property or liberty interest was deprived, held the Court, because nothing more than reputation was injured and no employment or similar deprivation resulted. As for the invasion of right of privacy, the majority opinion stated that the Court's privacy cases did not prevent a state from accurately publicizing a record of an official act such as an arrest for law enforcement purposes.[50]

In summary, the constitutional landscape in this area still needs more illumination, but these emerging principles may be discerned at this time:

1. In a rare case the citizen may withhold the information altogether from the government. This right, however, probably will never be extended beyond information that is at the heart of one of the enumerated guarantees in the Bill of Rights. (*Watkins v. United States*)
2. Other private information may constitutionally be compelled from citizens and third parties so long as the government has a reasonable need to learn the information and so long as the government adopts safeguards to protect the confidentiality of the information. (*Nixon v. Administrator; Whalen v. Roe*)
3. Accurate information about an individual, obtained from sources other than the individual, however embarrassing it may be, may constitutionally be disseminated so long as a legitimate purpose is served in the dissemination. (*Doe v. McMillan; Paul v. Davis*)

While the Supreme Court has moved deliberately in the informational privacy area, Congress has enacted specific legislation not designed to prevent collection but designed to prevent unwarranted dissemination and to increase the accuracy of information that is collected. Justice Miller's fears of Congress as the grand inquisition have long ago been confirmed, and administrative agencies beyond his imagination now hold inquisitions of their own. Collection of information is today a foregone conclusion, and the congressional focus has been on limiting its dissemination. The need for such limits nowadays has increasingly been recognized because of (1) the rapid growth of the American economy and the increasing mobility of Americans that has resulted in governmental and industrial dependency upon personal data bases; (2) the increasing use of computers to collect, collate, and retrieve personal data; and (3) the realization that such data bases may be abused, as was revealed during the Vietnam and Nixon era (such as the IRS's Special Services Staff created by President Nixon from 1968 to 1973 for the purpose of investigating the politically unwelcome, creating dossiers, and spying illegally on Americans by the intelligence agencies).[51]

As mentioned, Congress has generally adopted an approach in this area of requiring reports and information but enacting at least some safeguards to prevent unnecessary dissemination by federal agencies of certain information, even absolute bans on dissemination thereof to Congress or other agencies.[52] Moreover, the Federal Reports Act of 1942[53] requires that information obtained in confidence may be given to other agencies only in specific cases and, even then, must remain confidential in the hands of the recipient.

In 1974, the Privacy Act was enacted, establishing a right of access by individuals to their own agency files and prohibiting, with limited exceptions, all disclosures by the agency of those records.[54] This statute is probably the single most important enactment protecting the privacy of information on individuals held by federal agencies. (Congress has also enacted laws, set forth in the Appendix to this chapter, protecting against abuse of private information collected by the private sector and by local governments.)

III

After the *KQED* case, it probably no longer makes sense to address the conflict between the *constitutional* right of access and the constitutional right of privacy. It makes more sense to address the extent to which there are or should be constitutional or other privacy limits on disclosure under the FOIA or the Sunshine Act or on voluntary disclosures by the government.

Certain FOIA exemptions (such as exemptions four, six, and seven) are designed in part to exempt from mandatory disclosure those materials, such as personnel records, financial records, and investigation files, which could unduly invade the privacy of the subject. The many courts of appeals which have ruled on this are now divided over whether the FOIA *requires* that exempt material be withheld or merely permits it to be withheld.[55] The Justice Department now takes the position that release under the exemptions is discretionary. (This issue will undoubtedly be decided by the Supreme Court in *Chrysler Corp. v. Schlesinger,* awaiting oral argument.)

The nondisclosure provision of the Privacy Act, however, *is* mandatory.[56] That prohibition, unfortunately, only applies to records kept by name or identifying symbol and only to individuals. It does not restrict dissemination of corporate records or investigative files naming individuals, such as an investigation file on "communist infiltration in universities." Nor does it prevent any disclosure whatever, including disclosures of individual's files, required under the FOIA.

In short, there is plenty of opportunity under the present statutory framework for personal, embarrassing, financially sensitive, or confidential business information to be gathered by the government and then released to Congress, the press, or the public to the regret of the person or business submitting the information or simply one of the subjects mentioned in the requested materials. This has led to one of the major and unanticipated developments under the FOIA—the many "reverse FOIA suits" that have been brought to enjoin government disclosure of material about or submitted by the plaintiffs.

Usually, the plaintiffs in these "reverse" cases have been businesses seeking to prevent discretionary governmental disclosures of their trade secrets or their financial condition or business plans or capabilities. In some cases, plaintiffs seek to prevent discretionary disclosures under the FOIA of their trade secrets or business plans to their competitors which are really sought for competitive reasons. Preventing disclosures of this type, sought for competitive advantage, really does not interfere with the "right to know" about how well the government is working. In fact, some businesses are refusing to supply required materials to various agencies until confidentiality agreements or court orders sealing the records from FOIA disclosure are obtained. So it makes sense to protect this privacy interest by improving the privacy rights of submitters of information in such circumstances.[57]

On the other hand, "reverse" suits have been used to deny access to public interest groups seeking equal employment opportunity compliance reports and product and drug safety tests and reports, whose disclosure serves the public interest not only by advising the public, for example, of the safety of products they buy, but by allowing the public to assess how well the responsible agencies are enforcing laws respecting such matters. Here access does promote the "right to know." At the same time, there may well be legitimate expectations of privacy or property interests to be protected, especially when the information was turned over to the agency under an agreement that it would be kept confidential.

The same tension exists between the right to know and the right to privacy of employment, medical, or other sensitive information about individuals. Because individuals do not have the vast resources available to large corporations, the judicial contests thus far have typically been between only the party requesting disclosure under the act and the agency resisting disclosure on the ground that it would constitute an unwarranted invasion of personal privacy of the subject. The following are the type of cases that have arisen to date:

1. In *Department of Air Force v. Rose,* 1976,[58] the Air Force unsuccessfully resisted disclosures of case summaries prepared in connection with a cheating scandal at the Air Force Academy, even though the requesting party had agreed at the time of the request that the names of individual cadets should be deleted. The Supreme Court held that with the deletion of the individual cadets' names there would not be an unwarranted invasion of privacy under the act.

2. In *Tax Reform Research Group v. I.R.S.,* 1976,[59] the court sustained the I.R.S.'s deletion of the names of certain taxpayers on President Nixon's "enemies list" released by the Internal Revenue Service against a claim that the requesting party had a right to know the names.

3. In *Congressional News Syndicate v. Department of Justice,* 1977,[60] the Department of Justice sought to withhold the names of contributors and recipients of campaign contributions investigated by the Watergate Special Prosecution Force because of the opprobrium attached to those investigated as part of the Watergate inquiry. The court overruled this claim of privacy, in spite of the fact that the individuals at stake were not indicted, in view of the policy of the Federal Corrupt Practices Act that these names be made available to the public. The court held, however, that information as to the role, if any, played by these individuals who were not indicted was exempt.

4. In *Public Citizens Health Research Group v. Department of Labor,* 1977,[61] the plaintiff sought access under the act to information about the previous private sector employment and educational background of specified employees in the government for the ostensible purpose of determining whether or not their prior employment and background might have affected policy decisions made by them during their tenure

with the government. The court granted such limited disclosures, reasoning: "A person's employment and educational background, when subjective evaluations and other personal details have been redacted, is protected by privacy right, but not as weighty a privacy as is recognized when the facts about a person's family status or history are involved."

5. The Justice Department decided during 1975 that it would release a substantial portion of the Hiss and Rosenberg case files, even with respect to private materials pertaining to principal witnesses, except where the materials, if any, were of an intimate or personal nature and were wholly unrelated to the subject matter of the cases.[62]

In practice, the decision to release sensitive exempt information is solely within the discretion of the agency to which the request is directed and the individual does not get an opportunity, prior to dissemination, to persuade the agency or a court that dissemination should not be allowed. To be sure, most administrative agencies have now issued regulations implementing the access rights and restrictions under the FOIA and the Privacy Act. Significantly, however, while many of these regulations require predisclosure notice to companies *before* release of any trade secrets or confidential business information under the act, these regulations do not require predisclosure notice to any individual before sensitive matters about him or her (regardless of source) are disseminated.

The same procedures that have been adopted with respect to trade secrets and confidential business information would go a long way toward striking a satisfactory balance between the right to access and the right to privacy. A statute in the form of an amendment to the Privacy Act or regulations issued by each of the agencies should provide that a person who seeks to assert a privacy claim covering information filed with the agency should designate it as "exempt material" when it is first submitted to the agency. The agency would then determine whether or not such information was sufficiently private to defeat disclosure under the FOIA in those cases in which an FOIA request was made for disclosure, or when the agency itself simply wanted to determine whether or not the information deserved private treatment, or when the agency found that it was likely to have to disclose the information at some future date. Of course, when the agency receives the information pursuant to a confidentiality pledge by it not to disclose the information, the information should be automatically treated as nondisclosable by the agency.

Before an agency makes a determination regarding the disclosability of the information, it should advise the submitted party or the subject of the information so that they may provide comments to the agency on the privacy claim. Notice should also be given to the requesting party who seeks dissemination of the information so that the requesting party may also be heard on that question. Once a final determination regarding dissemination of the private material is made by the agency, any party aggrieved by the determination should be entitled to judicial review and preliminary relief against disclosure pending the judicial determination.

With respect to sensitive information submitted by others, but whose release would nonetheless injure a person's privacy, that person obviously would have no opportunity to designate it as confidential at the time it was received by the agency. Under such circumstances, the agency should be required to give notice to the subject prior to release of such information so that the victim of the disclosure would have an opportunity to persuade the agency that his or her privacy interests were paramount to the public interest of disclosure. Of course, if the agency had no reason to believe that particular information in the form to be released would be deemed confidential by any of the subjects mentioned therein, then dissemination would be permitted without any predisclosure notice. Thus if sensitive material could be safely released so long as the names of individuals are redacted, then predisclosure notice would not be necessary.

Finally, if a citizen challenges the release on privacy grounds, both the statutory and the constitutional standard would protect, at most, against "unwarranted" disclosures. "Unwarranted" presumes a balancing on a case-by-case basis of the competing needs. Other tests have been suggested and are summarized in Emerson, *The First Amendment and The Right To Know*,[63] but balancing seems inevitable. Significantly, however, a balancing test should still require the disclosure to be made in the way least destructive of the privacy interest, such as through redaction.

It is virtually impossible to fashion in advance hard and fast rules or even general principles for striking the balance as to what invasions are warranted or not. Many factors, however, can be identified: (1) whether access is sought for competitive or litigation needs, on the one hand, versus policymaking or governmental needs, on the other; (2) whether the victim of the requested disclosure is a public official whose official duties are drawn into question by the requested data; (3) whether there is reason to believe requested material that is defamatory is inaccurate; (4) whether the information was obtained in the first place pursuant to a confidentiality pledge; (5) whether, if disclosure is permitted, similar information will "dry up" in the future due to refusals of citizens to supply it (such as candid opinion by lawyers of the judicial qualifications of prospective judicial appointments); (6) whether the need to know and the need for privacy can both be substantially accommodated through redaction. These factors are not unlike those already being used by the federal courts in those cases where agencies resist FOIA disclosure on privacy grounds.

These limitations on government dissemination of private information, at least to the extent the constitutional right to informational privacy continues to develop, should apply not only to FOIA requests but also to dissemination made outside the FOIA by the executive, by Congress, by the courts, and by state and local governments.

Appendix: Recent Statutes on Informational Privacy in the Private Sector

In 1974, the Buckley Amendment was enacted, requiring colleges and universities receiving federal funds to allow parents and students certain access to students' records and to restrict dissemination of those records without parental consent.

In 1974, the Fair Credit Reporting Act was passed to regulate the right of access by consumers to consumer reports prepared by credit firms, to prevent credit reporting agencies from disclosing certain data to the government and others, and to require correction of inaccurate data upon request.

In 1974, the Fair Credit Billing Act prohibited creditors from reporting adversely to credit bureaus and others because of disputes with customers over the accuracy of bills, except in prescribed circumstances.

In 1976, the Sunshine Act was enacted to permit attendance by the public at agency and commission meetings, subject to certain exemptions including a privacy exemption. The act states that it is "the policy of the United States that the public is entitled to the fullest practicable information regarding the decisionmaking process of the federal government."

In 1976, the Tax Reform Act overruled a decision of the Supreme Court in *United States v. Miller*[64] and required the IRS in normal cases to give bank customers advance notice of the service of an IRS summons on a bank for production of the customers' bank records, so that the customer could challenge the scope of the summons.

A number of bills are now being considered in Congress that would create a more general statutory "right to financial privacy." (E.g., H.R. 8133, "Right to Financial Privacy Act of 1978," now incorporated into H.R. 13471 reported out by the House Banking Finance and Urban Affairs Committee.)

Notes

1. Pell v. Procunier, 417 U.S. 817, 839-40 (1974) (dissent).
2. Kurland, *The Private I*, U. of Chicago Magazine 7, 8 (Autumn 1976), cited in Whalen v. Roe, 429 U.S. 589, 599 n.24 (1977).
3. Public Utilities Commission v. Pollak, 343 U.S. 451, 469 (1952).
4. See generally, Gazelon, *Probing Privacy*, 12 Gonzaga L. Rev. 587 (1977).
5. E.g., EPA v. Mink, 410 U.S. 73, 105 (1973) (dissent); Gravel v. United States, 408 U.S. 606, 641-42 (1972) (dissent); Emerson, *Legal Foundation of the Right to Know*, 1 Wash. Univ. L. W. 1, 16 (1976).
6. Houchins v. KQED, Inc. 46 U.S.L.W. 4830 (June 26, 1978).
7. E.g., Branzburg v. Hayes, 408 U.S. 665, 684-85 (1972); Pell v. Procunier, 417 U.S. 817 (1974); Saxbe v. Washington Post Co., 417 U.S. 843 (1974).
8. Zemel v. Rusk, 381 U.S. 1, 16-17 (1965).
9. 5 U.S.C. sec. 552(b) (1).
10. EPA v. Mink 410 U.S. 73, 108 (1973) (dissent).
11. 43 Fed. Reg. 28805, 28955 (July 3, 1978).
12. 46 U.S.L.W. 4320 (April 18, 1978).
13. Id. at 4323.
14. J.A.G. Griffith, "Government Secrecy In the United Kingdom," in *None of Your Business* at 394 (Ed. N. Dorsen and S. Gillers 1974).
15. 18 U.S.C. sec. 793.
16. New York Times Co. v. United States, 403 U.S. 713 (1971); Near v. Minnesota, 283 U.S. 697 (1931).
17. Landmark Communication, Inc., v. Virginia, 46 U.S.L.W. 4389 (May 1, 1978).
18. 18 U.S.C. sec. 641.
19. EPA v. Mink, 410 U.S. 73, 83 (1973).
20. 418 U.S. 683, 710-13 (1974).
21. 418 U.S. at 712 n.19.
22. 498 F. 2d 725 (D.C. Cir. 1974).
23. 5 U.S.C. sec. 552a.
24. 429 U.S. 589, 607-608 (1977).
25. 389 U.S. 347, 350-51 (1968).
26. Kurland, *The Private I*, U. of Chicago Magazine 7, 8 (Autumn 1976), cited in Whalen v. Roe, 429 U.S. 589, 599 n.24 (1977).
27. 103 U.S. 168, 193-195 (1880).
28. Fairman, *Mr. Justice Miller and the Supreme Court* at 334 (1939).
29. 264 U.S. 298, 305-06 (1924).
30. 298 U.S. 1, 27 (1936).
31. United States v. Morton Salt Co., 338 U.S. 632, 652 (1950).
32. 431 F. Supp. 249 (E.D. Va. 1977).
33. 412 U.S. 306, 317 (1973).
34. Id. at 317.
35. 507 F. 2d 1116, 1122-23 (D.C. Cir. 1974).

36. 404 F. Supp. 352, 375 (D. Del. 1975).

37. 116 U.S. 616, 630 (1886).

38. 381 U.S. 479 (1965).

39. 354 U.S. 178 (1957).

40. Id. at 198-200.

41. 429 U.S. 589 (1977).

42. Id. at 605.

43. 433 U.S. 425, 455-65 (1977).

44. Id. at 529-30.

45. Id. at 535.

46. Id. at 457.

47. Id. at 455.

48. Id. at 504.

49. 424 U.S. 693 (1976).

50. Id. at 713.

51. See generally chapter 9 of the Report of the Privacy Protection Study Commission, *Personal Privacy in an Information Society* (1977).

52. See, e.g., Tax Reform Act of 1976, 26 U.S.C. sec. 6103: Census Act, 13 U.S.C. sec. 9; Drug Abuse Prevention and Treatment Act, 21 U.S.C. secs. 1102-1191; Child Abuse Prevention and Treatment Act, 42 U.S.C. secs. 5101-5106.

53. 44 U.S.C. sec. 3508.

54. 95 U.S.C. sec. 55a.

55. Compare, e.g., Westinghouse Elec. Corp. v. Schlesinger, 542 F. 2d 1190, 1197 (4th Cir. 1976), cert. denied, 431 U.A. 924 (1977) (mandatory nondisclosure) with Charles River Park "A" Inc. v. Department of Housing and Urban Development, 519 F. 2d 935, 941-43 (D.C. Cir. 1975) (permissive disclosure, but agency's decision to release information is still subject to judicial review under the APA for abuse of discretion).

56. 5 U.S.C. sec. 552a (b).

57. Cf. NLRB v. Robbins Tire & Rubber Co., 46 U.S.L.W. 4689, 4697 (June 15, 1978).

58. 425 U.S. 352 (1976).

59. 419 F. Supp. 415, 419 (D.C. Cir. 1976).

60. 438 F. Supp. 538, (D.C. Cir. 1977).

61. No. 76-886 (D.C. Cir. 1977).

62. See statement by Harold R. Tyler, Jr., deputy attorney general, August 17, 1975, reprinted in part in Center for National Security Studies, *Litigation Under The Amended Freedom of Information Act* at 44 (Ed. Marwick, 4th Ed. 1978).

63. 1 Wash. L. W. 1, 21-22 (1976).

64. 425 U.S. 435 (1976).

TWO

PROTECTION OF THE INDIVIDUAL
AGAINST HIMSELF
William Cohen

Justice William O. Douglas said on many occasions that the purpose of
the Bill of Rights was to take government off the backs of the people.
The mood of the American people in the last half of the 1970s is
characterized by growing anger that government is too much on their
backs—taking an increasing, and unnecessary, role in all aspects of their
lives. Given that public temper, one could expect to report confidently
that the outlook was good for increasing respect for individual liberty in
the United States.

That report, however, would be too simplistic, and too optimistic.
Americans may be no more tolerant today of the beliefs and life-styles of
those who differ greatly from themselves. Nor does popular opposition
to big government stem from a sharing of Justice Douglas' constant
positive faith in the capacity of all individuals to make basic choices in
the development of their personalities and the conduct of their lives. The
mood is, rather, negative—stemming more from growing individual
concerns of continuing deterioration in their own way of living, coupled
with an increasing conviction that government is a prime culprit
responsible for that deterioration. And there is no public consensus on a
philosophic principle that would define the proper sphere of individual
freedom from government control.

My topic requires me to assess the state of individual freedom in the
context of laws that are designed to protect the individual from his own
folly. Making that assessment requires, however, an impossible
definition of the philosophic principle of liberty marking the
appropriate areas of individual autonomy and legitimate government
concern. Those who regard all paternalistic laws as intolerable
interferences with individual liberty would assess the current state of
liberty in the United States as, at best, dismal. In various ways,
government controls, or attempts to control, the ingestion of drugs,
liquor, and tobacco. Government mandates the safety of the vehicles we

---

William Cohen is professor of law at Stanford University.

drive and, on occasion, as in the case of motorcycle helmets, mandates that individuals use safety devices. Government protects gullible consumers from misleading advertisements and unsafe or worthless products. Government protects those in need of medical care from medicinal drugs that are dangerous and even from those that are merely ineffective. Government mandates construction standards for our homes and work places. Government prohibits prostitution and gambling. The list is endless.

As I have defined my topic, it is narrower than the question whether, and when, paternalism is an appropriate government policy. Nor do I address the question whether free economic markets are a more effective means to control antisocial behavior than are coercive government regulations. The question I address is whether there are areas of human conduct that are so essentially within the realm of individual liberty that they are beyond the power of government to regulate and control. More particularly, my task is to deal with that area of human freedom in the context of government controls designed, in whole or part, to protect the individual against himself.

Nearly seventy-five years ago, the Supreme Court, in *Jacobson v. Massachusetts*, observed:

> There is . . . a sphere within which the individual may assert the supremacy of his own will, and rightfully dispute the authority of any human government—especially of any free government existing under a written constitution, to interfere with the exercise of that will.[1]

In the nineteenth century, John Stuart Mill lucidly defined his concept of the "sphere within which the individual may assert the supremacy of his own will." In "On Liberty," he said:

> [T]he sole end for which mankind are warranted, individually or collectively, in interfering with the liberty of action of any of their number is self-protection. That the only purpose for which power can be rightfully exercised over any member of a civilized community, against his will, is to prevent harm to others. His own good, either physical or moral, is not a sufficient warrant. He cannot rightfully be compelled to do or forbear because it will be better for him to do so, because it will make him happier, because, in the opinions of others, to do so would be wise or even right. These are good reasons for remonstrating with him, or reasoning with him, or persuading him, or entreating him, but not for compelling him or visiting him with any evil in case he do otherwise. To justify that, the conduct from which it is desired to deter him must be calculated to produce evil to someone else. The only part of the conduct of anyone for

which he is amenable to society is that which concerns others. In the part which merely concerns himself, his independence is, of right, absolute. Over himself, over his own body and mind, the individual is sovereign.

Mill's principle has its contemporary adherents. There are occasional decisions of state courts that have used Mill's theory as the basis for constitutional decision. For example, in 1968 a Michigan court of appeals held that state's motorcycle helmet law invalid, after quoting Mill *(American Motorcycle Ass'n. v. Davids).*[2] More recently, on the same rationale, some courts have invalidated state laws banning distribution of the controversial drug, laetrile.

However, just as Mill's principle was imperfectly practiced in his own nineteenth-century England, it has never been realized in the laws of the United States. In my own view, moreover, Mill's view is a false guide for defining the appropriate content of liberty in the United States of the late twentieth century. First, there are problems of definition. In an increasingly complex society, are there any aspects of human behavior that have *no* impact upon the welfare of others? *Jacobson v. Massachusetts* sustained compulsory vaccination because of the danger of epidemic. In 1969, the Oregon Supreme Court upheld its state's motorcycle helmet law on the rationale that an object hitting the unprotected head of a motorcyclist could cause him to lose control and endanger other motorists and pedestrians *(Oregon v. Fetterly).*[3] Similiar arguments could sustain such intrusive state measures as compulsory eugenic controls, and stripping parents of all responsibility for the upbringing of their children—without apparent violation of Mill's principle of liberty. More signficantly, no modern civilized state shows complete indifference to the plight of victims of their own folly. We will not permit the disabled, unhelmeted motorcyclist to die because he cannot afford medical care, nor will we permit his family to starve because his disablement flows from his own decision not to wear a helmet. The modern welfare state, because it pays the bills and picks up the pieces, can assert an interest in most human behavior judged to be self-destructive.

A second level of difficulty stems from the problem of competence. Mill conceded that a person was not competent to sell himself into slavery. Modern adherents of Mill's principle are willing to make exceptions for those unable to exercise free choice because of immaturity or mental defect. Compulsory education laws, and laws invalidating transactions of the mentally incompetent are only two among the most obvious examples of laws designed to control the choices of those judged incompetent to exercise normal adult judgment. The exception for incompetents once accepted, however, may be difficult to cabin. Prohibitions of false advertising are supported by the argument that consumers without pervasive expertise are unable to judge the merits of false claims. It is then but a series of small steps to argue that consumers need to be denied access to dangerous products and then to those products that are simply ineffective. Thus, supporters of the ban on sale of laetrile make plausible arguments that terminally ill cancer patients and their families, in their desperation, are fair game for charlatans selling worthless cures. Those who would continue to prohibit "voluntary" euthanasia argue that allowing the terminally ill to "die with dignity" may be equivalent to allowing their families to dispense with the financial and emotional burden of the victim by pressuring the seriously ill to accept death. Are alcoholics and drug addicts exercising free will when they continue their self-destructive behavior? In short, unless the exception to Mill's principle for those incompetent to make their own choices is closely contained, it threatens to swallow the principle.

A third objection to Mill's principle as a contemporary guide to defining human liberty is more basic. It is simply that the principle is wrong—that the just society is not indifferent to the plight of those who are victims of their own poor judgment. I agree with Judge (then Professor) Hans Linde, who wrote in *Oregon Law Review*:

> [N]o provision [in the Constitution] expressly proscribes a society that values the lives and health of its members and seeks to protect them against even self-inflicted harm. To hold that such objectives of public policy are impermissible would place an ironic twist on modern welfare legislation and on the Constitution under which it has been enacted. For it would mean that the impetus and object of all legislation must appear selfish, not as a matter of a naive cynicism about politics, but because the Constitution required it. Must the harm to be prevented by prohibiting the sale of impure food and drugs even beyond a risk of fraud, by prohibiting lotteries, by minimum standards in housing codes, by obligatory safety standards, always be explained as harm to others than the person directly protected? Under such a theory, the Constitution would demand the pretense that long, thankless battles fought from some of the most generous motives in modern politics really meant to serve the self-interest of the taxpayers or other third-party beneficiaries. It would take us back sixty years to the days when the humane impulse behind Oregon's pathbreaking law limiting laundresses to a ten-hour day had to be rationalized on the ground that "as healthy mothers are essential to vigorous offspring, the physical well-being of woman becomes an object of public interest." . . .

That theory conceived of society as a market and applied to it a rigorous philosophy of individualism and personal autonomy. The philosophy that the law should leave people alone unless their conduct harms others has, and one may hope will continue to have, much appeal. Applied to noneconomic issues, it is enjoying a dramatic revival among the young. It may be about to find expression in a new wave of legislative reforms in the criminal law and elsewhere. But there is also another view of society, less atomistic, that would not confine the actions of political man to pursuing the self-interest of economic man by other means. It would hold that we need not be indifferent to the fate of others—that "no man is an island," in Donne's famous words, for "any man's death diminishes me, because I am involved in mankind"—a philosophy with roots as ancient and honorable as radical individualism.

There can be no single choice between these views of legitimate social goals. The balance must be struck for each act of legislation, and we may divide bitterly over the legislative choice. The same generation that saw an intolerable invasion of personal freedom in a prohibition against yellow-dog contracts also imposed prohibition against alcoholic beverages. My present point is only that it is a legislative choice. We may value personal autonomy and fear well-meant paternalism. . . . But, as the Supreme Court keeps reiterating, no provision of the Constitution imposes the choice of social philosophy upon us.[4]

It is still true that, as indicated by Judge Linde, the United States Supreme Court has failed to give constitutional status to Mill's theory that the state may not regulate individual behavior that has no effect on third persons. In the last decade, however, a constitutional right of privacy has been recognized, which shields some areas of conduct from state regulation. The right of privacy has created a sphere of individual autonomy, but that sphere is not concentric with that which would exist if the Mill hypothesis were the rule of decision. The privacy right is narrower. It applies only to limited realms of individual autonomy. In the Court's latest statement, the list of areas of personal choice protected from unjustified government interference included marriage, pro-creation, contraception, family relationships, and child rearing and education (*Carey v. Population Services International,* 1977).[5] While that list does not purport to be exhaustive, the Court has not extended the contours of the right of privacy to include such areas of autonomy as drug, alcohol, and tobacco use, and private consensual adult sexual activities. On the other hand, the privacy right is broader in some respects than Mill's theory. Within the list of protected activities, autonomy has been constitutionally protected even when the interests of other persons are involved. Prior to viability, for example, the state cannot forbid abortion to protect the potential human life of the fetus.

The constitutional right to privacy has been applied to a wide range of situations. There are, of course, the celebrated decisions concerning contraception and abortion (for example, *Griswold v. Connecticut*, 1965).[6] Earlier cases decided under different constitutional theories have been reaffirmed, and reexplained as examples of the right of privacy. Thus, parents may not be compelled to send their children to public schools (*Pierce v. Society of Sisters*, 1925).[7] The state may not compel the sterilization of convicted criminals (*Skinner v. Oklahoma*, 1942).[8] More recent applications of the concept have invalidated laws that restricted the number of related persons who could live in a single-family household, and which required judicial permission for marriage of persons under a previous obligation to support children not in their custody.[9]

Beyond the right of privacy, the free exercise clause of the First Amendment may immunize some aspects of individual choice from state control. In *Wisconsin v. Yoder*, the Court decided that Old Order Amish children could not be required to attend school beyond the eighth grade.[10] The Court's opinion took pains, however, to state that secular objections to compulsory education would not provide a viable constitutional defense to a compulsory school attendance law. In 1964, the California Supreme Court, conceding there was no constitutional right to use peyote as a recreational drug, held that the free exercise clause prohibited punishing members of the Native American Church for using peyote in its "central role in the ceremony and practice" of the church *(People v. Woody)*.[11]

There is considerable controversy as to the range of autonomy protected by the constitutional right of privacy. One level of that controversy concerns the question whether the constitutional right has any basis in the text or history of the United States Constitution. In the birth control cases, Justice Douglas' opinion for the Court justified the right of privacy as falling within the penumbral protection of specific provisions of the Bill of Rights. Other Justices have found the right within the contours of the word "liberty" as used in the due process clauses of the Fifth and Fourteenth amendments. For Justice Black, however, it was clear that neither the constitutional text nor its history recognized a generalized right of privacy, and the concept marked an unconstitutional shift of power to the courts. There are many who continue to criticize the Supreme Court for attempting to protect aspects of personal liberty and autonomy that are not clearly reflected in the specific guarantees of the Bill of Rights, and who will insist, as did Justice Black, that generalized rights of individual autonomy must be protected, if at all, by the political processes. The ghost of economic due process—that body of Supreme Court cases of the first part of this century that gave constitutional dimension to concepts of economic liberty—continues to haunt the banquet table of constitutional law. Despite the fervor of Justice Black's protest, the right of privacy is now firmly embedded in the Supreme Court's jurisprudence. Current battles have stressed issues concerning the nature and scope of the right, rather than the question of its existence.

It is difficult to measure the competing state interests that will justify limits on individual choice in areas that concededly fall within the zone of constitutionally protected privacy. The right to rear children, for example, still must yield to the constraints of child labor and compulsory education laws. The recognition of a fundamental right to free choice in marriage does not mean the wholesale invalidation of all state laws restricting marriage and divorce. Most particularly, recognition of the abortion decision as falling within the constitutional protection of privacy did not resolve the more difficult question of the extent to which the abortion decision can be constrained. Having rejected the argument that a woman's choice of abortion was absolute, the Court was forced to cope with the question whether protection of the fetus was a sufficient basis for a broad ban on abortion. The West German Constitutional Court, at almost the same time, viewed the interest of the fetus to be itself protected by the German Constitution, and invalidated a permissive abortion law. And, in the United States, the abortion controversy continues unabated, with the debate centered on the unresolvable ethical and moral question whether human life begins at conception or at some other point during pregnancy.

A more fundamental difficulty has been to discover the nature of the interests that should fall within the right of privacy. For some, the privacy interests that the Court has recognized cannot be reconciled with autonomy claims that have been denied. My own view is that the existing list of protected interests has all the coherence of a list of irregular verbs. It is fair to say that the only organizing principle that will explain why, for example, the right to use contraceptives falls within the constitutional right of privacy while the right of unmarried persons to engage in private consensual sexual behavior does not, is the set of personal preferences of the judges who compose the list of preferred privacy rights.

A lesser criticism of the Supreme Court's performance in defining the parameters of the constitutional right of privacy is that the judges' list of areas of individual freedom only imperfectly reflects our own social mores, just as the Supreme Court's now-repudiated economic due process decisions continued laissez-faire economic theories as constitutional doctrine after they had been repudiated by public opinion. Some critics of the list of privacy rights complain that it is too narrow. Others complain that it is too expansive.

A broader, and more perceptive, description of the concept of privacy was offered by Justice Douglas, concurring, in the abortion cases.

[A] catalogue of these rights includes customary, traditional, and time-honored rights, amenities, privileges, and immunities that come within the sweep of "the Blessings of Liberty" mentioned in the preamble to the Constitution. . . .

First is the autonomous control over the development and expressions of one's intellect, interests, tastes and personality. . . .

Second is freedom of choice in the basic decisions of one's life respecting marriage, divorce, procreation, contraception and the education and upbringing of children.

Third is the freedom to care for one's health and person, freedom from bodily restraint or compulsion, freedom to walk, stroll or loaf.

Whether or not Justice Douglas' list is an appropriate standard for interpreting the Fourteenth Amendment, it provides for me a fair description of those rights of individual autonomy that will be respected by the truly free society. Troubling questions remain, since neither philosophical constructs nor general conceptions decide concrete cases. Justice Douglas conceded that the rights in his second and third categories were not absolute, but could be abridged on a showing of compelling state interests. Recognition of a right to care for one's health and person is only the first step in deciding controversies concerning motorcycle helmet laws, and laws banning the distribution of laetrile for therapeutic treatment.

I began by asserting that no inventory of the state of individual liberty could be completed without prior definition of the concept of liberty. It is, unfortunately, all too clear that all restraints on individual autonomy are not needless restrictions of liberty. And, it is all too unclear what principles should govern us in choosing the appropriate spheres of individual liberty and state concern. That dilemma has been present, however, throughout American history. We have always been a nation of idealists who have bemoaned the inability of our government to conduct itself consistently with any ideology. Just as Thomas Jefferson, during his presidency, was required to compromise his own philosophy of states' rights and limited federal power, our own conceptions of limited government power over the individual may be difficult to maintain in a world that becomes ever more complex, and a society that becomes ever more interdependent. Popular clamor for lesser governmental intrusions into our daily lives may be nothing more than romantic longing for simpler social structures of the past. Too often, our real choice is not whether we can lead our own lives as we wish, but whether we wish to surrender control to government or to concentrations of private power. Still, in our mass society with its pressures for conformity, questions of liberty continue to be asked in widely divergent situations, such as motorcycle laws; laetrile regulation; euthanasia; alcohol, drug, and tobacco regulations; and regulation of sexual behavior. In the absence of a clearer vision of the definition of individual liberty, the measure of our freedom may be the extent to which questions continue to be asked rather than whether or how they are resolved.

Notes

1. 197 U.S. 11 (1905).

2. 11 Mich. App. 351, 158 N.W. 2d 72.

3. 254 Ore. 47, 456 P. 2d 996.

4. Linde, *Without Due Process: Unconstitutional Law in Oregon,* Oregon Law Review 49 at pp. 178-181 (1970).

5. 431 U.S. 678 (1977).

6. 381 U.S. 479 (1965); Roe v. Wade, 410 U.S. 113 (1973).

7. 268 U.S. 510 (1925).

8. 316 U.S. 535 (1942).

9. Moore v. City of East Cleveland, 97 S. Ct. 1932 (1977); Zablocki v. Redhail, 98 S. Ct. 732 (1978).

10. 406 U.S. 205 (1972).

11. 61 Cal. 2d 716.

THREE

FREEDOM OF INQUIRY
IN THE SCIENCES

Leonard B. Boudin

I

Freedom of inquiry in the sciences is increasingly the subject of controversy.[1] This is caused by the large amount and high cost of research, particularly through government funding, the extraordinary advances in scientific discovery, the stake of drug and other business corporations in the products of such research, international rivalry in weaponry, and the benefits and risks of scientific research and experimentation.

The controversy has a wide range: DNA, psychosurgery, and research into the IQ differences *vel non* among the races. It includes the successful search by governments for increasingly terrible means of warfare and arises from the efforts of some groups to seek genetic, in addition to and sometimes rather than social, political, and economic causes of race riots and other manifestations of social upheaval.[2]

II

Restrictions upon scientific research have been advocated because of the newly found ability to change genetic behavior, the presumed dangers in man's altered conception of himself,[3] the physical risks to human subjects, the violation of their privacy, and the possibility of physical, chemical, and biological harm to the community.[4] The scientists and their supporters, in contrast, remind us that science, indeed all human thought, has flourished because of an absence of government control, that the exceptions have been dark moments in the history of civilization and that government regulation of science is presumptively evil; they reject the claim of danger to the community.[5] A basic premise, bluntly stated by Gerard Piel, publisher of *Scientific American,* is that "no limit can or should be set upon scientific inquiry" even where so-called national security[6] is involved.

Leonard B. Boudin is a partner in Rabinowitz, Boudin & Standard, New York.

III

Unquestionably, freedom to think, research, and publish has been a major factor in the acquisition of human knowledge and understanding. In our constitutional context, a democratic system of government depends upon the participation of knowledgeable citizens, and scientific research is an important source of that knowledge. Dr. Alexander Meiklejohn's great contribution to constitutional thought was his emphasis upon public affairs as the basic objective of the First Amendment.[7] This was reflected in the Supreme Court's decision in *New York Times v. Sullivan*,[8] which, as the great philosopher said, left him dancing in the streets.[9]

The citizen's right to know was the raison d'être of the early Supreme Court decisions in *Meyer v. Nebraska*[10] and *Pierce v. The Society of Sisters*,[11] which freed private school curricula from government control; true, property rights were also central in those decisions. However, the great passport case of *Kent v. Dulles*,[12] where Justice Douglas wrote the opinion for five justices, upheld the right to travel for the purpose of acquiring knowledge, not to improve one's material wealth. Similarly, *Lamont v. The Postmaster General*[13] upheld the citizen's right under the First Amendment to receive information from the so-called communist bloc.

Finally, Justice Douglas' opinion in *Griswold v. Connecticut*,[14] upholding the right to give and receive contraceptive advice and devices, declared that "the State may not, consistently with the spirit of the First Amendment, contract the spectrum of knowledge." Since much research is done in universities and other institutions of learning, academic freedom, the essence of the concurring opinion in *Sweezy v. New Hampshire*,[15] is also relevant.

IV

These brave statements of principle cannot disguise the realities of government control over scientific research. First, through its classification of documents and information, purportedly in the interests of national defense and foreign relations, the government conceals important scientific information.[16] Congressional hearings, law review articles, and executive orders have criticized the classification system repeatedly, to no avail. Second, the government itself employs thousands of scientists in the Defense Department and elsewhere, and therefore exercises a proprietary control over their research. Third, since the government is the major source of funding, it influences the course of scientific research throughout the country. The scientific community, therefore, has the responsibility to pursue research apart from political considerations. It must also resist, on moral and perhaps legal grounds, the denial of general research grants by government agencies, because the researcher may do some work in areas not to the government's liking.

V

Restrictions on research in areas such as terrestrial communication capable of disclosing a superior type of life on other planets cannot be justified on the ground that it may disorient our society.[17] DNA research has been criticized on the grounds that man has no right to affect his own evolutionary process.[18] These arguments are inconsistent with the practical and philosophical need for an unrestrained search for knowledge. The name of Galileo is a sufficient warning against such restrictions and the First Amendment is blind to the content or implication of knowledge. However, there is a constitutional difference between the acquisition and disclosure of knowledge, and the use of that knowledge. The latter, sometimes called "technology," is properly subject to government regulation, even though its source may not be censored.[19]

VI

The State does not have a substantial interest in protecting the scientist against the hazards to which he subjects himself. However, the scientist has no right to subject to physical danger other human subjects of his research or the community. This issue has been posed most starkly by the claim of opponents of DNA research—that a pathogenic virus may escape from the laboratory and adversely affect the human race.[20] In considering this claim, I accept Dr. Carl Cohen's admonition that DNA research must be considered under principles applicable to research in any sphere, and that it cannot be prohibited or regulated, except upon evidence of hazards contemplated by that principle.[21]

Mr. Piel has suggested that the DNA controversy "has its roots in deeper moral questions"—namely, should man "presume to seize the control of evolution that is now so nearly in his hands"?[22] Certainly, opposition upon this ground violates the historic canon of free scientific inquiry as well as the First Amendment. For the same reason, social scientists should have the right to seek proof that IQ differences exist among the races. However, any research may be restricted if it presents a danger to the community. Indeed, the great microbiologists led by Dr. James D. Watson were themselves responsible for the recent moratorium on DNA research in order to assess the dangers of possible contamination.[23] Today, Dr. Watson and many of his colleagues believe that the DNA regulations which followed their warning are unduly restrictive of research.[24]

The assignment of the probabilities of risk is a matter of scientific expertise; what to do in cases of risk is a matter of government policy. The government has the constitutional power and duty to regulate research which might affect public health and safety. This power is not subject to constitutional challenge despite the fact that the same government has created the risk of proliferation from nuclear weapons, conceals from its citizens information necessary for their welfare, and permits the devastation of our communities by, for example, private manufacturing companies and Liberian oil tankers.

Thus, while the First Amendment precludes regulation of research, it permits regulation of the technological aspects (including the methodology) of the research. The First Amendment implications do, however, impose upon the government that constitutional duty to employ the least intrusive means of regulations.[25] This principle probably requires that the federal government supersede all local regulation which might be too varied and burdensome. It might require the use of civil, rather than criminal, sanctions. Scientists are entitled to full due process hearings before being subjected to regulation, and the scientific community must be given a major role in the evaluation of risks and benefits. Since the public may be adversely affected by the research, informed laymen are entitled to participate in the decision-making process. Professor Cohen has argued that the burden of proof as to risks rests upon those who would make a claim of highly probable disaster;[26] Dr. Sissella Bok would place it upon the scientists.[27] Perhaps the placing of the burden should depend on the magnitude of the potential disaster.

VII

In addition to the rights of scientists, there is another important and opposing concern: whether scientific research, experiments and treatment, may violate the constitutional rights of the subject. This arises in the context of social science research on persons who are unaware that their privacy is invaded.[28] It occurs when sufferers from syphilis are deprived of drugs in order to determine the effects of deprival. In another case described by Dr. Bok, women applying to a family clinic for contraceptives were given either oral contraceptives or placebos.[29]

The most serious interference with individual rights occurs with the coercive use in prisons and mental institutions of psychotropic (mind-altering) drugs, electrical stimulation of the brain (ESB) by implantation of electrodes, psychosurgery, and other organic conditioning techniques to control sick or aberrant behavior. In other cases, these drugs have been used, notably by the CIA, to experiment upon subjects who were totally unaware of the experiment.[30] The literature with respect to the use of psychiatric hospitals for political dissidents in the Soviet Union is similarly disturbing.[31]

Such research and treatment attacks personal autonomy and integrity of thought. Justice Brandeis in his famous *Olmstead* dissent[32] said that "the makers of our Constitution ... recognized the significance of man's spiritual nature, of his feelings and of his intellect. . . . They conferred, as against the government, the right to be let alone—the most comprehensive of rights and the right most valued by civilized men." The great successor to his seat, Justice Douglas, more than any Justice ever to sit on the Court, was consistently and eloquently concerned with the concept of individuality.[33] More recently, Circuit Judge Shirley M. Hufstedler reminded us that "the personal interest to be protected by the right of privacy is in the individual's interest in preserving his essential dignity as a human being."[34]

The use of organic techniques to change personality, thought processes, and indeed, a person's character, violates the First Amendment right to thought processes and privacy as well as the Fourth Amendment right against unreasonable search and seizure. The most creative development of this theme may be found in the many writings of Professor Michael H. Shapiro of the University of Southern California Law Center.[35] His views were adopted by a Michigan Circuit Court in *Kaimowitz v. The Department of Mental Health*, which held that a patient involuntarily committed to a mental hospital cannot be subjected to psychosurgery:

> A person's mental processes, a communication of ideas, and the generation of ideas, come within the ambit of the First Amendment. To the extent that the First Amendment protects the dissemination of ideas and expressions of thought, it equally must protect the individual's right to generate ideas.[36]

Earlier, in *Stanley v. Georgia*, the Supreme Court had stated the fundamental principle:

> Our whole constitutional heritage rebels at the thought of giving government the power to control men's minds. . . . Whatever the power of the state to control public dissemination of ideas inimical to the public morality, it cannot constitutionally premise legislation on the desirability of controlling a person's private thoughts.[37]

These concepts of law and morality generally bar the use of organic therapies in the absence of informed consent. A judicial proceeding is the proper forum to determine whether such informed consent has been given as well as the medical soundness of the proposed theory.

These principles are now embodied in California legislation drafted by Professor Shapiro.[38] The basic statute declares that "all persons involuntarily confined have a fundamental right against enforced interference with their thought processes, states of mind, and patterns of mentation through the use of organic therapies. . . ."[39]

California law also subjects one "who lacks the capacity for informed consent" to organic therapy where it is established "it will be beneficial to the person, that there is a compelling interest in administering such therapy, and that there are no less onerous alternatives to such therapy."[40] However, even there, neither psychosurgery nor ESB may be imposed upon any person because of its drastic nature and irreversible effect.

I have some doubt as to whether any institutionalized person is capable of consent; the reward-punishment syndrome is implicit in his captivity. On the other hand, his right of personal autonomy entitles him to such treatment as he desires.[41] This dichotomy is probably best reconciled by the legislation which permits compelled treatment so long as it does not create an irreversible situation.

Brandeis' and Douglas' fear of big government is more justified today than ever before in our history. Advances in science have given new and dangerous weapons to governments for use against their citizens. Science fiction and Orwell's predictions have become reality. Our salvation can only come—if it is to come—in a framework of greater freedom of inquiry and greater freedom from government power.

Notes

1. See particularly Daedalus, *Limits of Scientific Inquiry,* Spring 1978; *Science Policy Implications of DNA: Recombinant Molecular Research;* Hearings, Subcommittee on Science, Research and Technology of the House Committee on Science and Technology, 95th Cong., 1st sess., March 1978 (herein after "Hearings"); Promise and Hazards of Recombinant DNA Research: Three Schools of Thought, Federation of American Scientists Public Interest Report, April 1976.

2. See *The IQ Controversy, Critical Readings* (J. Block and G. Dworkin, eds., 1976); Mark, Sweet and Ervin, *Role of Brain Disease in Riots and Urban Violence,* 201 J.A.M.A. 895 (1967).

3. Robert L. Sinsheimer, *The Presumption of Science,* Daedalus, supra, note 1, p. 23.

4. Daedalus, supra, note 1, passim; George Wald, testimony in Hearings, supra, note 1, March 29, 1977, pp. 62-87; Wald, *The Case Against Genetic*

Engineering, Current, Nov. 1976, p. 25.

5. See Daedalus, supra, note 1, passim; Mark M. Ptashone, *The Defense Doesn't Rest,* Current, supra, note 4, p. 30.

6. Piel, "Scientific Research: Determining the Limits," talk given under the auspices of the Resident Associate Program, Smithsonian Institution, June 14, 1977.

7. See, e.g., A. Meiklejohn, *Political Freedom* (1960), and *The First Amendment Is an Absolute,* 1961 Sup. Ct. Rev. 245, 255.

8. 376 U.S. 254.

9. Kalven, *The New York Times Case: A Note on "The Central Meaning of the First Amendment,"* 1964 Sup. Ct. Rev. 191, 221 n.36.

10. 262 U.S. 390.

11. 268 U.S. 510.

12. 357 U.S. 116.

13. 381 U.S. 301.

14. 381 U.S. 278.

15. 354 U.S. 234.

16. See, e.g., Thomas Franck and Edward Weisband, *Secrecy and Foreign Policy* (1974), passim.

17. See Daedalus, supra, note 1, passim.

18. Ibid.

19. Testimony of Thomas I. Emerson, Hearings, supra, note 1, May 25, 1977, pp. 886-890.

20. George Wald in Hearings, supra, note 4.

21. Carl Cohen, *When May Research Be Stopped?,* 296 New England J. Medicine, May 26, 1977, p. 1203.

22. Piel, supra, note 6.

23. *The Nobelist vs. the Film Star,* Outlook, The Washington Post, May 14, 1978, p. D-1.

24. Ibid.

25. Supra, note 19.

26. Supra, note 21, p. 1207.

27. Bok, *Freedom and Risk,* Daedalus, supra, note 1, pp. 115, 124.

28. Id. at 117.

29. Bok, *The Ethics of Giving Placebos,* 231 Sci. Amer. 17, November 1974.

30. U.S. Senate, Senate Rept. 94-755, 94th Cong., 2d sess.

31. I. F. Stone, *Betrayal by Psychiatry,* N.Y. Rev. of Books, February 10, 1972.

32. Olmstead v. United States, 216 U.S. 386.

33. Note, *Toward a Constitutional Theory of Individuality: The Privacy Opinions of Justice Douglas,* 87 Yale L.J. 1579 (July 1978).

34. Hufstedler, *The Directions and Misdirections of a Constitutional Right of Privacy.* Benjamin N. Cardozo Lecture, Association of the Bar of the City of New York (May 11, 1971), 26 Rec. A.B.C. N.Y. 546, 1971.

35. See, e.g., Shapiro, *Therapeutic Justification for Intervention into Mentation and Behavior,* 13 Duquesne L. R. 673, Summer 1975; Shapiro, *Who Merits Merit* and *Problems in Distributive Justice and Utility Posed by the New Biology,* 48 S. Cal. L. R. 318 (1974); Shapiro, *Legislating the Control of Behavior*

Control: Autonomy and the Coercive Use of Organic Therapies, 47 S. Cal. L. R. 237, 1974.

36. Civil Case No. 73-19434-A.W. (Wayne County, Mich. Cir. Ct., July 10, 1973), summarized at 42 U.S.L.W. 2063, July 31, 1973.

37. 394 U.S. 557.

38. *Deering's California Penal Code* sec. 2670 et seq.

39. *Deering's California Penal Code* sec. 2670.

40. *Deering's California Penal Code* sec. 2679 (B).

41. Estelle, Corrections Director, et al. v. Gamble, 429 U.S. 97.

PART TWO

FREEDOM AND LAW ENFORCEMENT

FOUR

CONTROL OF INTELLIGENCE AGENCIES

Thomas I. Emerson

The need to control the intelligence agencies has been evident for a number of years. Since the operations of intelligence agencies are normally concealed from public view the extent of the problem, although long suspected, did not appear in full force until recently. Beginning with the hearings of Senator Sam Ervin's Watergate Committee in 1973, however, the true picture began to emerge. Additional information was provided by the House Judiciary Committee in its proceedings on the impeachment of President Nixon, and, subsequently, extensive investigations were conducted by the Senate Select Committee under Senator Frank Church and the House Intelligence Committee headed by Representative Otis Pike. Other important sources of information have included investigative reporting, discovery in civil litigation, the Freedom of Information Act, and revelations by former members of the intelligence community.

The disclosure of what the intelligence agencies have been doing came as a stunning shock to most Americans. The record of their misdeeds seems to be unending. It includes political surveillance of hundreds of thousands of citizens and hundreds of organizations never charged with any violation of law; selective investigations and prosecutions directed at political enemies; campaigns of "preventive action" designed to disrupt and destroy groups or individuals through forgery, false accusations, fostering dissension, and the like; extensive use of plainly illegal methods such as unauthorized wiretapping and bugging, burglaries, mail opening, and even assault and violence; the creation of a police apparatus of dossiers, undercover agents, informers, and agent provocateurs; and, abroad, "covert actions," including the training of paramilitary organizations, attempted assassination, and other forms of violence. Most of these operations have been conducted without clear statutory authority and without supervision or oversight.

Plainly these activities present a serious challenge to American

Thomas I. Emerson is Lines Professor of Law Emeritus, Yale University.

democracy. The philosophy, tactics, and powers of the intelligence agencies as they have operated in the past point squarely in the direction of a police state. Although the agencies have apparently curbed these abuses somewhat in the last two years, there is no guarantee that they will not revert, especially in a period of crisis, to their past practices. Indeed the combination of events that led to the public exposure of intelligence agency operations may never occur again, and this may be our last opportunity to take effective action.

The full solution to the problem of controlling intelligence agencies in a modern, technological world is not easy to find and certainly not easy to put into practice. The roots of the difficulty go deep into the foundations of our society. Nevertheless, one thing seems clear. The abuses of the past have been possible, in part at least, because the intelligence agencies have been subject to virtually no constraints. Their functions have never been clearly formulated; their statutory authority has been absent or ill-defined; their operations have been unsupervised; and there has been no way, except in unusual circumstances, for the public to know what they are doing. Clearly an indispensable part of the solution is to develop a system of legal and public restraints.

Unfortunately, very little has been accomplished thus far. There has been much discussion and some concrete proposals, but virtually no action. The only significant achievement to date, apart from some internal reform in the agencies themselves, has been the creation of permanent committees on intelligence in the Senate and in the House, authorized to draft legislation and to maintain oversight. The major task remains to be done.

The Constitutional Structure and the Role of the Courts

In devising a legal system to control the intelligence agencies we must start with the constitutional structure and the role that our judicial institutions can play. The First Amendment, the Fourth Amendment, and other provisions of our Bill of Rights provide protection to individual citizens against many of the practices that the intelligence agencies have engaged in. Likewise various statutes and regulations, enforced through the judicial process, establish additional safeguards. At the present time, however, a serious challenge has been posed to, and important gaps exist in, this system of judicial protection.

The major challenge, and one that casts an ominous shadow over the whole constitutional structure, is the claim of "inherent powers" in the president to override constitutional and statutory restrictions in the interest of "national security" or in the conduct of foreign affairs. Many presidents have asserted such powers on various occasions in the past. The climax was reached, however, during the Nixon administration, when illegal wiretapping, break-ins, mail openings, and various "preventive actions" and "covert operations" were justified in the name of "national security." Subsequent administrations, while more moderate in tone, have continued to put forward claims of inherent power in the president to conduct intelligence operations without regard to ordinary constitutional or legislative controls.

The United States Supreme Court, in a decision of far-reaching significance, has definitely rejected the claim of inherent presidential power to ignore constitutional or statutory limitations in the area of "domestic intelligence." In *United States v. United States District Court*, decided in 1972, the Court held that the government could not engage in wiretapping, in violation of the requirements of the Fourth Amendment and the applicable statute, despite the contention that such action was necessary in order to protect "national security." Justice Powell, speaking for a unanimous court, put the underlying constitutional considerations this way:

> These Fourth Amendment freedoms cannot properly be guaranteed if domestic security surveillances may be conducted solely within the discretion of the executive branch. The Fourth Amendment does not contemplate the executive officers of Government as neutral and disinterested magistrates. Their duty and responsibility is to enforce the laws, to investigate, and to prosecute. . . . But those charged with this investigative and prosecutorial duty should not be the sole judges of when to utilize constitutionally sensitive means in pursuing their tasks. The historical judgment, which the Fourth Amendment accepts, is that unreviewed executive discretion may yield too readily to pressures to obtain incriminating evidence and overlook potential invasions of privacy and protected speech.

The Supreme Court also struck down claims to inherent presidential powers in the Pentagon Papers case, where the government attempted to enjoin the *New York Times*, the *Washington Post*, and other newspapers from publishing classified documents on the Vietnam war; in the Nixon tapes case, where President Nixon argued that "executive privilege" gave him unrestricted power to withhold information from other branches of government; and in the steel seizure case, where President Truman took over the steel mills on grounds of "national security." The constitutional principles expressed in the *United States District Court* case are thus applicable not only to the Fourth Amendment but to the First Amendment and other safeguards of the

Constitution. They thus preclude claims of inherent powers to disregard constitutional and statutory protections where "domestic intelligence" is concerned.

In *United States v. United States District Court,* however, the Supreme Court left undecided the question whether the same principles applied where the intelligence agencies were concerned "with the actions of foreign powers or their agents," that is, the so-called foreign intelligence area. The Carter administration, in the espionage prosecution against David Truong and Ronald Humphrey for transmitting information to Vietnamese authorities, and in other cases, is vigorously contending that the executive branch is empowered to ignore constitutional and statutory limitations in the "foreign intelligence" area. For reasons to be set forth later, it is impossible to disentangle operations in the "domestic intelligence" field from operations in the "foreign intelligence" field. Thus the constitutional question that will ultimately be decided by the Supreme Court is of major significance. A ruling that constitutional and statutory limitations can be disregarded in "foreign intelligence" operations would deal a mortal blow to any effort to bring the operations of the intelligence agencies within the rule of law.

Apart from matters of constitutional structure, the courts are of course available for the enforcement of constitutional and statutory rights of the individual against illegal actions of the government. The principal forms of such judicial relief are criminal prosecutions against government officials, civil actions by individuals against the government and its officials, and the exclusion in judicial proceedings of evidence obtained by unlawful methods. All these forms of redress are useful, and indeed crucial to any effective system of control. But all have important drawbacks.

Criminal prosecutions are brought by government officials against other government officials only with extreme reluctance and, in the case of the intelligence agencies, only under rare circumstances. Thus, despite the disclosure of the thousands of violations of law, only one prosecution of three officials of the Federal Bureau of Investigation has so far been instituted. Moreover, claims based on the Nuremberg defense (the contention that government officials who follow orders are immune from prosecution) have been vigorously pressed and are unresolved. In addition, the absence of clear statutory prohibitions against some of the practices of the intelligence agencies has further inhibited prosecution.

Civil remedies, in the form of suits for damages, injunction or other relief, are available in many circumstances. But again there are many problems, including claims of government immunity, the difficulty of persuading judges and juries to hold government officials liable, the inability to obtain crucial information from intelligence agencies, high costs, excessive delays, and small recoveries. As to the exclusionary rule, it is useful only in the exceptional case where the government brings a prosecution, and the rule itself is under heavy attack from high quarters.

Many of these difficulties in resorting to the judicial process can be alleviated. Thus gaps in statutory protection can be filled, defenses based on governmental immunities eliminated, provision made for the payment of attorney's fees in civil litigation, and the like. All of these efforts to improve the judicial remedy, however, require legislation.

One further series of issues related to the judicial process remains to be considered. There are a number of points at which the courts could apply or extend existing constitutional principles to meet some of the novel problems that have arisen with the extraordinary growth of intelligence activities in our society. On the whole the courts have failed to seize these opportunities. Thus, the First Amendment would clearly seem to prohibit the intelligence agencies from engaging in forms of political surveillance that chill or inhibit freedom of expression and association. Nevertheless the Supreme Court, at least as to the surveillance program of U.S. Army intelligence, refused relief, on the ground that the persons bringing the action had not shown sufficient injury to give them standing to raise the constitutional issues. Similarly, although the intelligence agencies make widespread use of informers to infiltrate political organizations, the Supreme Court has declined to rule that such tactics constitute a search and seizure of information within the meaning of the Fourth Amendment. The Supreme Court has likewise refused to extend protection against agents provocateurs by bringing up to date antiquated rules relating to police entrapment. In addition the Court has not been willing to penetrate the veil of secrecy with which the intelligence agencies surround themselves. Thus, despite the plain provision of the Constitution requiring "a regular statement of account of the receipts and expenditures of all public money," the Court has refused to require that the budget of the Central Intelligence Agency be made public. All of these decisions reveal an unnecessarily timorous attitude on the part of the courts in dealing with the intelligence community.

Taken as a whole, the judicial branch of government performs an indispensable function in the effort to keep the intelligence agencies within constitutional and civilized bounds. Unfortunately the courts have been slow to recognize the implications of the growth and expansion of intelligence activities within our society. Equally important, the courts need aid from the legislature in order to improve both their substantive and procedural performance.

Self-control

The executive branch of government, including the intelligence agencies themselves, have made some efforts at reform. In February 1976 President Ford issued an executive order imposing some restrictions on the operations of the intelligence agencies in the area of "foreign intelligence." This was succeeded by an executive order promulgated by President Carter in January 1978 that reorganized the intelligence bureaucracy and somewhat modified the Ford restrictions. In March 1976 Attorney General Edward Levi issued guidelines for the FBI dealing with the initiation and conduct of investigations in the "domestic security" area. Guidelines concerned with other aspects of FBI operations were made public in January 1977. Foreign counter-intelligence guidelines have also been issued but are secret and not available to the public. Partly as a result of these restrictions and partly in response to public pressures accumulating from the steady stream of exposures, the FBI, the CIA, U.S. Army intelligence, and other agencies have curtailed some of their most objectionable activities.

These measures are welcome and should be encouraged. They are, however, clearly not sufficient to solve the basic problems. In the first place the limitations imposed by the executive orders and the guidelines do not go far enough. Without attempting to analyze them in detail, it suffices to say that, giving them the most favorable interpretation, they do not conform to the basic principles for controlling the intelligence agencies as set forth in detail below. For example the Carter executive order authorizes electronic surveillance without obtaining a warrant. On a less favorable interpretation, they would permit the agencies to engage in the very practices that have been most severely criticized, including political surveillance, preventive action such as the FBI Cointelpro program, and even violations of law. In the second place they are based upon, and embody, the theory that the president has inherent powers to conduct "national security" investigations without regard to constitutional limitations, an inadmissible premise. Thirdly, reform of the bureaucracy by the bureaucracy can achieve only limited goals. Among other things, the restrictions imposed are subject to broad interpretation by the agencies themselves, allowing many opportunities to escape the intended impact; adequate outside checks are not provided; and implementation by criminal or other sufficient sanctions is not afforded. Finally, and most important, the limitations are subject to withdrawal, abandonment, or neglect at any time at the whim of the executive authorities. There is no assurance whatever that they would remain in force or be adhered to in times of stress, the very point at which they would be most needed.

For these reasons there is broad agreement that more must be done than internal executive reform. The crucial ingredient is legislation.

Principles of Legislation

Before discussing detailed legislative proposals it is imperative to consider the underlying premises upon which effective legislation must be based. In the light of past experience, six fundamental principles may be stated.*

1. *The intelligence agencies must be confined to the collection, analysis, and proper dissemination of information; they should not engage in "preventive action" or "covert action."*

The proper function of the intelligence agencies is to collect information, analyze it, and disseminate it to those who need it. When intelligence agencies go beyond this point they are inevitably operating outside the rule of law.

The most glaring examples of improper practices by the intelligence agencies are the FBI "preventive action" programs and the CIA "covert actions." Both were designed to harass and destroy, through illegal methods that did not stop short of violence, individuals, groups, and even governments who were perceived as political opponents. Whether conducted at home or abroad such operations constituted nothing less than guerrilla warfare.

The most notorious FBI "preventive action" program was Cointelpro. It was directed not only against radical groups such as the Communist Party and the Socialist Workers Party, but against black groups such as the Southern Christian Leadership Conference, liberal groups such as the National Committee to Abolish the House Un-American Activities Committee, and even Antioch College ("the vanguard of the New Left"). The tactics employed included dissemination of derogatory information from investigative files, spreading of false rumors, mailing of poison pen letters, obtaining dismissal from employment, falsely denouncing members of an organization as informers, promoting street warfare between rival groups, assaults, and other forms of violence. It was, as William C. Sullivan, former assistant to Director J. Edgar Hoover, testified, "a rough, tough, dirty business. . . . No holds were barred."

The FBI, in addition to Cointelpro, engaged in numerous other

---

*These principles were originally set forth in more abbreviated form in an article prepared for *Human Rights*, to be published in fall 1978.

"preventive actions." Dr. Martin Luther King, Jr., was the target of one. Using the excuse that two members of Dr. King's staff had left-wing connections, the FBI tapped his telephone, bugged his quarters, distributed derogatory information about him, spread the rumor that he had a Swiss bank account, attempted to have his supporting funds cut off, tried to stop publication of his articles and books, and made plans to find a "suitable" successor. The campaign included an anonymous letter to Dr. King suggesting he commit suicide.

The CIA "covert actions" conducted abroad included bribery, obtaining publication of false information, training paramilitary groups, attempted assassination, encouraging terrorism, and organizing plots to overthrow governments. These operations not only violated international law but had serious domestic consequences in the United States, such as the spreading of false information and the corruption of academic, religious, and journalistic institutions.

Under no circumstances do these practices have a place in a civilized community. If allowed to carry on such activities the intelligence agencies become a state within a state, totally beyond public control. Nothing could be more dangerous for a democratic society or for the development of an international law.

It is highly doubtful that "preventive action" is of any value in promoting national security. Quite the contrary, such tactics are almost certainly counterproductive. The principal results are the discrediting of law enforcement, an increase of tensions within the society, the polarization of political viewpoints, and a reluctance to use the machinery of law and politics to resolve conflicting claims. The same may be said, in international terms, of "covert actions" abroad.

2. *In performing their function of gathering information the intelligence agencies should be confined, so far as any data involving political activities is concerned, to the collection of information that has a direct and immediate relation to a violation of law or is necessary to the administration of a law.*

Even if the intelligence agencies are limited to the collection, analysis, and dissemination of information, their operations can have a detrimental and even disastrous effect upon individual rights, particularly freedom of expression. When the government collects information that relates to the political beliefs, opinions, associations, or activities of a citizen, the very process of investigating and maintaining the data is inhibiting. The questioning of friends, neighbors, employers, and others; the compiling of dossiers and lists; the creation of an apparatus of agents, informers, and possibly agents provocateurs; the potential use of the information for reprisals or selective prosecution—all tend to repress free expression and may destroy it altogether. Hence any system of controls must be built-in protection for First Amendment rights. The most effective method of affording this protection is to limit the authority of intelligence agencies, so far as the collection of data pertaining to political activities is concerned, to information that is directly and immediately related to the enforcement or administration of the law.

More specifically this means that the FBI, which has no jurisdiction outside the area of the criminal law, and which has been one of the chief offenders, must confine its operations to matters where there is reason to believe, based on concrete and articulable facts, that a violation of the criminal law has taken place or is about to take place. Counterintelligence operations should be limited to the enforcement of the espionage, treason, sabotage, and similar laws. Other intelligence agencies deal with the administration of regulatory laws: their authority to gather information, where there would be any effect on First Amendment rights, should be confined to the particular law over which they have jurisdiction. Similar restrictions should apply to the CIA insofar as it conducts its activities within the United States or deals with American citizens abroad. The gathering of general "domestic security intelligence" or "foreign intelligence" that would impair First Amendment rights should be outlawed.

Imposition of such restrictions on the intelligence agencies would, of course, require careful definitions and a drawing of difficult lines. A number of borderline situations would be certain to arise. The provisions establishing jurisdictional limitations would therefore have to be reinforced by other measures specially designed to protect First Amendment rights. These include repeal of the speech crime laws (such as the Smith Act), which open wide avenues of inquiry into political expression, development of specific standards for initiating investigations, time limits on the duration of investigations, and various methods of assuring accountability and oversight.

If the nonpolitical standard of jurisdiction is not followed, the First Amendment rights of citizens are bound to be infringed and the whole intelligence apparatus becomes a vehicle for controlling public opinion and inhibiting political, social, and economic change.

3. The improper practices of which the intelligence agencies have been guilty in the past should be carefully defined and specifically prohibited.

In seeking to control the intelligence agencies it is not sufficient merely to grant them "charters" setting forth their affirmative authority to conduct intelligence operations, leaving it to be implied that they are not to engage in other activities. Nor is a general prohibition against other conduct an adequate protection. The abusive practices that have been characteristic of the intelligence agencies in the past should be strictly defined and specifically prohibited, subject to criminal and civil penalties. It should be made explicit that such practices will not be tolerated in a free society.

Conduct which should be expressly forbidden by statute includes:

Political surveillance. Political surveillance consists of the collection, maintenance, or dissemination of information, or other investigative activity, relating to any person's beliefs, opinions, associations, or other exercise of First Amendment rights. As already noted, the intelligence agencies, particularly the FBI and the CIA, have engaged in this type of activity on an enormous scale. Such conduct is incompatible with the guarantees of the First Amendment and should be expressly forbidden.

Selective investigation. Selective investigation consists of investigatory activity undertaken in whole or in part because an individual or organization has engaged or is engaging in legitimate political expression. It involves the use of governmental powers for illegal purposes. Modern society is extremely vulnerable to such misuse of government authority, and the intelligence agencies are particularly prone to engage in such tactics. The practice should be prohibited by express provision of law.

Preventive action and covert action. These activities have already been discussed. Not only should the intelligence agencies be given no authority to engage in such conduct, but they should be specifically forbidden to do so.

Problems will of course arise under these provisions in drawing the line between authorized and unauthorized investigative activities. But such problems are by no means insuperable. Over a period of time, as individual cases are decided, the concepts of "political surveillance," "selective investigation," "preventive action," and "covert action" will take on more specific meaning and a body of common law will develop. The important thing is to start that process in motion.

It is also true that much of the conduct prohibited is already a violation of constitutional guarantees. Nevertheless it is important to embody the prohibitions in statutory form. In the first place the official statement by the legislative branch that the conduct in question is prohibited makes it far more likely that the courts will reject any claims by the executive branch that the "inherent powers" of the president justify such activity. Moreover, the existence of legislation provides an incentive for lower officials to resist pressures to employ illegal methods and would encourage "whistle blowing." In addition, civil actions by persons whose rights have been infringed will be placed on a firmer basis. Finally, the enactment of specific legislation emphasizes the moral commitment of the nation to root out practices so destructive of the democratic process.

4. *The more intrusive techniques utilized by intelligence agencies should be subject to judicial supervision through a warrant procedure.*

Traditionally the intelligence agencies have engaged in various practices which, while not wholly illegitimate, nevertheless particularly intrude upon privacy or other individual rights. Any effective system of controls should make special provision against abuse of these intrusive methods. The most common technique for affording this protection is judicial supervision through the requirement of a court-approved warrant.

The warrant procedure should be mandated in at least the following situations:

Wiretapping and bugging. There are strong arguments for prohibiting the intelligence agencies from engaging in wiretapping or bugging at all. Such practices involve a grave invasion of privacy and amount to the very kind of general search that the Fourth Amendment was designed to prohibit. Nevertheless, if wiretapping and bugging are allowed they should be subject to the warrant procedure. The Omnibus Crime Control and Safe Streets Act of 1968 already provides for a warrant in all cases concerned with "domestic intelligence." The government has construed the statute, however, as not forbidding electronic surveillance in "foreign intelligence" matters, under presidential "inherent powers"; in this area the intelligence agencies continue to use wiretapping and bugging without obtaining a warrant. The Supreme Court, as previously noted, has left open the question of the government's authority to do this. This gap should be closed by legislation. As will be discussed shortly, there is no convincing reason for distinguishing between "domestic" and "foreign" intelligence with respect to this issue.

Informers. Again, there are good reasons for prohibiting the use of informers by the intelligence agencies where directed against an individual or organization exercising First Amendment rights. If the practice is not forbidden, however, it should be rigidly controlled through the warrant procedure. The employment of informers to gain the confidence of an individual or to infiltrate an organization constitutes a serious infringement of personal or organizational privacy. It should be permitted only under judicial supervision.

Searches of private records. Investigative searches of private records, such as bank records, personal tax records, employment records, health records, telephone call records, and the like infringe upon both First and Fourth amendment rights. They expose to government scrutiny vast amounts of information about a person's private and political life. The practice of the intelligence agencies to inspect such records in the hands of third parties, such as banks or telephone companies, should be limited to circumstances where the agency can convince a court of its necessity. Even then the person concerned should receive notice and an opportunity to contest, except in criminal investigations where a search warrant is obtainable.

Mail covers. Mail covers, that is, the obtaining of information from the outside cover of mail, are also an intrusive technique and should require a warrant. The actual opening of mail is already subject to the requirement of a warrant (except mail coming into the United States from abroad).

The warrant procedure is by no means a complete guarantee against abuse by the intelligence agencies. In many cases, perhaps most, the process tends to be a formality. Nevertheless the warrant device does require that the intelligence agency set forth formally and offically the basis for using an intrusive technique. And there always is the possibility that, over a period of time, judges and lawyers can make the warrant requirement into a more effective safeguard.

5. *The collection of "foreign intelligence" within the borders of the United States and with respect to American citizens abroad should be subject to the same safeguards as the collection of "domestic intelligence."*

In recent years, apparently since the Supreme Court decision in the *United States District Court* case, the government has attempted to develop a distinction between "domestic intelligence" and "foreign intelligence." "Foreign intelligence" is defined broadly as the collection of information (and the conduct of covert operations) concerning any foreign power (including a foreign government, organization, or person), concerning national defense or foreign policy, or concerning counterintelligence. The term is sometimes defined more narrowly to refer to the collection of intelligence (and the conduct of covert operations) with respect to activities conducted by or on behalf of a foreign power. The government's contention is that in the area of "foreign intelligence" the inherent powers of the executive branch are greater, the constitutional limitations are lesser, and the legislative restrictions required are fewer. The Ford and Carter executive orders and various legislative proposals embody this doctrine.

The distinction is unsound and the conclusions drawn from it are dangerous. The position is based upon the assumption that, in the area of "foreign intelligence," the rights of Americans (citizens and permanent resident aliens) are less involved than in the area of "domestic intelligence." With the exception of operations conducted abroad not related to American citizens, the assumption is unfounded.

As to the intelligence operations within the United States it is impossible to draw a line, so far as the impact upon American individuals and associations is concerned, between foreign and domestic intelligence activities. In the first place the area covered by the concept of "foreign intelligence" is virtually unlimited. Almost everything that happens within the United States affects the national defense or our relations with foreign countries. Even in its narrow form the concept could be interpreted to cover much of the political activity that takes place in the United States. Secondly, whatever the scope of the area involved, the intelligence agencies cannot engage in operations in that sector that do not infringe upon the First Amendment, Fourth Amendment, and other rights of Americans. The targets of intelligence operations cannot be limited to non-Americans and the range of investigatory activities cannot be confined to them. On the contrary the power conferred on the intelligence agencies would reach to every American who was a member of an organization that had any connection with a foreign power. It would likewise extend to any American who possessed information that was of interest to a foreign power, a category that includes virtually every scientist in the country. Even the most limited form of "foreign intelligence" activity imaginable, a wiretap on a foreign embassy, would inevitably involve surveillance of Americans.

Furthermore, reliance upon the extended powers of the president in the area of foreign affairs is misplaced. The reason that the president is deemed to have greater inherent powers in the conduct of foreign relations is because effectiveness in such matters requires a single head, demands a capacity for immediate decision, and requires flexibility. These factors do not apply to the conduct of intelligence operations within the United States, whether "foreign" or "domestic" in nature.

As to American citizens abroad, the Supreme Court has held that they still retain their rights under the American Constitution. There is no reason why, in dealing with officials of their own country, they should not have the same rights as they would have within the United States.

For these reasons it is not permissible to make different rules for the conduct of "foreign intelligence" and "domestic intelligence." Except for activities in foreign countries that do not affect American citizens, the standards of protection for Americans, not foreigners, should govern.

6. *Adequate controls to enforce legislation governing the intelligence agencies require measures that will provide accountability, internal oversight, and external oversight.*

Enactment of legislative controls over the intelligence agencies is one thing; implementation of them is another. Control of any bureaucracy is difficult, but control of the intelligence bureaucracy is particularly hard to achieve. The intelligence agencies operate under a cloak of secrecy. They develop powerful tendencies, as the career of J. Edgar Hoover demonstrates, to go their own way. Government officials, including the courts, are reluctant to criticize, expose, or penalize, fearing that such intervention may harm the national security. In short, the intelligence community tends to become a sacred cow, untouchable by normal methods of control.

In order to overcome these difficulties, legislation must embody a variety of devices, operating at the following three levels.

Accountability. Accountability requires a system of record-keeping and reporting. Significant decisions, such as the decision to initiate an investigation, should be recorded in writing, with the facts and reasons given, by the official responsible. Ad hoc and periodic reports should be required. The objective is to create a "paper trail," by which individual responsibility can be assigned and the basis for review made available.

Internal oversight. Internal oversight should extend beyond the ordinary methods of supervision by superior officials in the line of authority. The best method of securing an independent check of performance is probably an inspector-general system. In addition, departmental heads or similar officials should exercise oversight through control of the budget and other devices.

Outside oversight. Some method of oversight by persons totally outside the agency and its department is essential. Legislative committees have a power base from which to maintain such oversight. While they have not been very effective in the past it may be possible to improve their performance. A board of overseers composed of prominent persons outside the government, if given an adequate staff, could perform an adequate oversight function. And the General Accounting Office, which is independent of the executive branch and possesses a staff trained in investigating the government bureaucracy, might be most effective of all. Any such oversight agency should, of course, have full access to all agency operations and complete power to investigate complaints or institute an inquiry on its own motion.

Other aids to implementation are also available. These include special procedures in cases affecting First Amendment rights, imposition of time limits on the conduct of investigations, extension of the civil service to FBI and CIA employees, provision for special prosecutors, and measures to increase the effectiveness of civil suits brought against officials violating constitutional or statutory rights.

It should be added that this machinery for securing compliance with legislative restrictions can operate successfully only in a context marked by the maximum possible openness, including publication of budgets, protection for "whistle-blowers," encouragement of investigative reporting, and a public concern to know what is going on.

Proposed Legislation

Legislation to control the intelligence agencies has been under discussion for well over two years. The principal measures pending are: (1) H.R. 6051, the Federal Intelligence Activities Control Act, a comprehensive bill drafted by a group headed by the American Civil Liberties Union; (2) S. 1556/H.R. 7308, the Foreign Intelligence Surveillance Act, a bill regulating electronic surveillance in the "foreign intelligence" area; (3) S. 2525/H.R. 11245, the National Intelligence Reorganization and Reform Act, a bill drafted by the Senate Intelligence Committee dealing with all aspects of "foreign intelligence"; and (4) proposals under consideration by a subcommittee of the Senate Judiciary Committee for the creation of "charters" for the agencies operating in the "domestic intelligence" field.

H.R. 6051

H.R. 6051, introduced in April 1977 by then Representative Herman Badillo and ultimately sponsored by over a score of members of the House, conforms very closely to the six principles set forth above, and indeed in some respects goes beyond them. It defines and prohibits "political surveillance," "preventive action," and "selective investigations or prosecutions"; and it repeals various speech crime statutes. With respect to methods of investigation it prohibits electronic surveillance altogether, limits the use of informers by forbidding intelligence officials to allow an informant to pose as a member of a group engaged in First Amendment activities, and requires a warrant procedure for inspection of records or the use of mail covers. The name of the Federal Bureau of Investigation is changed to the Federal Bureau of Criminal Investigation (FBCI) and its function is limited to investigation of violations of criminal law. The name of the Central Intelligence Agency is changed to the Foreign Information Service and it is prohibited from engaging not only in "covert actions" but in any clandestine espionage activities, except in time of war.

H.R. 6051 also contains numerous provisions dealing with administration and implementation. Thus it sets forth in detail the procedures to be followed by the new FBCI; provides for accountability, supervision, and oversight of FBCI operations; creates criminal penalties and civil liabilities for violation; and requires open budgets for the FBCI and the Foreign Information Service. In addition the bill contains various ancillary provisions. It amends the Freedom of Information Act to limit secrecy in intelligence operations; establishes criminal penalties for "official deceit"; attempts to protect "whistle blowing"; and creates a system of temporary special prosecutors.

H.R. 6051 sets a high standard of strict controls. In outlawing all electronic surveillance and in forbidding the CIA to engage in any clandestine operations in peacetime, it apparently goes beyond what most members of Congress are willing to support. In any event it has received little attention. No hearings have been held or scheduled.

S. 1556/H.R. 7308

S. 1556/H.R. 7308, the Foreign Intelligence Surveillance Act, deals only with the use of electronic data in "foreign intelligence" operations, the area left open by the Supreme Court's decision in the *United States District Court* case. While thus relatively narrow in scope, the bill nevertheless raises several issues of crucial importance to the entire problem. In its progress through the Senate, S. 1556 has been the subject of extensive discussion and negotiation between members of Congress of different political persuasions, the Department of Justice, the intelligence agencies, interested organizations, and the general public. As a result it has become a sort of testing ground for legislation to control the intelligence agencies. In the form in which it reached the Senate floor, S. 1556 received broad support and passed the Senate in April by a vote of 95 to 1. Its counterpart, H.R. 7308, passed the House on September 7, containing some changes from the Senate version. The bill was sent to conference.

The Foreign Intelligence Surveillance Act is limited to electronic surveillance conducted in the United States; it does not apply to operations abroad. "Electronic surveillance" includes wiretapping, bugging, and other use of mechanical equipment to intercept communications. Different rules are applicable to "United States persons" (defined as American citizens and permanent resident aliens) and to foreigners.

As to "United States persons" the bill authorizes electronic surveillance, after securing a court warrant, in order to obtain "foreign intelligence information" from a "foreign power," or from an "agent of a foreign power." "Foreign intelligence information" is broadly defined to include information that is necessary to the "national defense," the "conduct of foreign affairs," or protection against "clandestine intelligence activities" of a foreign power or an agent of a foreign power. Obviously this definition of "foreign intelligence information" brings a wide range of activities within the coverage of the statute. There is virtually no limit to information necessary to national defense, foreign relations, and counterintelligence.

There are, however, limits upon the individuals or organizations that can be targeted. Electronic surveillance can be used only against a "foreign power" or an "agent of a foreign power."

The term "foreign power" is defined to include not only a foreign government or a foreign political organization but "an entity which is directed or controlled by a foreign government." Since the United States government has always contended that the Communist Party of the United States is dominated and controlled by a foreign government, and indeed the Supreme Court has upheld that finding, it would appear that political organizations with foreign connections could be made the target of electronic surveillance whether or not they were suspected of any violation of law.

The term "agent of a foreign power" is more narrowly defined. It includes any person (individual or organization) who (1) knowingly engages in "clandestine intelligence gathering activities" (undefined) for or on behalf of a foreign power which "involve or may involve" a violation of a criminal statute; and (2) any person who "aids or abets" or "conspires" with another person in such activities. This provision embodies a "criminal standard"; that is, only a person who is suspected of violating a criminal law may be targeted for electronic surveillance. It should be noted, however, that the standard is couched in weak terms: it is sufficient if the activity not only does involve but "may" involve a law violation. Moreover, the criminal standard applies only to the initial target; it does not protect innocent third parties who may be in communication with the target.

Foreigners (non–United States persons) are governed by a different standard. They may be targeted for electronic surveillance if (1) they are an "officer or employee" of a foreign power, or (2) the circumstances of their presence in the United States "indicate" that they "may" engage in "clandestine intelligence activities contrary to the interests of the United States," or (3) aid or abet or conspire to do so. Thus the criminal standard is not extended to foreign students, academics, journalists, or other foreign visitors.

The Foreign Intelligence Surveillance Act establishes elaborate procedures for obtaining a warrant. These are designed to prevent abuses against targeted individuals and organizations and to minimize the impact upon third parties whose communications are intercepted.

The procedural provisions, however, contain a number of weaknesses, some of which are inherent in the nature of electronic surveillance. Thus notice of interception need not be given and judicial review is limited because it takes place ex parte, in camera, and the persons aggrieved are not represented. Moreover, any information obtained, even though the search was not based on "probable cause," may be used as evidence in a criminal prosecution for any crime, whether related to national security or not.

The bill declares that its provisions "shall be the exclusive means" by which electronic surveillance may be conducted in the United States. Furthermore it repeals the provision of the 1968 act, which reserves to the president any claimed powers he may have to engage in electronic surveillance without regard to statutory authority. These provisions would make it more difficult for a president to assert "inherent powers" to act alone in the interests of "national security." The Carter administration has expressed its willingness to abide by this mandate. Whether future presidents will continue to claim "inherent powers," despite express legislative prohibition, remains to be seen.

Taken as a whole the Foreign Intelligence Surveillance Act is a substantial improvement over the bill as originally proposed. It contains some good features, such as the rejection of "inherent powers" and the acceptance, at least in part, of the criminal standard. It also contains objectionable features, some of which may be inevitable in any legislation allowing electronic surveillance. Moreover, viewed as an alternative to the present situation, in which the executive branch conducts electronic surveillance regardless of constitutional and statutory restrictions, its enactment would represent progress. The question whether any electronic surveillance should be allowed, however, still calls for an answer.

S. 2525/H.R. 11245

S. 2525, called the National Intelligence Reorganization and Reform Act of 1978, is the work of the Senate Intelligence Committee. The same bill has been introduced in the House as H.R. 11245. Hearings are in progress in the Senate but no action has been taken in the House.

The bill undertakes to provide the statutory basis for all intelligence activities concerned with the conduct of foreign relations and the protection of national security against dangers from abroad. It establishes the administrative framework for the intelligence agencies, authorizes various intelligence activities, imposes certain limitations, and provides machinery for internal controls, external oversight, and judicial review. The present draft is a long, complex bill, consisting of seven titles and 263 pages. Only a very brief and somewhat cursory summary is possible within the limits of this chapter.

Various sections of S. 2525 establish the scope of authority for intelligence agencies to collect information. The initial area open to them is vast. Thus one provision authorizes the gathering of "information pertaining to capabilities, intentions, or activities of any foreign government in the fields of espionage, other clandestine intelligence collection, covert action, assassination, or sabotage, or pertaining to such government's own efforts to protect against the collection of information on its capabilities, intentions, or activities." Within this area there is no limitation on the collection of "publicly available information." Thus the intelligence agencies are free to compile dossiers on individuals or organizations engaged in political expression or political activities.

The gathering of information that is not "publicly available" is subject to certain limitations, including restriction to information concerning "clandestine activity" that "involves or may involve a violation of the criminal laws of the United States." Upon analysis, however, these limitations prove illusory. Thus "may involve" is wide open and, moreover, not subject to judicial scrutiny as it is in the case of electronic surveillance legislation. Furthermore, there are a number of exceptions to the limitation, including one that permits the collection of information concerning any person who "possesses information or material" that might be the target of any clandestine intelligence activity on behalf of a foreign power. This provision by itself would open virtually the entire scientific community to surveillance. In short, the bill wholly fails to meet the criminal standard.

Other sections of the bill deal with the methods authorized for the collection of information. At least four major features of these provisions raise serious questions. First, the bill authorizes a series of intrusive techniques that may be utilized even when a person is not charged with or suspected of any violation of law. The techniques include examination of tax records, "physical surveillance" (shadowing), use of "covert human sources" (informers), mail covers, and requests for information from confidential records pertaining to employment, education, medical care, telephone calls, and financial matters. Second, the bill provides for "unconsented physical searches" (break-ins), after obtaining a court order, in situations that would not justify a traditional search warrant. Third, informers may be used to infiltrate an organization, provided that participation in the affairs of the organization is "confined to the collection of information" and does not "influence the lawful activities of the organization." Both are unrealistic conditions; the mere casting of a vote, for example, "influences" the affairs of the organization. Fourth, one section of the bill specifically authorizes officers and agents of the intelligence agencies "to commit any violation of the criminal statutes of the United

States" provided the conduct does not involve acts of violence, does not violate other provisions of the bill, and is necessary to protect against espionage, sabotage, international terrorist activity, or assassination. This provision, empowering government officials to commit illegal acts, is unprecedented in American law.

In addition to the collection of information, S. 2525 authorizes the intelligence agencies to engage in preventive action in connection with activities concerned with espionage, clandestine intelligence collection, covert action, sabotage, terrorism, and similar activities of a foreign government; and in connection with the efforts of a foreign government to protect against the collection of information on its capabilities, intentions, or activities. The powers conferred are vague and amorphous, and subject to few limitations. Their use on a major scale, however, is clearly contemplated.

The CIA is also authorized to carry on "covert action" abroad, now to be called "special activity in support of foreign policy objectives." That term is defined as activity that is "(A) designed to further official United States programs and policies abroad, and (B) planned and executed so that the role of the United States Government is not apparent or acknowledged publicly." Some limitations are imposed, including a prohibition against activity that has as its object or is likely to result in support of international terrorist activities; mass destruction of property; creation of food or water shortages, floods, or epidemics; "the violent overthrow of the democratic government of any country"; and torture. Most of these limitations, however, may be waived by the president when there is "a grave and immediate threat to the national security."

S. 2525 contains some provisions limiting the conduct of the intelligence agencies in the exercise of the powers conferred. Thus no agency may pay or provide valuable consideration to "any United States person following a full-time religious vocation" to engage in intelligence activities or provide information; this is also subject to presidential waiver. Similar restrictions, but not subject to waiver, are imposed on the use of journalists. There is also a general prohibition against interference with the exercise of constitutional and statutory rights, which is apparently qualified by the authority, noted above, to engage in illegal acts. There are no provisions, however, that affirmatively and specifically forbid the intelligence agencies to engage in most of the abuses that have characterized their operations in the past, such as political surveillance, selective investigations, break-ins, and similar conduct.

The administrative provisions of S. 2525 constitute the most effective portions of the bill. Accountability is secured through requirements that certain activities be authorized in writing and through a system of reporting. Oversight is provided within the agencies by creating the offices of general counsel and inspector general, and outside the agencies by the General Accounting Office, the Intelligence Oversight Board, and congressional committees. Judicial review is available through criminal penalties and civil suits. Whistle blowing is given some protection.

Even here, however, there are deficiencies. The oversight provisions rely too heavily upon obtaining reports of failure to comply with the provisions of the bill, rather than upon routine inspections. The criminal sanctions extend only to illegal searches and unauthorized human experimentation. And the civil sanctions provide only for the recovery of damages and make no provision for injunctions.

In general, S. 2525 falls far short of meeting the standards embodied in the six principles set forth above. As it stands now its effect would be largely to give statutory authorization for many of the past practices of the intelligence agencies against which legislative protection is needed.

Charters for Agencies Engaged in Domestic Intelligence Operations

The Subcommittee on Administrative Practices and Procedures of the Senate Judiciary Committee has undertaken to draft "charters" for the intelligence agencies operating in the domestic intelligence field. Hearings have been held but thus far no draft of legislation has been made public. The Department of Justice is apparently urging the preparation of comprehensive law enforcement legislation that would delay the adoption of investigative controls. The work of the subcommittee should be followed closely but no specific appraisal is possible at this time.

Other Related Issues

A number of issues have risen that, although they have wider ramifications, also bear upon the problems of controlling the intelligence agencies. The more important ones should be noted briefly.

Government Secrecy

One of the major difficulties in controlling the intelligence agencies lies in the secrecy surrounding their operations. Much of what they do must, of course, remain concealed, at least temporarily. But secrecy always breeds abuse, renders oversight ineffective, and prevents public scrutiny. Plainly openness should be sought and secrecy held to a minimum.

Secrecy in intelligence activities is, of course, part of a larger problem of secrecy in government generally. During the mid-1970s significant advances were made in opening up government operations to public view. Legislative committees became more active, government employees and former employees more willing to disclose information, and the Freedom of Information Act was amended to make it more effective. In the last two years, however, strenuous efforts have been made to reverse this favorable trend.

One feature of these countermoves has been the attempt by the government to interpret existing espionage laws as imposing criminal penalties upon persons who disclose any national defense or classified information, thereby in effect creating an official secrets act. The Truong-Humphrey prosecution is based on this contention. Another aspect of the campaign has been the call for legislation to make unauthorized disclosures by government employees a criminal offense. A third feature has been the expanding use of contracts of silence imposed upon government employees, and the enforcement of such contracts through civil suits seeking injunction or damages. In the *Snepp* case the government is attempting to obtain substantial damages on the basis of such a contract even though it admits that no classified information was revealed.

Another effort to reduce openness in government centers around the Freedom of Information Act. That legislation has been particularly useful in obtaining an inside view of the workings of the FBI and the CIA. Now proposals are being put forward to curtail the amount of information that the intelligence agencies must disclose under the Freedom of Information Act. Enactment of such legislation would be a severe blow to efforts to establish civilian control over the intelligence community.

Budgets

The budgets for the CIA and other national intelligence operations have never been made public. Each year appropriations are concealed in appropriations for other agencies and even most members of Congress do not know how much money the national intelligence agencies have or how they spend it. This takes place every year despite the provision of the Constitution, already mentioned, that "a regular statement of account of the receipts and expenditures of all public money shall be published from time to time."

In May 1977 the Senate Intelligence Committee, without objection from the Carter administration, voted 9 to 8 to make the total amount of the national intelligence budget public. Even this modest proposal never reached the floor of the Senate or the House. There is no good reason why the American people should not know the total amount of national intelligence appropriations, just as they know the total of our defense appropriations. Moreover, while the issue is more arguable, there are strong reasons for insisting that the basic details of these budgets be made public also.

Government Immunity

It has long been a precept of Anglo-American law that, while the government itself was sovereign and could not be sued in the courts, government officials were liable in their individual capacity for actions done in violation of law. Civil suits against government officials have never been a simple or easy way for individual citizens to secure redress against governmental malpractices. Yet they have had a significant impact in keeping government officials within legal bounds. In this modern age the doctrine of individual liability is indispensable to maintaining some vestige of control over a huge, impersonal bureaucracy—it is especially useful in the case of the intelligence agencies. One particular feature of value has been that discovery proceedings in the course of such litigation have been a fruitful source of information about intelligence operations.

The doctrine imposing personal liability upon government officials for violation of law is now under serious attack. The courts have tended to develop theories of complete or partial immunity that have more and more isolated government officials from vulnerability to civil suits. Various legislative proposals have been advanced to accomplish the same result. Thus S. 1, an earlier version of the bill to reform the Federal Criminal Code, included provisions that amounted to a Nuremberg defense, granting immunity where the government official acted under orders of a superior. S. 2525, discussed above, would allow immunity where an employee of an intelligence agency relied upon a written order or directive or upon the opinion of legal counsel.

The most immediate threat to the doctrine of individual liability is pending legislation, primarily the product of the Department of Justice, that would amend the Federal Tort Claims Act. S. 3314/H.R. 9219; while providing for recovery against the United States itself for violation of constitutional rights, it would relieve individual government officials of liability if those officials believed that their actions were within the scope of their duties and were thought by them to be lawful. S. 3314, but not H.R. 9219, includes provisions for internal disciplinary proceedings as a substitute for the curtailment of civil liability; clearly such a system, administered by the bureaucracy itself, can hardly take the place of resort to court action. The net effect of this legislation, if enacted, would be to virtually eliminate any personal responsibility or accountability by government officials for their illegal acts.

Terrorism

One of the principal arguments against imposing limitations on the operation of the intelligence agencies is that strict controls would render the intelligence agencies incapable of protecting the nation against political terrorism. The argument has been persuasive to some people but it has little substance. In the first place, political terrorism in the United States is not now a pressing problem and it may never become one. In the second place acts of terrorism are violations of existing federal and state laws. The intelligence agencies would not be restricted in their investigation of such acts, except to the extent that they are required to conform to constitutional mandates. Thirdly, the ability of the intelligence agencies to anticipate or prevent terrorism has not been significant; such acts of terrorism as have occurred in the United States, such as the assassination of President Kennedy and Dr. Martin Luther King, Jr., were not foreseen by the intelligence agencies. Nor is their capacity for prevention likely to increase, short of establishment of a police state. Finally, terrorism is a phenomenon that must be forestalled or dealt with by measures far removed from the activities of the intelligence agencies. Indeed, abusive practices by the intelligence agencies will in the end only undermine public confidence in the government and accentuate rather than retard resort to terrorist acts.

Information Systems

A major threat to privacy in the United States arises out of the development of interlocking computer banks, making data upon every aspect of the life of every citizen readily available to the government and to others. The problem, of course, goes far beyond the operations of the intelligence agencies. The important point for our purposes is that control over information systems be divorced, so far as possible, from intelligence operations. The intelligence agencies have enough power as it is, without adding to their capacity for invading privacy.

State and Local Intelligence Agencies

The activities of state and local intelligence agencies must not be overlooked. Many state and local agencies have been guilty of the same abusive practices as the federal agencies. Indeed, more people have undoubtedly been affected by their activities than by those of the federal agencies. In general the same principles of control apply to the state and local intelligence agencies as to the federal; and the same problems of initiating such controls are present.

Model legislation for the control of state and local intelligence agencies has been drafted by the Center for National Security Studies. It has been considered by several city legislative bodies but thus far has not been adopted by any.

Conclusions

Bringing the intelligence agencies under control is one of the major problems confronting the American people today. Unfortunately the propitious time is running out. The vivid memories of intelligence agency abuses, and the feelings of outrage, are beginning to fade. Opponents of control are seeking delay, knowing time is on their side. One can only hope that the issues will be moved to a conclusion during the next session of Congress.

FIVE

DUE PROCESS OF LAW
AND GOVERNMENTAL INVESTIGATIONS
Peter M. Kreindler

As the years pass the power of government becomes more and more pervasive. It is a power to suffocate both people and causes.
— *Douglas, dissenting in* Branzburg v. Hayes, *408 U.S. 665, 724 (1972).*

The Grand Jury: From Knight to Serf

The Constitution recognizes but one accusatory body. Under the Fifth Amendment, "no person shall be held to answer for a capital, or otherwise infamous crime, *unless* on a presentment or indictment of a Grand Jury." This fundamental right stands side-by-side with other bedrock protections secured by the Constitution for one charged with an offense against the State: the ban against double jeopardy, the privilege against self-incrimination, and the guarantee of due process of law.

Original Concept

The constitutional status of the grand jury bespeaks "the high place it held as an instrument of justice."[1] As wrested from King John at Runnymeade, the grand jury was to stand between the accuser and the accused, the Crown and the defendant, to assure that a criminal trial was a response to a well-founded belief that the defendant may have committed a crime and was not the vehicle for baseless persecution. A body of laymen, acting independently of prosecutor and judge, free of technical legal and evidentiary rules, was to interpose a communal judgment before the oppressive weight of criminal prosecution could be brought to bear on the individual. The basic function of the grand jury remained the same for the next five centuries and was carried forward into the Constitution as one of the principal institutional safeguards of personal and political liberty.

In *Wood v. Georgia* (1962), Chief Justice Warren stated that the grand jury "has been regarded as a primary security to the innocent against hasty, malicious and oppressive persecution; it serves the invaluable function in our society of standing between the accuser and the accused,

Peter M. Kreindler is a member of Hughes, Hubbard & Reed, Washington, D.C.

whether the latter be an individual, minority group, or other, to determine whether a charge is founded upon reason or was dictated by an intimidating power or by malice and personal ill will."[2] In that case, the Supreme Court reversed the contempt conviction of a local Georgia sheriff for allegedly "obstructing" a grand jury investigation. The local judge had impaneled a grand jury to investigate "an inane and inexplicable pattern of Negro bloc voting," and the sheriff had responded with an open letter to the grand jury deploring the judge's instructions to the jury as "race agitation" and imploring the jury not to "let its high office be a party to any political attempt to intimidate the negro people in the community." Rather than obstructive, the Supreme Court found the sheriff's letter fully supportive of the grand jury's function.

While the Court since that time has alluded to the grand jury's historic role, the Court has done so only to pay it lip service. In *Branzburg v. Hayes* (1972), for example, the Court referred to the "dual function of determining if there is probable cause to believe that a crime has been committed and of protecting citizens against unfounded criminal investigations."[3] But far from advancing the values served by the Fifth Amendment, *Branzburg* added significantly to the inquisitorial powers of the grand jury by upholding the right of the grand jury, despite the First Amendment, to require newsmen to testify about confidential sources—in this case in the context of an investigation of the Black Panthers. As I discuss below, *Branzburg* is part of a quickening trend of sacrificing individual freedom guaranteed by the Bill of Rights— whether it be the freedom of press, speech, or association of the First Amendment, the ban on unreasonable searches and seizures of the Fourth Amendment, or the self-incrimination clause of the Fifth Amendment—to the understandable desire to solve more crimes and secure more convictions. It is when that desire turns to zealousness, and when prosecution is but a euphemism for persecution, that the grand jury must step into the breach.

Expansion of Prosecutorial Control

As late as 1974 the Court proclaimed that the "Grand Jury's historic functions survive to this day."[4] But judges and prosecutors alike for years have acknowledged that this view of the grand jury has long been outmoded. No longer independent, the grand jury is hardly more than a rubber stamp for the decisions of the prosecutor, whether in summoning witnesses or returning indictments. As Justice Douglas has put it, "the grand jury, having been conceived as a bulwark between the citizen and the Government, is now a tool of the Executive."[5] While the Supreme Court in recent years has done little to stem the demise of the grand jury as a protector of the accused, the cause of the demise was endemic to the very nature and constitution of the grand jury, as long as it is operated under its traditional procedures.

Whether in England at the time of the Magna Carta or in the eighteenth-century colonial America, the grand jury was composed of local citizens, well versed in the affairs of their compatriots. It was no difficult task for them to weigh charges brought before them. They often could appraise the merits of a proposed prosecution from their own knowledge or from information gleaned from their neighbors. Under those circumstances, the jurors could bring an independent view to bear on the matters laid before them. The secrecy of their proceedings supported their independence by shielding them from the influence of the Crown or State.

Today, it is the rare case, indeed, when grand jurors have the faintest familiarity with the facts of the crimes they are asked to investigate. The grand jury's geographical responsibility covers large areas, and the jurors' legal "neighbors" and "peers" are no more than strangers. The laws to be applied are complex, often leaving judges and lawyers in doubt as to their meaning and application. In these circumstances the jurors are captives of the prosecutor, wholly dependent upon him for the evidence brought before them and for the interpretation of the laws they are to uphold. While grand jurors theoretically retain the power to act independently—for example, to summon witnesses on their own—the stranglehold of the prosecutor as a practical matter is unrelenting, and the "independence" of the grand jury alluded to by the courts is little more than a fiction. In short, any experienced prosecutor can obtain an indictment of whom he wants, when he wants it. Secrecy, rather than shielding the grand jurors from undue influence, now permits the prosecutor to work his will without effective oversight by the courts and cuts off the jurors from additional sources of information that might be invaluable to informed, responsible deliberation.

This is not to say that abuse of the system is rampant. While an occasional prosecutor in the run-of-the-mill cases may be overbearing or overzealous,[6] the majority of grand jury investigations are straightforward, conducted in good faith, and pose no danger to the fundamental rights of the accused. But there is grave danger in the area of political dissent. It was not so long ago that the Nixon administration, through the Internal Security Division of the Department of Justice, launched its carefully planned assault on the anti-Vietnam war movement and disparate dissident organizations. One grand jury investigation after another was opened, all coordinated from Washington. Their targets ranged from the Weathermen to the Catholic Left to those responsible for publishing the Pentagon Papers.

Conspiracy was the watchword, and the family and friends of the putative defendants, as well as reporters and academics sympathetic to the antiwar movement, were swept into the dragnet of subpoenas and interrogations that probed associations and beliefs far more than the details of specific substantive offenses.

As two observers commented at the time, the investigations raised the specter that "the grand juries were being groomed to replace the moribund and powerless congressional anti-subversive committees as instruments of harassment and of domestic political intelligence."[7] We now know that their observations were more insight than hysteria. The government's attempts to prosecute the conspiracy indictments resulting from the grand jury investigations met with remarkably little success. This interlude of grand jury abuse is looked back upon with virtually universal condemnation.

The opportunity for abuse stems in large measure from the one-sided accusatorial role of the grand jury. Its proceedings are rarely, if ever, punctuated by any of the procedural safeguards that have characterized our adversary system of justice. While other aspects of the criminal justice system have kept pace with developing notions of due process, the grand jury remains in the same state in which it was spawned in 1787. Witnesses are not entitled to be accompanied by counsel; they are not provided transcripts of their testimony; targets have no right to confront or cross-examine their accusers or to present exculpatory evidence.

The typical response to charges that the grand jury has become a latter-day Star Chamber is that any defendant has the opportunity to vindicate himself at trial. Anyone who has been touched by the criminal justice system, however, knows that acquittal at a trial is small consolation for the anguish and cost of defending against an indictment. Moreover, even a "not guilty" verdict cannot expunge the inevitable stigma that attaches to an indictment. Nor is there much room for pride in the trial jury's grudging finding, latent with negative implications, that there is less than proof beyond a reasonable doubt that you are a criminal. "The risk of prosecution," Justice Douglas has said, "is not a risk which the wise take lightly."[8]

The grand jury is no longer simply a sounding board for the prosecutor's case, used to give the requisite approval to an indictment framed by evidence obtained through traditional law enforcement means. Instead, it has been used increasingly as an investigative tool of the prosecutor, brought into play where classic police techniques have been unavailing. Thus, at the same time that the grand jury, as a result of changing sociological circumstances, has quiescently ceded its histori- cal function as a shield against prosecutorial overreaching, it is being forced into the role of an active, but unwitting adjunct to the prosecutor's investigatory activities. It is no revelation that the grand jury subpoena, more often than not issued by the prosecutor without the grand jury's knowledge, has become an integral part of criminal investigations. Prosecutors, lacking independent compulsory process, have resorted to the grand jury for police and intelligence purposes. During the Vietnam war, the grand jury "emerg[ed] as the 'chosen instrument' of [the Nixon] Administration strategy to curb dissent."[9] The burgeoning use of the grand jury subpoena threatens fundamental values of individual freedom and privacy, however, because of the recent circumscription of the Fourth and Fifth amendments. As Justice Douglas warned long before the Nixon administration abuses, without the right of privacy, "the Fourth Amendment and the Fifth are ready instruments for the police state that the Framers sought to avoid."[10]

Elimination of Safeguards against Abuse

The lower courts in recent years had responded to a growing sense that grand jury procedures permitted prosecutors to take unfair advantage of their targets, and the courts had begun to impose certain minimal procedural protections. They had required prosecutors to advise witnesses of their rights, just as the Warren Court in *Miranda* had required police to do when interrogating suspects. They had required prosecutors to advise a witness who was a target of the investigation of his impending status as a defendant so that he could more keenly assess the consequences of his testimony. Failure to give the warnings could lead to suppression of the witness' testimony or dismissal of the indictment. Courts also had barred a prosecution for perjury before the grand jury where the prosecutor had called the witness with the purpose of eliciting perjurious testimony.

In a series of three rulings the Burger Court reversed each of the reforms.[11] These decisions signify an abrupt halt to a trend in the lower courts to apply generalized notions of due process to the grand jury, leaving it clear that a witness' protection before the grand jury is limited to the express commands of the Fourth Amendment and the self-incrimination clause of the Fifth Amendment. At the same time, however, the Supreme Court has been forging an increasingly narrow and begrudging interpretation of the Fourth and Fifth amendments. This is a far more serious concern in light of the evolving nature of the grand jury.

It has never been seriously disputed that the proscription of unreasonable searches and seizures and the privilege against self-incrimination apply in the grand jury context. In *Hale v. Henkel* (1906), for example, the Supreme Court held that the Fourth Amendment limits

the permissible scope of grand jury subpoenas requiring the production
of documents:

> While a search ordinarily implies a quest by an officer of the law, and a
> seizure contemplates a forcible dispossession of the owner, still, as was
> held in the *Boyd* case, the substance of the offense is the compulsory
> production of private papers, whether under a search warrant or a
> *subpoena duces tecum*, against which the person, be he individual or
> corporation, is entitled to protection.[12]

Hale v. Henkel also made clear that, at least in the absence of immunity,
a witness could not be compelled to testify before the grand jury if his
testimony would implicate him in criminal activity subject to
prosecution.

Boyd v. United States (1886)[13] was then the seminal case delineating
the reach of the Fourth and Fifth amendment protections that *Hale v.
Henkel* subsumed within the contours of grand jury proceedings. *Boyd*
marked out a substantial zone of privacy to be free from governmental
intrusion. Under the Fourth Amendment it held that the government
could not seize a person's documents unless it had a superior right to
possession and title—for example, if the documents were contraband.
This gave rise to the so-called mere evidence rule: search warrants
could not be issued for items that were simply evidence that a crime had
been committed, and a person's private papers, if they were not
themselves the instrumentalities of crime, could not be seized. Under the
Fifth Amendment, the Court held that the use of such documents against
a person without the person's permission compelled the person to be a
witness against himself in violation of the self-incrimination clause.

Reaffirming its decision in *Boyd*, the Court thirty-five years later
found it impossible

> to add to the emphasis with which the framers of our Constitution and this
> court . . . have declared the importance to political liberty and to the
> welfare of our country of the due observance of the rights guaranteed by
> these two Amendments. . . . It has been repeatedly decided that these
> Amendments should receive a liberal construction, so as to prevent
> stealthy encroachment upon or "gradual depreciation" of the rights
> secured by them, by imperceptible practice of courts, or by well-
> intentioned but mistakenly over-zealous executive officers.[14]

Regrettably, the "depreciation" of these rights and the concomitant
sacrifice of individual liberty and privacy have come, not only at the
hands of errant or overreaching prosecutors, but also by deliberate
decision of the Supreme Court. Although the process of erosion to some

extent has been a steady one, starting as early as last century, it has accelerated in recent years.

In 1896 the Court first held that the privilege against self-incrimination pertains only when a person may subject himself to criminal prosecution as a result of his testimony. Thus, a person can be compelled to declare his involvement in criminal activity, even if his declaration exposes him to public obloquy and civil disabilities, through the simple expedient of granting him immunity.[15] The Court's holding was echoed again in 1956[16] and, most recently, in 1972 when the Court in a well-publicized and highly controversial decision held that so-called use immunity, rather than "transactional" immunity, suffices.[17] To Justice Douglas, however, who registered among the dissenters in the last two of the three cases, the self-incrimination clause "is not only a protection against conviction and prosecution, but a safeguard of conscience and human dignity and freedom of expression as well. . . . Oppression occurs when infamy is imposed on the citizen by the State."

The Fifth Amendment protection against use of a person's own documents as part and parcel of the government's case also has all but evaporated. In *Couch v. United States* (1973), the Court held that the privilege applies only when the court's process compels the accused to give testimony. There, the Court held that a taxpayer could not object to a subpoena addressed to her accountant covering her personal tax records. The Court, however, seemingly reaffirmed the long-standing protection against compelled production by the accused herself. In reaching its decision, the Court emphasized that "inquisitorial pressure or coercion against a potentially accused person, compelling her, against her will, to utter self-condemning words or *produce incriminating documents* is absent."[18]

Nonetheless, just three years later, relying on cases requiring the giving of blood samples and handwriting and voice exemplars, the Court has indicated that even production of incriminating papers by the accused does not fall within the privilege, unless the compelled act of production is itself testimonial.[19] That is, a person can be required to disclose documents that implicate him criminally so long as his implicit representation that the documents are his is not a necessary part of the government's case. Thus, for example, under the Court's rationale, if a handwriting expert could identify the documents as authored by the accused, the accused's "admission" that the documents were his would not be necessary to introduce the documents into evidence.

The Court's holding technically reaches only business, rather than personal papers, but the underlying premise of the decision has no limitation in terms of the character of the documents involved. It would appear to extend to "a personal diary containing forthright confessions of crime."[20] Justice Marshall, in a surprising concurrence in the Court's judgment, expressed confidence that lower courts will be quick to find "inherent" testimony in the production of private papers so that they would remain beyond the prosecutor's reach. Justice Brennan was not so sanguine. The trend is sufficiently clear that one can conclude, with unsettling confidence, that Justice Brennan's prediction will prove to be far closer to truth. To Justice Brennan, the decision is a "portent . . . of a serious crippling of the protection secured by the privilege."[21]

The most significant aspect of the Court's decision—because of the far-reaching effects it will undoubtedly have on the lower courts—was the categorical denial that the Fifth Amendment serves any privacy interest beyond the express limitation on "compelled testimonial self-incrimination":

> The Framers addressed the subject of personal privacy directly in the Fourth Amendment. They struck a balance so that when the State's reason to believe incriminating evidence will be found becomes sufficiently great, the invasion of privacy becomes justified and a warrant to search and seize will issue. They did not seek in still another Amendment—the Fifth—to achieve a general protection of privacy but to deal with the more specific issue of compelled self-incrimination.[22]

Throughout his tenure on the bench, Justice Douglas, sensitive to the commitment to fundamental liberty that underlay the Fifth Amendment, eschewed this parochial approach. He perceived that "those who wrote the Bill of Rights believed that every individual needs both to communicate with others and to keep his affairs to himself. That dual aspect of privacy means that the individual should have the freedom to select for himself the time and circumstances when he will share his secrets with others and decide the extent of that sharing."[23] Speaking even of the limited intrusion on privacy sanctioned by *Couch*, he voiced the fear that the Court's approach would quickly "stultify the exchange of ideas that we have considered crucial to our democracy."[24] The danger of now committing one's thoughts and ideas to paper is self-evident. The dilemma, of course, is that the pace and complexity of life require written discourse—discourse that all of the parties intend to be private.

The Court's focus on the Fourth Amendment as a privacy refuge offers little solace to the grand jury witness. The "mere-evidence rule" met its demise ten years ago,[25] and all documents, of whatever character, are now subject to subpoena. The Court's recent pronouncement in *Fisher* suggests that the courts will restrict "subpoenas which suffer from 'too much indefiniteness or breadth in the things required to be "particularly described." ' "[26] The Court's statement, however, may be most notable for its omission of any reference to *Hale v. Henkel,* which held that some "necessity" or "evidence of . . . materiality" must be shown to justify a subpoena requiring the production of documents. One searches the cases in vain for any meaningful review of grand jury subpoenas by the courts to assure that their scope is justified by the needs of the grand jury or that there is probable cause for an intrusion into a person's records. Indeed, in *United States v. Dionisio,* the Supreme Court cautioned against requiring any "preliminary showings" that "impede [the grand jury's] investigation and frustrate the public's interest in fair and expeditious administration of the criminal laws."[27]

In *Dionisio,* the Court held that a grand jury subpoena requiring a person to appear solely to give testimony is not subject to any Fourth Amendment constraints because it does not result in a seizure. At least one lower court has questioned whether, in light of this decision, the Fourth Amendment retains any vitality at all as applied to the grand jury.

The story of the Court's about-face would not be complete without referring to *United States v. Calandra.*[28] The holding is simple: a witness before the grand jury may not refuse to answer questions on the ground that they are based on evidence seized in violation of the Fourth Amendment. The decision is one of several of the Burger Court restricting the exclusionary rule, ostensibly because barring use of the illegally seized evidence would not be a substantial deterrent to future Fourth Amendment violations. The Court added, however, that questions addressed to the witness do not themselves trench on the individual's privacy because a "witness has no right of privacy before the grand jury." The Fourth Amendment violation, according to the Court, is "fully accomplished by the original search without probable cause. Grand jury questions based on [that] evidence involve no independent governmental invasion of one's person, house, papers, or effects, but rather the usual abridgment of personal privacy common to all grand jury questioning." No amount of semantics or double-talk can undercut the inescapable conclusion that the intrusion by the grand jury into the witness' personal affairs would not have been possible but for the illegal police action.

Calandra, at the same time that it trumpets the importance of the grand jury as a shield against the executive, undercuts the grand jury's ability to perform that function. After *Calandra,* a grand jury can be induced to rely on evidence that the prosecutor ultimately will not be able to use at trial. Moreover, the grand jurors may never be aware that the prosecutor does not have the "air-tight" case he has presented to them. *Calandra* thus opens the door for an indictment to be used not to begin a prosecution that the government believes it can win, but to harass and intimidate defendants who he may believe are guilty but cannot convict.

Need for Reform

The carefully drawn balance of the Bill of Rights, in which the grand jury played a central role, has given way to the popular call for more effective law enforcement. The aphorism that "the public has a right to every man's evidence" has been the opening wedge and driving force behind the decline of the First, Fourth, and Fifth amendments as effective limitations on the government's investigatory powers, and where constitutional rights must be weighed against the power of the State, the scales are tipping against the Bill of Rights. The time has come to redress the balance and restore the grand jury to its historic role, as well as to reinstate privacy as a protected value.

There is a growing sensitivity to the need for grand jury reform that extends beyond the traditional ranks of civil libertarians. Several bills were introduced in the last Congress that served as a focal point for debate. Principal changes proposed by these bills include (1) mandatory instructions to grand jurors informing them of their rights and responsibilities; (2) expanded rights of witnesses, including the right to have counsel present in the grand jury room and the right to have subpoenas quashed in specified circumstances; (3) elimination of nonconsensual immunity; and (4) the general availability of grand jury transcripts.

The Department of Justice predictably has objected to most of the reforms with the repeated refrain that the changes would transform the grand jury from an investigative/charging body into a guilt-determining body and that increased judicial oversight would impede grand jury investigations and delay the ultimate disposition of criminal cases. Instead, the department urges that appropriate reforms be instituted administratively. To this end, the department has issued guidelines to federal prosecutors, which, among other things, establish as a general rule that: (1) witnesses should be advised of their basic rights; (2) "targets" should not be subpoenaed, but should be notified of their status and given the opportunity not to appear; (3) a prosecutor should not present evidence that he knows was obtained in violation of the accused's constitutional rights; and (4) prosecutors should present evidence that directly negates guilt.

These reforms are laudable, and their importance should not be downplayed. The difficulty, of course, is that the guidelines are hortatory only and contain numerous exceptions that can be invoked at the sole discretion of the government. Basic institutional reform, with appropriate judicial oversight, remains necessary to restore the constitutional balance. Moreover, meaningful reform can be accomplished without imposing intolerable burdens or restraints on the grand jury. The outlines of a legislative program follow.

1. Basic instructions to the grand jury by the impaneling judge should be standardized, informing the jurors of their constitutional responsibilities, not only to indict when there is probable cause, but also to act as an independent check on abuses by the prosecutor. The instructions should encourage grand jurors to exercise effective oversight of the proceedings. To facilitate this oversight, subpoenas should be issued only with the concurrence of the grand jury.

2. Witnesses should be advised of their rights, and they should be allowed to be accompanied by counsel in the grand jury room for purposes of advice and consultation. Since a witness already has the right to leave the room to consult counsel, the continued exclusion of counsel can serve only to permit the intimidating atmosphere of the grand jury room to chill his right or to permit high-handed inquisitorial tactics to go unchecked. The counterargument that counsel will engage in obstructionist tactics is a makeweight; courts can be granted the summary power to exclude counsel if he abuses his right to be present.

3. Prosecutors should be barred from using against a person evidence that has been obtained in violation of his constitutional rights. A witness, however, should not be permitted to refuse to answer questions on this ground—that course would lead to interminable minitrials to determine whether the evidence had been obtained illegally, which would unduly delay grand jury proceedings. Instead, it would be a sufficient remedy to dismiss an indictment whenever it was shown that the prosecutor knowingly used such evidence.

4. Witnesses should be granted the right to quash subpoenas calling for the production of private papers that implicate First Amendment or privacy interests, unless the grand jury can demonstrate that its "need" for the documents outweighs the intrusion on these fundamental interests. As we know from the Nixon tapes cases, this is a balance that the courts traditionally have drawn, and the judicial protection should be available to common citizens as well as to presidents. Any delay in grand jury proceedings resulting from this limited judicial review will be more than justified by the safeguarding of the core values of the Bill of Rights.

Courts already have the power to quash unreasonable or unduly burdensome subpoenas, but any legislation should make clear that they are expected to exercise effective oversight of grand jury subpoenas—to insure, for example, that they are not used to harass or intimidate people or to obtain evidence for other proceedings.

5. Immunity should be conferred and testimony compelled only when a witness consents. In the majority of cases, of course, witnesses are all too happy to secure immunity, and, thus, the new limitation would not be a significant restraint on the government's power to obtain testimony. It is in the other cases—where the witness is likely to decline immunity on the grounds of either political or moral principles—that First Amendment values and basic human dignity are at stake and that it is unseemly, to say the least, to confront the witness with the choice of abandoning his principles or suffering the consequences of contempt. Moreover, history has shown that many individuals faced with this choice will go to jail rather than compromise their principles. Thus, we have cheapened the self-incrimination clause without substantial gains in useful testimony.

6. Individuals who have been identified as targets should not be subpoenaed and, in the absence of a special need for secrecy such as a demonstrable danger of flight or retaliation, they should be notified of their status and given the opportunity to appear before the grand jury. Targets also should be given the opportunity to make a written presentation to the foreman of the grand jury suggesting witnesses to be called, avenues of inquiry to be followed, or additional sources of exculpatory evidence. The grand jury could then exercise its own judgment as to the evidence that appropriately should be considered before returning an indictment. Finally, after the prosecutor has decided to seek an indictment of an individual, the individual should be given the opportunity, through counsel, to make a brief oral presentation to the grand jury.

It is these reforms in particular that would free the grand jury from total dependence on the prosecutor as a service for evidence and other information and would permit the grand jury to make an independent judgment as to the proper course and scope of its investigation. While there undoubtedly would be situations in which it would be inappropriate to inform a person of his status as a target—for example, when the target might flee—the independence of the grand jury will be maintained only if that judgment is made by a court and not by the prosecutor.

7. All grand jury proceedings should be transcribed, and, after an indictment has been returned, the defendant should be provided a complete transcript (with the exception of the jurors' actual delibera-tions), including any statements by the prosecutor to the jurors summing up his case or explaining the applicable law.[29] This would serve two essential purposes. First, if a prosecutor knows that his conduct will be subject to scrutiny, he will be less likely to engage in improper tactics, either in examining witnesses or guiding the grand

jury in its deliberations. Second, availability of the transcript will permit judicial review so that indictments secured through deliberate and blatant abuse of the grand jury can be appropriately dismissed. Secrecy of the transcript, on the other hand, serves no real purpose in the majority of cases. It is mere poppycock to suggest, as some have, that disclosure of the transcript will lead to a plethora of new or additional pretrial motions that will significantly delay any trial. District judges have shown themselves more than competent to sift the frivolous from the meritorious and to get on with the cases before them.

*   *   *

I have dealt at some length with the development of the subpoena power in the context of the grand jury. The evolving principles, including the limitations on the right of privacy, apply equally to congressional and administrative investigations, which, as we will see below, play an increasingly important role in the federal investigative scheme.

Administrative Investigations: The Civil Analog to the Grand Jury?

The mushrooming complex of federal regulatory programs and the advent of agencies to administer them have led to an extensive enforcement framework. Regulatory violations, in addition to criminal exposure, may lead to civil fines, forfeitures, or a host of injunctive penalties.

Dangers of Administrative Investigations

Building upon the Administrative Procedure Act, the courts have imposed well-defined restraints on agencies to assure that due process is afforded during the adjudicative stage of any enforcement proceedings. The courts, however, have been reluctant to interfere with or impose upon agency proceedings in the precomplaint or investigative/charging stage. Under the "exhaustion" doctrine, courts normally will not review agency action until all administrative remedies have been pursued. Accordingly, judicial review is generally not available until after a final agency order has been entered. By that time, of course, any procedural challenges to the conduct of the underlying investigation are largely moot: either the respondent has been exonerated, or he has been found guilty, in accordance with the mandated adjudicative procedures. Any violation of his rights either has been "cured" or "cleansed."

Even when the courts have reviewed the conduct of administrative investigations, they have held that traditional safeguards associated with due process are reserved for proceedings that determine liability.

They have balked at the prospect of limitations that would "make a shambles of the investigation and stifle the agency in its gathering of facts."[30] In short, the ability to defend oneself in an adjudicative hearing, if charges are brought, has been deemed sufficient protection.

Agencies, however, possess enormous power to secure their ends merely with the threat of enforcement and without the formal steps that lead to reviewable sanctions. The costs of defending an enforcement action, both in terms of money and manpower, and the fear of adverse publicity resulting from a public proceeding, give the agency leverage to induce those threatened with enforcement to accede to the agency's demands on an informal basis. The agency, with little cost to its ultimate goals, can thus short-circuit the procedures of a formal enforcement action that afford some check on arbitrary power. Similarly, the "prospect" of an adjudicative proceeding is no comfort to the individual smeared by a fact-finding inquiry unrelated to any enforcement intentions.

Moreover, the investigation preceding the initiation of charges can itself be both burdensome and oppressive. There are at least two distinct possibilities for abuse and, in both cases, victory in a subsequent enforcement proceeding is far from an adequate remedy. First, investigations can be used to harass and intimidate for purely political or personal reasons. One well-publicized example will suffice. The Nixon administration maintained an "enemies list," a collection of political rivals and philosophic critics of President Nixon, which was used as a basis for initiating Internal Revenue Service audits and investigations.

Second, when an enforcement mechanism is in place, those charged with the duty of enforcement have the irresistible impulse to justify their existence. As a consequence, they may investigate for the sake of investigation, whether or not substantial federal interests are at stake, or whether or not there is reasonable cause to believe that a violation has been committed.

Failure of Judicial Oversight

The lifeblood of the administrative investigation, like the grand jury proceeding, is the subpoena, and if there is to be any meaningful, independent oversight of administrative investigations, it must come through control over the subpoena power. Administrative subpoenas are not self-enforcing and noncompliance will not result in sanctions unless and until there is a court order directing compliance. Thus, courts necessarily become involved in the investigative process. Unfortunately, they have largely abdicated their responsibility.

Initially, the courts had ruled that administrative subpoenas could be issued only in the context of adjudicative proceedings or where there was probable cause to believe that there were regulatory violations. Those limitations have given way, however, to the perception that the investigating arm of an administrative agency is "analogous to the Grand Jury," able to investigate "merely on suspicion that the law is being violated, or even just because it wants assurance that it is not."[31] The only limitations on the subpoena power that ostensibly remain are the requirements that the inquiry fall within the agency's jurisdiction and that the subpoena be "sufficiently limited in scope, relevant in purpose, and specific in directive so that compliance will not be unreasonably burdensome."[32]

Just as with grand jury subpoenas, the courts have dashed any hope that this formulation imposes meaningful restraints on an agency's information-gathering powers. The standard inquiry when a subpoena is challenged is whether the information sought is "plainly incompetent or irrelevant to any lawful purposes," a virtually insurmountable burden for the person seeking relief in light of the courts' expansive concept of relevance.

In reality, the courts have done nothing more than insure that the subpoena on its face meets the threshold requirements of particularity and relevance, without probing either the purpose or the contours of the agency's investigation. The failure to require any justification for invoking the court's power to enforce the subpoena and the presumption that the agency is acting for a valid purpose have combined to render judicial review largely a pro forma exercise. Professor Davis, the dean of administrative law, has described the evolution in vivid terms that are reminiscent of the history of the grand jury subpoena:

> The story of the development of the administrative power of investigation is rather dramatic. As regulation has expanded and intensified, the administrative quest for facts and more facts has gained momentum and has seemingly become an irresistible force. This force has collided with what at first were apparently immovable constitutional principles concerning privacy, searches and seizures, self-incrimination, and freedom from bureaucratic snooping. The constitutional principles remained firm for a time but gradually weakened and crumbled. The force proved irresistible. Remnants of the constitutional principles are left standing, but only to an extent clearly consistent with permitting administrative agencies freely to secure factual materials needed to carry out the programs they administer.[33]

Need for Judicial Scrutiny

The analogy to the grand jury, of course, is far from perfect. The institutional restraint of the grand jury, however imperfect, is lacking in the administrative context. Accordingly, the courts must reassert their authority to insure that administrative subpoenas reflect a responsible and rational exercise of investigative power. The agency should first be required to demonstrate that there is good cause for the subpoena. That showing could take one of two forms: either (1) that the agency has reason to believe that a regulatory violation has occurred and that the subpoena is in pursuit of evidence relating to that violation, or (2) that the subpoena complies with reasonable agency guidelines for the conduct of investigations. Although the investigative power should not be tied to situations where the agency has preexisting evidence of violations, when the agency ventures beyond that self-limiting circumstance into the realm of "spot checks" or general investigations, it should do so pursuant to substantive guidelines establishing general investigative priorities and plans. Those guidelines will act as a check on the arbitrary, irrational, or simply misguided ad hoc use of the investigative power. If there are deviations from the guidelines, or any other reason to believe that the subpoena power is being abused, the courts should be adamant in satisfying themselves that the subpoena has been issued for a proper purpose.

Second, the courts must once again balance the interests of the agency against the rights of the individual. Whenever a subpoena trenches upon valid privacy interests, the courts should demand a showing that the intrusion is justified by actual needs of the investigation, and not simply by the investigator's desire to pursue all leads and avenues of inquiry, no matter how peripheral to the central issues before him and no matter how duplicative of prior efforts. All too often subpoenas are issued in a scatter-gun approach, without any thought to whether less intrusive means are available or whether the evidence is at all essential to the investigation.

Finally, in order to provide advance protection against abuse and to provide the courts with a meaningful framework for oversight, all agencies should be required to formalize internal procedures for the initiation and conduct of investigations and the preferring of charges. Two goals are of paramount importance. Investigative decisions should not be confined to the discretion of one person. At a minimum, there must be a quasi-independent body within the agency to review alleged abuses at the request of aggrieved parties. In addition, enforcement should not be instituted without first giving the subject of the investigation notice of the charges and the opportunity to argue that formal enforcement proceedings are not warranted. The formal decision whether to institute proceedings should then be made by an individual who has not had principal day-to-day responsibility for the conduct of the investigation. Many agencies have procedures of this type, and experience has shown the burdens imposed on the investigative process are far outweighed by the beneficial effects of traditional due process protections.

Congressional Investigations—Are They a License To Condemn?

Of all governmental investigations, the congressional inquiry raises perhaps the deepest concerns. Sam Ervin, the colorful senator who chaired the Senate's Watergate hearings, has remarked that it can be an "instrument of justice." But he has also warned that it can be "freedom's scourge . . . it can debase our principles, invade the privacy of our citizens, and provide a platform for demagogues and the rankest partisans."[34] One could catalogue the numerous congressional investigations that have uncovered governmental corruption and provided an impetus for corrective action and needed reform. The Watergate hearings spring to mind. But the specter of the McCarthy era, when the rallying cry of "Fifth Amendment Communist" destroyed the lives of individuals and congressional hearings "were legislative trials where public obloquy was the punishment,"[35] is a constant reminder of the ever-present threat to fundamental rights.

Special Problems

While congressional investigations are subject to the same abuses that intermittently have characterized grand jury and administrative investigations, there are differentiating circumstances that separate them out. Unlike grand jury investigations and most administrative investigations, which are conducted in secret, congressional investigations are largely conducted through public hearings that often receive widespread publicity.

Although no formal charges that can result in government sanctions are lodged against individuals as a result of the investigations—a factor that at first blush might seem to alleviate cause for concern—it is blinking reality to suggest that this is a meaningful distinction. Congressional "fact finding" can be just as effective as an indictment in labeling a person as a wrongdoer and can have practical repercussions equally serious. As Justice Douglas has said, "we should all be painfully aware of the potentially devastating effects of congressional investigations. There are great stakes involved when officials condemn individuals by name."[36]

Moreover, formal charges, whether criminal or civil, are followed by a trial at which the panoply of due process rights is afforded and the individual may exonerate himself before a neutral tribunal. While trials may not be a complete answer to abuses in the charging process, they go a long way toward alleviating any lasting effects. Congressional hearings do not provide that opportunity.

Far from being a neutral tribunal, congressmen by profession are politicians. In a moment of understated candor, the Supreme Court has observed that "it would be somewhat naive to assume that [congressmen] would be wholly objective and free from considerations of party and politics and the passions of the moment."[37] And, unlike prosecutors and administrative officers who must answer to their superiors on a day-to-day basis, there is no such supervision of congressmen.

Finally, and perhaps most significantly, the courts are constitutionally precluded from granting effective relief against congressmen. Under the speech and debate clause, the courts may not assume jurisdiction over congressmen or their aides in any matter involving the performance of legislative acts. Thus, for example, the courts may not enjoin implementation of a congressional subpoena, even if the subpoena violates the First Amendment;[38] nor may they enjoin the publication and distribution within Congress of a needlessly defamatory report;[39] nor may they enjoin the use of private papers, seized illegally in violation of the Fourth Amendment, even if the papers are clearly irrelevant to the legislative inquiry.[40]

Justice Douglas instinctively recoiled at this reading of the speech and debate clause. His rhetorical questions, posed in response to the 1951 holding that the courts could not probe the motives of a legislative committee, have proved prophetic:

> We are apparently holding today that the actions of those committees have no limits in the eyes of the law. May they depart with impunity from their legislative functions, sit as kangaroo courts, and try men for their loyalty and political beliefs? May they substitute trial before committees for trial before juries? May they sit as a board of censors over industry, prepare their blacklists of citizens, and issue pronouncements as devastating as any bill of attainder?[41]

Judicial Oversight of Subpoenas

Nevertheless, the courts retain some residual oversight when Congress seeks the courts' aid in enforcing congressional process. Congress, although it has the power to imprison contumacious witnesses, in recent years has looked to the courts to punish those who challenge its authority. The federal courts, according to Justice Douglas, will not "sit as push-button mechanisms to fine or imprison those whom Congress refers to the United States Attorney for prosecution.... A court will not lend its hand to inflict punishment on a person for contempt of a congressional committee where the proceeding was *fundamentally unfair*."[42]

The precise role of the courts remains unclear, however. In *McGrain v. Daugherty*, the landmark decision upholding the inherent investigative power of Congress, including the subpoena power, the Supreme Court limited the investigative power to subjects on which "legislation could be had." The power of inquiry, according to the Court, did not extend into "private affairs."[43] That has proved to be no limitation at all, of course, for there are presently few, if any, aspects of our daily lives that are not a proper subject for federal legislation.

The Court again confronted the scope of congressional inquiries in *Watkins v. United States.*[44] Watkins, who was called before a Subcommittee of the House Un-American Activities Committee, freely answered questions addressed to his own affiliation with the Communist Party, but refused to confirm whether others were members. He was convicted of contempt.

The Supreme Court reversed the conviction on narrow grounds, holding that the committee's jurisdictional resolution was too vague to permit Watkins to judge whether the questions asked were pertinent to the committee's inquiry. Nonetheless, the Court said that it had "no doubt that there is no congressional power to expose for the sake of exposure," characterizing investigations conducted "solely for the personal aggrandizement of the investigators or to 'punish' those investigated 'as' indefensible." Unfortunately, these broad pronouncements as a practical matter may be no more than rhetorical flourish, for the Court carefully added that it was not its function to test the motives of congressmen: "Their motives alone would not vitiate an investigation which had been instituted by a House of Congress if that assembly's legislative purpose is being served." The sole test of the committee's purpose apparently was to be the formal statement of its jurisdiction.

The Court also recognized the necessity of an accommodation between the needs of Congress for information and the individual's interest in privacy. It was not willing to assume that every congressional investigation is justified by a public need that outweighs any private rights affected. "To do so would be to abdicate the responsibility placed by the Constitution upon the judiciary to insure that the Congress does not unjustifiably encroach upon an individual's right to privacy nor abridge his liberty of speech, press, religion or assembly."

Any hope that there were teeth in the Court's pronouncement was short-lived. Two years later the Court affirmed the contempt conviction of a university professor for refusing to answer questions about his affiliation with the Communist Party.[45] Applying the balancing test of *Watkins*, the Court held that the importance of dealing with the Communist threat was paramount. The Supreme Court has once again recently adverted to the balancing test,[46] and one can hope that with the perspective of history the courts, if called upon to apply it, will be more skeptical, not so much of claims of the importance of legislative programs and the necessity of supporting investigations, but of the asserted need for individual witnesses or documents.[47]

In addition, it is time to rethink the assumption that the motives of legislators are sacrosanct. The importance of a legislative inquiry cannot be assessed in the abstract. The purposes for which it is undertaken must play a role in any balance to be drawn. As long as motives go unquestioned, legislative investigations will be a fertile ground for the abuse of individual rights, either to serve partisan interests or to pander to public opinion.

Need for Self-Restraint

No matter what standard of review the courts apply, the courts cannot offer a complete solution. Aside from the restraints of the speech or debate clause, review for many individuals comes too late. A subpoena may not be challenged in court until after the witness has refused to obey and been cited for contempt. Few will risk a contempt conviction in the hope that the courts will provide a safe harbor. Most will give in to congressional demands long before the courts are in a position to intervene.

In these circumstances, there is a premium on legislative self-restraint. Basic guidelines that would prevent some of the abuses of the past seem obvious and, indeed, have been followed by some committees in the past, albeit on a sporadic basis:

1. Whenever hearings focus on the alleged wrong-doing of an individual, if at all practicable, the individual should be given the opportunity to present evidence and to cross-examine those who testify against him.

2. Witnesses who indicate that they will plead the privilege against self-incrimination either should not be called or should be allowed to claim the privilege in executive session.

3. Witnesses should not be granted immunity and required to testify without their consent.

4. Due consideration should be given to the rules requiring, in the case of the House, and permitting, in the case of the Senate, testimony that will charge a person with a crime or tend to defame him to be taken in closed session.

5. And finally, more heed must be paid to fundamental rights of the First, Fourth, and Fifth amendments.

As disappointing as it may be to those who cherish the courts as the guardian of our basic liberties, "self-discipline and the voters must be the ultimate reliance for discouraging or correcting [legislative] abuses."[48]

* * *

Much of the Bill of Rights was a direct response to the injustices of ecclesiastical inquisitions and the Star Chamber. The grand jury was entrusted with the sole power to prefer serious criminal charges, and individuals were guaranteed due process of law, with specific limitations on the investigative and inquisitorial tactics of the Crown that had been most abhorrent. According to Madison,

> If they [the Bill of Rights] are incorporated into the Constitution, independent tribunals of justice will consider themselves in a peculiar manner the guardians of those rights; they will be an impenetrable bulwark against every assumption of power in the Legislative or Executive; they will be naturally led to resist every encroachment upon rights expressly stipulated for in the Constitution by the declaration of rights.

When Justice Douglas took the bench in 1939, the grand jury remained the principal federal investigative body. The New Deal was a watershed, however, leading in the years to follow to expanded legislative horizons and the flourishing of administrative agencies. As a result, congressional committees and administrative bureaucracies have proliferated at alarming rates, so much so that one observer has described congressional inquiries as the "daily fare of American life." Administrative investigations certainly do not take a back seat.

Having watched this development for more than thirty years on the bench, Justice Douglas harbored grave doubts about whether Madison's prediction had been fulfilled. "As the years pass," Justice Douglas wrote, "the power of government becomes more and more pervasive. It is a power to suffocate both people and causes." To be sure, the worst abuses have been isolated, but it is the subtle erosion of our fundamental rights that presents the greatest threat to individual freedom and liberty. A renewed commitment to those rights is overdue.

Notes

1. Costello v. United States, 350 U.S. 359, 362 (1956).
2. 370 U.S. 375, 390 (1962).
3. 408 U.S. 665, 686-87 (1972).
4. United States v. Calandra, 414 U.S. 338, 343 (1974).
5. United States v. Mara, 410 U.S. 19, 23 (1973) (dissenting opinion).
6. Judge Frankel, a United States District Judge, and Gary Naftalis, formerly a federal prosecutor from the prestigious United States Attorney's office in the Southern District of New York, in a comprehensive discussion of the grand jury,

tell of an incident where a prosecutor, after berating a witness before the grand jury, refused the witness' request to consult with a lawyer before being compelled to answer further questions. The prosecutor refused, instructing the foreman of the grand jury to require the witness to answer. M. Frankel and G. Naftalis, *The Grand Jury: Institution on Trial* 64-66 (1977).

7. Donner and Cerruti, *The Grand Jury Network: How the Nixon Administration Has Secretly Perverted a Traditional Safeguard of Individual Rights,* The Nation 5, 9 (January 5, 1972).

8. Ullman v. United States, 350 U.S. 422, 444 (1956).

9. Donner and Cerruti, supra, at 5.

10. Warden v. Hayden, 387 U.S. 294, 325 (1967) (dissenting opinion).

11. See United States v. Mandujano, 425 U.S. 564 (1976); United States v. Wong, 431 U.S. 174 (1977); United States v. Washington, 431 U.S. 181 (1977).

12. 201 U.S. 43, 76 (1906).

13. 116 U.S. 616 (1886).

14. Gouled v. United States, 255 U.S. 298, 303-04 (1921).

15. Brown v. Walker, 161 U.S. 591 (1896).

16. Ullman v. United States, supra.

17. Kastigar v. United States, 406 U.S. 441 (1972). Transactional immunity bars prosecution for the transaction that is the subject of the immunized testimony. Use immunity permits prosecution for the transaction, but bars use of the immunized testimony or any leads obtained from the testimony in such a prosecution.

18. 409 U.S. 322, 329 (1973).

19. Fisher v. United States, 425 U.S. 391 (1976).

20. Ibid., 425 U.S. at 415, n.1 (Brennan, J., concurring).

21. Ibid., 425 U.S. at 414.

22. Ibid., 425 U.S. at 400.

23. Warden v. Hayden, 387 U.S. 294, 323 (1967) (dissenting opinion).

24. Couch v. United States, supra, 409 U.S. at 342 (dissenting opinion).

25. Warden v. Hayden, supra.

26. Fisher v. United States, supra, 425 U.S. at 401, quoting Oklahoma Press Publishing Co. v. Walling, 327 U.S. 186, 208 (1946).

27. 410 U.S. 1, 17 (1973).

28. 414 U.S. 338 (1974).

29. The traditional reasons for maintaining the secrecy of grand jury transcripts have no bearing in the vast majority of cases. There may be circumstances, however, in which full, or even partial disclosure of the transcript would have deleterious effects. Again, that conclusion should be reached by the court and not the self-interested prosecutor.

30. Hannah v. Larche, 363 U.S. 420, 440-48 (1960).

31. United States v. Morton Salt Co., 338 U.S. 632, 642-43 (1950).

32. See v. City of Seattle, 387 U.S. 541, 544.

33. K. Davis, 1 Administrative Law Treatise sec. 3.01, at 160 (1958).

34. J. Hamilton, *The Power to Probe: A Study of Congressional Investigations,* Introduction, p. xii (1976).

35. Ibid., at 81.

36. Doe v. McMillan, 412 U.S. 306, 329 (1973).

37. United States v. Brewster, 408 U.S. 501, 520 (1972).

38. Eastland v. United States Servicemen's Fund, 421 U.S. 491 (1975).

39. Doe v. McMillan, supra.

40. McSurely v. McClellan, 521 F. 2d 1024 (D.C. Cir. 1975).

41. Tenney v. Blandhove, 341 U.S. 367, 382 (1951) (dissenting opinion).

42. Hutcheson v. United States, 369 U.S. 599, 640 (dissenting opinion).

43. 273 U.S. 135, 173-74, 177 (1927).

44. 354 U.S. 178 (1957).

45. Barenblatt v. United States, 360 U.S. 109 (1959).

46. Eastland v. United States Servicemen's Fund, supra, 421 U.S. at 509-10, n. 16.

47. Compare Senate Select Committee on Presidential Campaign Activities v. Nixon, 498 F. 2d 275 (D.C. Cir. 1974), where the Court held that the Ervin committee did not have a pressing need for the Nixon tapes justifying an intrusion of executive privilege.

48. Tenney v. Brandhove, supra, 341 U.S. at 378.

SIX

GOVERNMENTAL INSPECTIONS
IN THE INTEREST OF SECURITY:
SEARCHING THE INNOCENT

Jerome B. Falk, Jr.

Until recently, few would have questioned the assertion that the Fourth Amendment bars an official search of one's person, home, or office unless the requisite level of suspicion has been created by the individual's own conduct. More judicial opinions than anyone would care to read review and sift the circumstances which may permit a search and those which are insufficient to do so. But nearly all of these decisions allowing a search share a common theme: something in the conduct of the individual gave rise to a legally sufficient level of belief that the person was in possession of stolen property, drugs, weapons, or other indicia of criminality which justified an official intrusion into the private precincts of the individual. That individuating circumstance, that requisite level of suspicion, we call "probable cause," except where the intrusion is limited to the lesser invasion of privacy known as the "protective frisk" or "pat search," where under recent decisions a lesser degree of suspicion—"reasonable suspicion"—is said to suffice.[1] But the common denominator of these decisions was the conduct of the person searched. Thus the Supreme Court said only recently that "some quantum of individualized suspicion is usually a prerequisite to a constitutional search or seizure."[2] As a consequence, one whose conduct appeared to be wholly innocent could reasonably expect to spend his or her days within the boundaries of the United States without ever experiencing the indignity of a search of the person, home, or office.

In recent years, this requirement—that searches occur only on the basis of individuating circumstances—has been eroded. In the non-

Jerome B. Falk, Jr., is a member of Howard, Prim, Rice, Nemerovski, Canaday & Pollak, San Francisco. He adds this biographical note: No former law clerk of Justice Douglas', and surely not one writing for proceedings which bear his name, could safely ignore the Justice's admonition that those with a self-interest in their subject make full disclosure (Douglas, *Law Reviews and Full Disclosure*, 40 Wash. L. Rev. 227, 1965). I was counsel in two of the cases mentioned in this paper: *Williams v. Alioto* and *Zurcher v. The Stanford Daily*. Nevertheless, the reader may be assured that any comments on the Zurcher decision will be more restrained and polite than the circumstances warrant.

criminal context, health inspections of private dwellings based upon area-wide standards have been upheld, even though nothing specific is known about the individual dwelling.[3] Likewise, administrative inspections of business may be performed upon a showing that reasonable legislative or administrative standards permit the search, even though there is no reason to suspect the business establishment of law violation.[4] These decisions did require a warrant, however, and must be understood in light of the undeniable reality that health and regulatory inspections of this kind simply could not be made if the traditional "probable cause" standard were applied. Health inspectors may be able to establish that rats or some other kind of disease sources are likely to be present in a particular neighborhood, but seldom can they make such a showing as to a particular dwelling.

Another case eroding the requirement that individuating circumstances predicate search or seizure is *United States v. Martinez-Fuerte.* There the Court upheld the maintenance of a fixed checkpoint in an interstate highway more than sixty-five miles from the Mexican border. All traffic is briefly stopped and visually screened; a small percentage of cars are diverted to an inspection area for questioning of the driver and further visual inspection of all that is in open view. Although probably not a search, the Court conceded that this detention is a "seizure" within the Fourth Amendment. It was also conceded that neither the initial stop of all traffic nor the diversion of some cars is based upon probable cause or "reasonable suspicion" as defined in *Terry.* Nevertheless, the Court thought that the public interest in detecting illegal aliens outweighed what it perceived as the minimal impairment of personal rights caused by the checkpoint procedure.

Another—and to my mind the most severe of all—departure from the requirement of individuating circumstances is the decision in *Zurcher v. The Stanford Daily.*[5] There the Supreme Court upheld a search, pursuant to warrant, of a newspaper office conducted for the purpose of locating and seizing photographs believed to have been taken by the paper in the course of gathering the news. The District Court and the Court of Appeals for the Ninth Circuit had held the search unconstitutional because there was no probable cause to believe that the *Daily* or its staff had engaged in any criminal activity or would refuse to comply with a subpoena. The Supreme Court disagreed:

> The critical element in a reasonable search is not that the owner of the property is suspected of crime but that there is reasonable cause to believe that the specific "things" to be searched for and seized are located on the property to which entry is sought.

Although the Court's opinion asserted that this has always been so, Justice Stevens' dissent exposed the error of that statement. Prior to 1967, he pointed out, decisions of the Court had forbade a search for "mere evidence" and limited the power of search and seizure to contraband, weapons, and the fruits of crime such as stolen property. There will ordinarily be the requisite probable cause to believe that one in possession of illegal narcotics or stolen property has engaged in criminal conduct; thus understandably, so long as "mere evidence" could not be searched for or seized, the cases provided little or no occasion to consider whether citizens whose conduct was for all appearances wholly lawful might nevertheless be searched. In 1967, the Court repudiated the "mere evidence" rule,[6] opening the way to the use of the search power to searches of those in possession of documentary evidence such as occurred in the *Zurcher* case. *Zurcher*'s response was to conclude that innocence is irrelevant to the State's power of search.

The practical consequences of this decision are disturbing. Although most of the public reaction—almost uniformly adverse—has been directed to the press/First Amendment aspects of the case, its ramifications do not end there. If the only requirement of the Fourth Amendment for the issuance of a search warrant is probable cause that the individual possesses, or the office contains, documentary or other tangible evidence relevant to a criminal prosecution, many others will be vulnerable to such searches despite their undoubted innocence of any criminal wrongdoing. The files of a lawyer, for example, often contain information that will be of interest to law enforcement activities.[7] Bank records of persons under criminal investigation may often be useful to law enforcement. Also potentially useful in criminal investigations are records maintained by physicians, psychiatrists, telephone business offices, accounting firms, employment agencies, credit bureaus, large employers, private investigators, security services, or any other place where confidential personal or financial information relating to many persons is routinely kept. Such records may, of course, be *subpoenaed*.[8] But a subpoena exposes to official scrutiny only the files or documents sought, and then only after the person or entity to whom it is directed has had an opportunity to seek judicial relief. A search is different in kind, for it precludes any attempt to seek judicial oversight and, more importantly, exposes to police scrutiny an entire office or file room. A search of the offices of a lawyer or doctor, for example, breaches the privacy not only of the person whose file is sought, but also the privacy of the lawyer or doctor who is innocent of wrongdoing and of every other client or patient whose file may be examined in an effort to locate the materials sought.

This departure from concern with individuating circumstances as a basis for search has occurred elsewhere under the insistent pressure of perceived necessity. The most widely experienced example is, of course, the airport antihijacking procedures first instituted in the late 1960s, which reached full flower in the early 1970s. Initially, focus on individuating circumstances was retained. Courts were called upon to review frisks and baggage searches of individuals who possessed characteristics described in a "profile" developed by the Federal Aviation Administration said to have been based upon characteristics common to hijackers.[9] Other decisions focused upon the suspicious conduct of a potential passenger said to have risen above the normal manifestations of anxiety of persons anticipating the terrors of jet flight and airline food.[10]

But these efforts to accommodate existing Fourth Amendment principles—and their focus upon individuating circumstances—to the exigencies of the airport search were not entirely successful. Neither conformity to the FAA profile nor the other kinds of suspicious conduct, such as displays of nervousness or the presence of bulging pockets, will ordinarily rise to the level of probable cause. While it may constitute "reasonable suspicion" for a brief stop and protective pat search under *Terry v. Ohio, Terry* does not authorize the more severe intrusion upon privacy which occurs when one's pockets, purse, or hand baggage is searched. And even as the doctrinal limitations of traditional Fourth Amendment analysis were proving troublesome, the inadequacies of a screening procedure dependent upon isolating some persons for inspection out of a huge body of air travelers became apparent.

The consequence was an almost complete departure from reliance upon individuating circumstances as the basis for search. *All* passengers are now screened. Each passenger who wishes to enter the gate must pass through a magnetometer which is adjusted (in theory, at least) to detect an abnormal quantity of metal on the person. If it is triggered, then the person is asked either to submit to a personal search, to a closer inspection of the person with a hand-held magnetometer, or to remove objects of metal from the pockets and pass again through the magnetometer. In addition, all hand baggage is inspected; in larger airports, this is now accomplished with an x-ray device, but in smaller facilities (and where the x-ray machine raises questions), this may be done by hand.

These procedures have, with some limitations, been uniformly upheld by the courts. The decisions are, however, far from uniform in their analysis. All of the decisions reflect a shared—and entirely reasonable—perception that blowing up airplanes is an unacceptable way to make a point or to express one's individuality. But there the commonality of decisions ends.

Some courts have thought that airport searches may be justified by reference to the "administrative search" cases.[11] Here these courts argued, as in the inspection of regulated businesses or of homes for health purposes, the purpose is primarily civil and not criminal. Other courts have thought that in light of the danger to transportation and human life posed by hijackers, an analogy to the cases authorizing routine search at international borders is appropriate.[12] Other courts have thought the "pat search" rationale of *Terry v. Ohio* applicable, even where the search went beyond a protective frisk but includes inspection of hand luggage.[13] Other courts have simply concluded that under all the circumstances airport searches without probable cause or reasonable suspicion are "reasonable" and hence permissible under the Fourth Amendment.[14] Finally, some courts have held that by presenting one's self and hand luggage at the gate, the traveler "consents" to the search—at least where posted signs clearly explain the search requirement and the alternative (of not traveling or checking all hand baggage) is reasonably apparent.[15]

Some courts have endeavored to impose limitations on this sweeping power of search. Some decisions have required that the individual passenger be free at all times to terminate the inspection process and leave the terminal; for example, a passenger who activates the magnetometer must be free to abandon his travel plans and avoid either a search of his person, pockets, or hand luggage.[16] Some courts have insisted that this opportunity to withdraw be clearly communicated,[17] but the courts have differed in their assessment of the adequacy of signs which merely state that those who attempt to board the aircraft will be subject to search.[18] A few decisions have required that a passenger who activates the magnetometer be given a further opportunity to pass through the device after removing metallic objects from his pockets before being subjected to a more intrusive frisk or personal search.[19] And the search of hand baggage must be confined to an inspection for weapons or explosives; inspection of a small envelope is impermissible.[20]

At a minimum, then, the courts permit the screening of every passenger by a magnetometer. Likewise, they permit the x-ray of every hand bag; indeed, they permit the actual inspection of all carry-on baggage (apparently without regard to the alternative of x-ray inspection), at least so long as the passenger is aware of the alternative of terminating his travel plans.

A litigant or lawyer wishing to challenge these procedures in a federal or state court would in all likelihood be confronted with a similar kind of inspection at the courthouse door. In response to incidents and threats directed at the judicial branch, many courts have required screening of all who would enter. The procedures are often less sophisticated than those in use at airports: while some courts have magnetometers, many do not, and attorneys, litigants and spectators may be personally pat-searched. Few if any courts have x-ray machines, so briefcases and packages are inspected by hand. For example, until recently the Supreme Court of California required each person attending court to submit all briefcases for inspection and to be thoroughly frisked by a guard, including a patting and touching of the upper thighs, armpits, and other relatively sensitive parts of the body. Although these practices generated widespread adverse public reaction and considerable private gambling among the bar, they have seldom been challenged and never successfully.[21]

Although no one will deny the imperative of protecting the judicial system against interference and harassment, the courthouse cases may well involve an even more serious compromise of Fourth Amendment principles. While there is a federal constitutional right to travel, it is far from clear that there is a constitutional right to travel by a particular means—aviation—and the traveler can indeed avoid all but the minor intrusion of passing through a magnetometer by checking all hand baggage. In contrast, one who visits a courthouse has an absolute constitutional right to do so, at least where the purpose is to attend a criminal proceeding to which the right of public trial attaches;[22] attorneys have a professional obligation to attend court; and witnesses are compelled to attend by subpoena. Moreover, there is no way by which one, such as an attorney, may avoid the search of necessary hand baggage or briefcases.

Troubling as these developments are, they pale in comparison to the massive invasion of privacy rights which occurred on the fabled streets of San Francisco in April 1974. The city had experienced a series of terrible, inexplicable, and savage murders by an unknown assailant. Massive police efforts had developed few clues, except for a determination of the type of pistol used and a general description and two composite sketches of the suspect. Tensions were exacerbated by the circumstances that all of the victims were white and the killer was known to be black. The investigation was given the code name Zebra and was, of course, highly publicized. Understandably, fear and anger stalked the City of St. Francis.

On April 17, the chief of police announced that new "stop and search" procedures would be observed. Officers, who had been provided with the composite drawings and a description, would stop all black men who met this "profile." Suffice it to say that the profile was exceedingly general. It was not required that persons to be stopped had done anything unusual or suspicious. Officers making a stop were authorized to "pat search" or "frisk" the detained individual.

In nine days, more than 600 black males were stopped, and many were frisked. The United States District Court for the Northern District of California found that the profile was sufficiently general that if the program were not restrained, countless additional black males would be stopped and frisked. It held that such forcible stops and pat searches could not be justified by *Terry v. Ohio*, because a profile of such generality that it describes so many persons cannot constitute "reasonable suspicion" within the meaning of *Terry*. The District Court's preliminary injunction was never reviewed on the merits by the Court of Appeals, for by the time an appeal was perfected by San Francisco the matter was moot.[23]

While the Zebra stop and search operation was particularly egregious, the constitutional issues presented by such cases are difficult. The Zebra case raised the spectre of racism; and the scope of the searches—and the exceedingly inadequate basis for performing them—was breathtaking. One wonders, however, whether in an emergency of similar gravity a similar operation could not be constructed which would pass constitutional muster. Would it, for example, be impossible for the police to formulate a "profile" with a greater scientific basis and somewhat greater precision than used in San Francisco? And would a court be able to intervene *in advance*, by simply reviewing the specificity of the standards, if it did not have the benefit of experience such as the District Court had in *William* (i.e., a record of an average of more than sixty stops per day under the profile)? And what if the operation were confined to a particular neighborhood where the suspect was known to reside or be present?

Fourth Amendment rights are uniquely fragile because they may be infringed if it is "reasonable" to do so. In times of national or local emergency, when the public cries out for action, will the courts and the Fourth Amendment impose a significant limitation? One might conclude from the *Williams* case that the answer may well be affirmative, for there a United States District Judge did indeed act, and act decisively. But there is substantial room for concern. In the first place, the Zebra case may well be atypical. The judge before whom it was litigated is a jurist of uncommon independence and courage. He was presented, as noted, with a unique record: six hundred stops in nine days. Moreover—and this may well be a decisive point of distinction— the Zebra stop and search operation made little sense from a law enforcement standpoint: the killer was unlikely to patrol the streets with a concealed weapon of the type known to have been used by the Zebra killer so long as the Zebra stop and frisk operation continued. In contrast, consider what one commentator has described as the "relatively mercurial speed with which the courts [in the airport search cases] have been dismantling many traditional Fourth Amendment concepts."[24] In those cases, where the inspection program has nearly brought to a halt incidents of airplane hijacking, the judicial response has been supportive. What protections, then, can we expect from the Fourth Amendment if a crisis of major proportions prompts an even more severe disregard of "traditional Fourth Amendment concepts"?

A not improbable example of what may lie ahead has been suggested by those concerned with the implications of plutonium recycling.[25] The proposed recycling of wastes from uranium fueled reactors will permit the extraction of plutonium from those wastes for use as additional fuel. Plutonium would be a breathtaking hazardous substance in the hands of a terrorist, for it is exceedingly toxic: a large number of fatalities would result if a small quantity were dispersed in the air. It has a half-life of 24,400 years. It can easily be transported in airtight containers which require only light shielding. And it can be used to fabricate a nuclear weapon with readily available technology. The risk of the theft of large quantities of plutonium is great, for it is estimated that by the year 2020 there will be more than one hundred thousand shipments per year of plutonium, primarily by truck on the public highways. Development of a system of breeder reactors will result in the generation of enormous quantities of plutonium, estimated by the AEC to net thirty thousand tons by 2020.

A plutonium theft would, therefore, pose a threat to public safety of the gravest order. Unhappily, its detection will not be easy. Because its radiation consists primarily of alpha particles which are effectively shielded with little difficulty, it can easily be stored in containers so that it cannot be detected through the use of geiger counters and like devices.

The consequence is that law enforcement in the plutonium age will be compelled to resort to old-fashioned methods of search. Will the Fourth Amendment stand as a barrier to whatever the authorities may require in an effort to recover a quantity of stolen plutonium? Will, for example, a door-to-door search of an entire neighborhood or even an entire city be permitted? Arguably, the warrant requirement might yield in the face of an emergency,[26] but what of the requirement that there be probable cause of a specific individual's wrongdoing or that items to be seized are located in a particular place? The relaxation of this requirement of individuating circumstances in the context of routine health and business premises inspections, in the "checkpoint" case, and in the airport search cases suggests that the court will find a way to authorize what would in fact be the most serious departure from Fourth Amendment standards ever sanctioned.[27]

The author of *Policing Plutonium* concludes that the impairment of Fourth Amendment principles which would necessarily occur as a consequence of plutonium recycling is itself a reason not to engage in such a program. That is a subject beyond the present scope of this chapter. But we have seen and experienced enough in the past ten years to know that our technologically advanced age and our inability to resolve social tensions and unrest have combined to pose a severe threat to traditional Fourth Amendment values. What is especially striking is the willingness with which most of us uncritically and without complaint accept these incursions. We pass quietly through the magnetometers and past the x-ray devices; we meekly hand over our purses, toilet article kits, and briefcases for inspection before routinely boarding an airplane; and we even submit, unhappily but quietly, to a frisk as a necessary condition of entering an American court-room.

If the choice is between such indignities and mass murder or terror, then presumably most of us will willingly bear the price of a loss in human privacy and dignity. But at the least we ought to be absolutely sure that the methods used are genuinely necessary and that the intrusions upon privacy are not one whit greater than required. As the review of the cases dealing with airport and courthouse searches suggests, this has not uniformly occurred.

For example, the magnetometer is less intrusive than an x-ray machine; and an x-ray machine is less intrusive than a personal inspection. Surely there is no justification for personal body searches when a magnetometer can be obtained and used at modest cost. In the same vein, no personal pat search should be permitted simply because a magnetometer has been activated unless and until the individual has been given a chance to remove all metal from the pockets and passed through a magnetometer once again. Likewise, there is no justification for inspection of briefcases or hand baggage when modern technology has provided an alternative—the x-ray machine—which can detect weapons with a less severe intrusion upon personal privacy. Finally, routine searches ought not to be tolerated unless there is a demonstrated need. The need for courthouse security in one area and at one time is not a justification for the universal erection of systems for doorway inspection at every courthouse. It is true that there have been all too many bombing attempts in major areas, and perhaps that really is sufficient justification for a security program at the Supreme Court of the United States, or elsewhere during a major, controversial trial. But the words "court" or "public building" are not yet synonymous with great danger and terrorism. Not every institution of government is so beleaguered as to justify this kind of twentieth-century moat.

If we are to be led into Mr. Orwell's *1984,* at least let us not go passively, but kicking and screaming to the last.

Notes

1. See, e.g., Terry v. Ohio, 392 U.S. 1 (1968).
2. United States v. Martinez-Fuerte, 428 U.S. 543, 560 (1976).
3. Camara v. Municipal Court, 387 U.S. 523 (1967).
4. See Marshal v. Barlow's Inc., 56 L. Ed. 2d 305 (1978).
5. U.S. 56 L. Ed. 2d 525 (1978).
6. Warden v. Hayden, 387 U.S. 295 (1967).
7. Such files of course contain information which is protected by the attorney-client privilege. But not everything in a lawyer's file is privileged; in any event, the Court in *Zurcher* said in response to a similar assertion of privilege: "Fifth Amendment and state shield law objections that might be asserted in opposition to compliance with a subpoena are largely irrelevant to determining the legality of a search under the Fourth Amendment." While it is arguable that this language was not intended to foreclose an argument that lawyer's offices may not be searched because that would offend privileges rooted in the Sixth Amendment right to counsel (but cf. Andreson v. Maryland, 427 U.S. 963 [1976]), it at least strongly suggests that state law based privileges will be ignored in assessing the constitutionality of such a search.
8. See, e.g., Fisher v. United States, 425 U.S. 391 (1976); Couch v. United States, 409 U.S. 322 (1973); United States v. Miller, 425 U.S. 435 (1976).
9. See United States v. Lopez, 328 F. Supp. 1077 (E.D.N.Y. 1971).
10. See, e.g., United States v. Lindsay, 451 F. 2d 701 (3d Cir. 1971) (suspicious conduct and bulging pockets); United States v. Fern, 484 F. 2d 666 (7th Cir. 1973); United States v. Homberg, 546 F. 2d 1350 (9th Cir. 1976); United States v. Skipwith, 482 F. 2d 1271 (5th Cir. 1973).
11. See, e.g., United States v. Davis, 482 F. 2d 893 (9th Cir. 1973); People v. Hyde, 12 Cal. 3d 158 (1974).
12. See, e.g., United States v. Skipwith, 482 F. 2d 1272 (5th Cir. 1973); United States v. Moreno, 474 F. 2d 44 (5th Cir. 1973).
13. See, e.g., United States v. Homberg, 546 F. 2d 1350 (9th Cir. 1976); United States v. Epperson, 454 F. 2d 769 (4th Cir.).
14. See, e.g., United States v. Edwards, 498 F. 2d 496 (2d Cir. 1974); People v. Hyde, 12 Cal. 3d 158, 170 (1974) (Wright, C.J., concurring).
15. See, e.g., United States v. Doran, 482 F. 2d 929 (9th Cir. 1977); United States v. Edwards, 498 F. 2d 496 (2d Cir. 1974) (Oakes, J., concurring); contra, United States v. Homberg, supra; United States v. Kroll, 481 F. 2d 884 (8th Cir. 1973) (search cannot be justified by "consent" as traveler cannot be compelled to choose between constitutional right of privacy and constitutional right to travel); United States v. Albarado, 495 F. 2d 799 (2d Cir. 1974).
16. See, e.g., United States v. Davis, supra; People v. Hyde, supra. The Fifth Circuit has decisively rejected this requirement. See United States v. Skipwith, 482 F. 2d 1272 (5th Cir. 1973).
17. See, e.g., United States v. Meulner, 351 F. Supp. 1284 (C.D. Calif. 1972).
18. Compare United States v. Davis, supra (suggesting that such signs may make the right to withdraw self-evident) with United States v. Ruiz-Estrella, 481 F. 2d 723 (2d Cir. 1973) (signs insufficient).

19. See, e.g., United States v. Albarado, 495 F. 2d 799 (2d Cir. 1974); contra, United States v. Sloacum, 464 F. 2d 1180 (3d Cir. 1972). There is authority striking down the search of *checked* baggage without probable cause even though the search of the passenger was permissible. United States v. Palazzo, 488 F. 2d 942 (5th Cir. 1974).

20. United States v. Kroll, supra.

21. See, e.g., McMorris v. Alioto, 567 F. 2d 897 (9th Cir. 1978) (upholding use of magnetometer and actual inspection of attorney's briefcase); Downing and Kunzig, 454 F. 2d 1230 (6th Cir. 1972); Barrett v. Kuzig, 331 F. Supp. 266 (M.D. Tenn. 1971). See generally Comment, 21 U.C.L.A. L. Rev. 797 (1974).

22. Admittedly, that statement oversimplifies a complex area of constitutional law. But while any given individual arguably may be excluded from attending a particular criminal trial, and while all may in limited circumstances be excluded, it is clear that the right of public trial prohibits the exclusion of all members of the public from all trials.

23. Williams v. Alioto, 549 F. 2d 136 (9th Cir. 1977).

24. Comment, The Courthouse Search, supra at 813.

25. See Comment, *Policing Plutonium: The Civil Liberties Fallout,* 10 Harv. Civ. Rights-Civ. Liberties L. Rev. 369 (1975); Comment, *The Plutonium Society; Deterrence and Inducement Factors,* 41 Albany L. Rev. 251 (1977).

26. See Camara v. Municipal Court, supra at 539; North American Cold Storage Co. v. Chicago, 211 U.S. 306 (1908).

27. Compare Lankford v. Gelston, 364 F. 2d 197 (4th Cir. 1966) (injunction against warrantless search of private homes after the search of more than three hundred homes, primarily occupied by blacks, in effort to locate fleeing killer of police officer).

PART THREE

FREEDOM AND GOVERNMENTAL
EXPENDITURES
TO ADVANCE THE COMMON GOOD

SEVEN

GOVERNMENT GRANTS TO EDUCATION AND THREATS TO ACADEMIC FREEDOM

William Reppy, Jr.

In 1958 the federal government spent $300 million to support education at all levels. By 1976 federal expenditures in aid of institutions of higher education alone totalled $9.7 billion (while an additional $10.4 billion was spent to aid other educational institutions). This total federal outlay has so increased that the Department of Health, Education and Welfare has calculated that "federal programs will provide 30 percent of all support of higher education" in 1978.

Numerous federal agencies are charged with distributing this enormous flow of money for higher education. HEW—primarily through the Office of Education—handles about three-fourths of the federal aid, followed by the National Science Foundation, Department of Agriculture, Department of Defense, Energy Research and Development Administration, and National Aeronautics and Space Administration, each controlling from 9 to 2 percent of the total federal funds flowing to higher education. Recipients include giant universities, small colleges, and technical institutes, both private and state-operated. (Heading the list of recipients on the basis of federal money received is the once-private Howard University, located in Washington, D.C.)

Federal funds are not, of course, simply handed over to institutions of higher education to be expended as the administrators see fit; rather, the federal government makes grants conditional on institutional compliance with specific standards. The largest chunk of the federal pie is earmarked for student financial assistance: scholarships, loans, work-study funds, etc. The amount expended for research and development at institutions of higher education is almost as large—$2.419 billion in fiscal year 1976. These funds are federally restricted for use in a wide variety of studies and projects, including top-secret national defense research, modern foreign language instruction, studies in mining and mineral fuel conservation, and law school clinical programs.

Devices for policing the method of expenditures of federal funds

---

William A. Reppy, Jr., is professor of law at Duke University.

budgeted for education also vary. Practices range from the placement of a federal watchdog-in-residence (e.g., when a laboratory associated with a university obtains a large, classified national defense research project), to inspections of the institutions by review committees, to the requirement of filing with federal agencies lengthy forms detailing the manner in which the terms and conditions of grants have been fulfilled.[1]

The extensive and still mushrooming involvement of the federal government in higher education—traditionally the responsibility of state and local governments and private endowments and eleemosynary corporations—has evoked shrill cries of protest from academia and words of warning from top federal officials. In an address to educators in August 1978, HEW Secretary Joseph Califano spoke of "dependence by our schools upon the federal government." Some institutions, he said, had become "dangerously dependent," with some private schools receiving almost 100 percent of their operating budgets from the United States. Califano's concern was not limited to the probable financial collapse of such institutions in the event a tightening of the national budget cut the flow of federal funds to higher education. The secretary was also alarmed by the possibility that government control accompanying such grants was interfering with the core of academic freedom. "The setting of academic standards . . . [and] planning of the curriculum [have] always been a state and local matter. Will [they] remain so?"

This paper explores the secretary's fears from the writer's outlook as an educator in a professional school and a researcher concerned with constitutional law principles. First it considers, briefly, the scope of the academic freedom concept as perceived by educators and by the courts. Second, examination is made of selected regulations and conditions that have, in the late 1970s, accompanied some federal grants to higher education. These conditioned grants have been particularly disturbing to professors and administrators of higher education institutions, forcing many to speak out on the propriety of current funding requirements. Focus is almost exclusively on the federal grant process, since the funding involved therein has a greater impact on academic freedom than other grants that could be viewed as intruding into an area of education not the granting entity's responsibility.[2] This portion of the paper also considers a number of direct federal controls over higher education institutions (i.e., not tied to grants or federal contracts), such as enforcement of civil rights acts provisions against discrimination on the basis of race and gender, since the government can, any time it wants to, attempt to utilize the condition-to-grant mechanism as an additional or alternative means of achieving the same federal goal. (This is quite common today: compliance with the antidiscrimination statutes, regulations, and executive orders is usually one condition for the receipt of federal funds by a college or university, even though such funds are to be used for projects having little relation to practices in hiring, admissions, etc.)

The next section of this paper assesses the extent to which conditions on federal grants have interfered with academic freedom. To this end, government controls that are essential to achieve the purposes of the expenditures are distinguished from controls which could be readily eliminated. Additionally, the benefits of obtaining the funds are weighed against the threats to academic freedom arising from the federal controls. This section of the paper also considers what remedies are available if it is concluded that the interference with academic freedom is now (or may become) excessive. Refusing the money is the simplest yet most extreme solution. This paper considers more palatable alternatives such as court action based on constitutional principles limiting the power of the federal government and political action aimed at Congress and the executive agencies.

My conclusions are: (1) at present, federal interference in academic freedom, even when the concept is most broadly defined, is, with very few exceptions, not unreasonable, if one starts with the assumption that government would be remiss in its duty to the taxpayer if it turned money over to colleges and universities to be spent at the institutions' pleasure without any control; (2) excessive and unreasonable interference in the future is possible but unlikely because of political pressures from state governments and academia; (3) the United States Constitution seems to provide almost no basis for relief if Congress decides deliberately to take over much of the administration of state and private institutions of higher education through the conditions-on-grant process.

The Scope of the Contemporary Concept of Academic Freedom

In the evolution of the concept of academic freedom, focus was initially on the rights of the individual involved—usually the individual teacher or researcher, occasionally the administrator, and less frequently the student. The core freedom of the individual is the freedom to inquire, study, and speak out as to his or her conclusions and beliefs without fear of reprisal through discharge, demotion, loss of pay or research support, etc.[3] As applied, academic freedom stood for the proposition that the teacher should be able to structure his class presentation in a manner he preferred, direct class discussion into issues he deemed important, and publish his views without censorship or discipline. This branch of the freedom has frequently been recognized by the courts, as in *Barenblatt v. United States,* 1959:

[I]nquiries cannot be made into the teaching that is pursued in any of our educational institutions. When academic teaching-freedom and its corollary learning-freedom, so essential to the well-being of the Nation, are claimed, this Court will always be on the alert against intrusion. . . .[4]

The concept of academic freedom as a protection of the individual was extended to shield him in his extrainstitutional political and personal life. He was protected from discipline by the institution employing him for taking an unpopular stand on public issues or for following a nonmajoritarian life style (e.g., for "living in sin" with a member of the opposite sex), at least so long as criminal laws were not violated and no harm to students or colleagues could be demonstrated. The requirement of taking a loyalty oath—which several statutes tried to impose in various modes, including making oath a condition to receipt of a government grant for research—came to be generally perceived as a violation of this aspect of academic freedom. Similarly, job disqualification for political party membership was viewed as a violation of the individual's academic freedom. Thus, in *Sweezy v. New Hampshire*, 1957, where the state sought to investigate the party affiliation of a university lecturer, Chief Justice Warren said:

> To impose any strait jacket upon the intellectual leaders in our colleges and universities would imperil the future of our Nation. No field of education is so thoroughly comprehended by man that new discoveries cannot yet be made. Particularly is that true in the social sciences, where few, if any, principles are accepted as absolutes. Scholarship cannot flourish in an atmosphere of suspicion and distrust. Teachers and students must always remain free to inquire, to study and to evaluate, to gain new maturity and understanding; otherwise civilization will stagnate and die.[5]

In recent years, as the perceived threat of government intereference in higher education has shifted from the political witch-hunting of the McCarthy period to governmental seduction of the institution as its vehicle for social engineering through the regulatory process, the concept of academic freedom has further broadened. University of California President David S. Saxon said at a seminar on academic freedom in Berkeley in 1976: "[T]he focus of academic freedom is shifting—from individual rights to institutional and collective rights and responsibilities." Brigham Young University President Dallin H. Oaks sees a close relationship between the branch of academic freedom protecting the institution itself and the traditional concern with individual rights:

> Teachers should realize that an institution which lacks freedom from

government interference in the management of its educational functions cannot protect its faculty from government interference in theirs.

In sum, administrative decision making is an integral part of the educational process necessarily requiring protection from outside interference under the academic freedom concept. The university should be able to plan the curriculum, formulate standards for admitting students, employ the teachers its administrators find most competent, fix an appropriate wage for them, etc., without governmental restrictions on the exercise of such authority. University of Michigan President Robben W. Fleming, for example, defines the right of the university to select its own personnel as one of the "most sensitive of all areas" of academic freedom.

The prong of the academic freedom concept that protects institutional decision making was recognized in the recent *Bakke* decision, involving the freedom of a university to formulate its own standards governing the admission of medical students. In the controlling opinion, Justice Powell stated:

> Academic freedom, though not a specifically enumerated constitutional right, long has been viewed as a special concern of the First Amendment. The freedom of a university to make its own judgments as to education includes the selection of its student body. . . . "It is the business of a university to provide that atmosphere which is most conducive to speculation, experience and creation. It is an atmosphere in which there prevail 'the four essential freedoms' of a university—to determine for itself on academic grounds who may teach, what may be taught, how it shall be taught, and who may be admitted to study."[6]

Examination of the literature in the last three years on academic freedom and government interference in higher education discloses a belief of many educators that the freedom must include a further protection against bureaucratic red tape—the filling out and filing of form after form after government form. Teachers, it is contended, should be able to teach full time and not have to give over large chunks of their working day to such red tape; administrators should be able to devote their time to policymaking. The government "reporting requirement," says Fleming, imposes a heavy burden on members of the academic community at all levels, and, he notes, faculty members "can hardly be said to be working at their highest skill in the completion of forms." Although I am not aware of a decision by a court adopting this freedom-from-red-tape aspect of the academic freedom concept, for purposes of assessing government control of higher education through the grant process it seems sufficient to observe that the educators themselves consider their being scooped up into the whirlwinds of bureaucracy a violation of academic freedom. (Whether the Constitution offers any relief is a quite different inquiry, the contours of the First Amendment and academic freedom not being identical.)

The Methods of Contemporary Governmental Interference with Higher Education

In the 1950s defenders of academic freedom were primarily concerned with governmental efforts to enforce political orthodoxy at institutions of higher education. Individual rights of faculty members were also the primary concern during the 1960s and early 1970s, as examples surfaced of apparently unreasonable governmental restrictions on the dissemination of research results funded in whole or in part by the government. Presently, almost no educators fear political witch-hunting. Although secrecy-censorship disputes occasionally arise with regard to classified research, the primary threat to academic freedom is perceived to be the federal government's seizing of the college and university as an instrument for social engineering.

In analyzing how this phenomenon is being achieved, one can classify the governmental impact on higher education as direct versus indirect in two different respects. First, the analysis must distinguish between regulation that is direct in the sense that it is not just a condition to receipt of grant money, and regulation that comes along with the acceptance of federal funds. For example, Congress would seem to have the power under the Thirteenth or Fourteenth amendments (unquestionably it has such power vis-à-vis state institutions) to impose a direct regulation requiring that all institutions of higher education, whether or not they receive a penny of federal funds, refrain from discrimination on the basis of race in hiring and in admission. Similarly, as the Constitution confers on the federal government the war and defense power, the United States has the authority to clamp a lid of secrecy on any research project which gets into militarily sensitive areas (e.g., the parapsychologist who inadvertently discovers a technique for determining by brain wave analysis who is or is not a foreign spy), whether or not the project is federally funded or conducted at an institution receiving federal funds.

On the other hand, while Congress is empowered to enforce some regulations directly on educational institutions, certain of these regulations—such as those against sex-based discrimination—have instead been enforced primarily through the spending power. Compliance becomes a condition of receiving federal monies or government contracts. However, many of the do's and don't's addressed to educators through the spending power as grant conditions concern matters not subject to direct regulation. Thus, by no stretch of the federal commerce power or any other federal power could Congress order the nation's law schools to offer a clinical course in trial practice using actual rather than simulated cases; nor could it require dental schools to have practicing dentists rather than regular faculty members teach certain community dentistry courses. Instead, Congress must use indirect means to regulate in these ways, advising institutions that if they want federal money, compliance with federal directives is a necessary prerequisite.

The second direct versus indirect interference dichotomy looks at the impact on the institution. A regulation that tells the institution precisely what administrative or educational decision it is to make—as with the legal clinic and family dentistry examples above—can appropriately be called direct regulation. Indirect regulation interference is of numerous types. The availablity of grant funds often determines what areas and what types of research will be performed and who will be hired to do it. When an act of Congress and the accompanying federal agency regulations simply make a limited amount of money available for some broad purpose, the institution nevertheless can learn what precise details in its program will please the bureaucrat in charge of disbursing funds by observing which applications from other institutions are being granted or denied, noting comments from peer review committees that inspect the school's facilities, etc. Finally, indirect interferences in educational institutions are manifested in the form-filing, red tape requirements outlined above, for these bureaucratic demands necessarily divert time and funds away from education.

There follows a survey of some of the devices—mainly now in effect but some at the proposal stage—which have excited most of the discussion by educators in the journals and specialized press serving the profession. They are mainly of two types: (1) impact-direct regulations (e.g., rewriting the curriculum or admissions standards) that are regulatory-indirect (i.e., a condition of receiving funds which can be avoided by turning down the money); and (2) impact-indirect requirements (e.g., creating a mass of paperwork) that are regulatory direct (i.e., must be met whether or not the institution takes federal money). Since the federal government can at any time attempt to enforce these rules either additionally or alternatively as conditions on federal grants, examples of the regulatory-direct interference are considered in this paper.

Direct Interference through the Spending Power

The most blatant federal interference with direct impact on academic freedom has involved American professional health-study schools: medical, dental, veterinary, etc. Regulation began rather innocently in 1965 with congressional provision for capitation grants (so much per student) to medical schools that would meet certain conditions for increased enrollment. The goal was to produce more American doctors. In a recent article in *Change* magazine, Stanford University Vice-President for Public Affairs Robert M. Rosenzweig reports that American medical schools were all apparently willing to make these changes in admissions practices. When the capitation grants were accepted, the number of students studying medicine, as Rosenzweig notes, almost doubled. Additionally, many medical schools became dependent on these federal grants, currently at $2000 per student per year. According to Rosenzweig, "the capitation grants came to constitute a significant fraction of the operating budgets of most medical schools, and the prospect of doing without them was not at all pleasing." That prospect arose in October 1976 when President Ford signed into law legislation affecting the capitation grant scheme which contained Section 771(b)(3) of the Health Professions Educational Assistance Act, known to many as the "Guadalajara Amendment." The amendment's purpose was to facilitate the transfer of American medical students studying abroad, many at a medical school in Guadalajara, Mexico, to United States medical schools. Thus, in order to keep the flow of federal money coming, America's 117 medical schools had to alter their admissions standards by accepting an assigned quota of American citizen transfer students from foreign institutions without regard to the possibility that the transfer students failed to meet admission standards. Pleas to President Ford from university presidents to veto the bill were unavailing.

Depending on which media report one reads, fifteen to nineteen medical schools declared that they would forego federal capitation grants rather than allow Congress to supplant their admissions standards. It is significant to note that the other one hundred or so medical schools were apparently so dependent on the federal funds as to be willing to go along with the Guadalajara Amendment.

In any event, the hue and cry from academia was enough to persuade Congress in December 1977 to greatly alter the amendment. As a result of these changes, medical schools may apply their usual admissions standards and still qualify for capitation grants if they make an effort to increase third-year enrollment by 5 percent (one year only, 1978-79).[7] Apparently all medical schools are going along with the *new* Guadalajara Amendment.[8]

Left unchanged in the 1976 version of the Health Professions Educational Assistance Act was the presence of federal intervention in the curriculum planning of medical schools accepting capitation grants. At least 50 percent of first-year resident positions would, by 1980, have to be for physicians in family medicine, general internal medicine, and general pediatrics (reflecting the congressional policy attempting to shift new doctors into areas of general practice and out of narrow specialties). According to a 1977 House report, this requirement produced no flap from academia because in fact the medical schools had already achieved the 50 percent goal.

On the other hand, provisions in the same 1976 legislation affecting the curriculum at dental and other nonmedical health professions schools have come under criticism. For example, most dental schools taking federal funds under the act have, to qualify for the funds, added to their curriculums a six-week clinical course conducted away from the dental school in "areas geographically remote" from the campus or in areas where "medically underserved populations reside." The course instructors must be "practicing dentists."[9] Similarly, schools of pharmacy are required to have their students take a course entitled "clinical pharmacy," which includes four specified curricular components.

Nor did veterinary school curriculum and admission standards escape federal interference. Those schools taking federal grants under the Health Professions Assistance Act must satisfy HEW that they have clinical training which "emphasize[s] predominantly care to food-producing animals or to fibre-producing animals, or to both types." And "at least thirty percent of the enrollment of full-time first year students in such schools will be comprised of students who are residents of States in which there are no accredited schools of veterinary medicine."[10] (There have been similar tamperings with the admissions processes in grant-taking schools of optometry, podiatry, and pharmacy.)

In addition, the federal government has also decided to dabble in curriculum planning for law schools. Under 20 U.S.C. sec. 1136, grants of up to $75,000 per law school are available for programs which "provide clinical experience to students in the practice of law." Funding has been quite limited, and the act gives preference to programs "providing such experience, to the extent practicable, in the preparation and trial of cases." HEW has construed "cases" to mean real cases, not simulated trial situations, thus disqualifying from assistance clinical trial practice courses at many excellent law schools that choose not to abide by the federal view of how law school clinical instruction should operate.[11]

In the area of research, the House of Representatives has indicated its intention to decide what are approved and nonapproved subjects by passing an amendment to an appropriations bill precluding the expenditure of federal funds on research at a named university on the subject of how marijuana use arouses sexual desires. Another area for possible federal control over research concerns experimentation in recombinant DNA, an acidic combination altering the genetic structure of life forms. The National Institute of Health "guidelines" establish standards for recipients of NIH grants which prohibit certain types of experiments unless risk of harm is shown not to exist. The guidelines also call for committees drawn from the university community to approve research proposals and monitor compliance.[12] It appears that some congressmen consider this effort insufficient, for bills curtailing recombinant DNA research have been introduced in the House and Senate. Lobbying for such government intervention to regulate research are strange coalitions of left-wing and conservative elements. A group entitled "Science for the People" has demanded a cutback in all funding to institutions engaged not only in recombinant DNA studies but also in research into the relationship between IQ and racial or genetic traits. Others seek to halt the study of the XYY syndrome because results might influence social policy and the research distracts attention from problems of racism and poverty.[13]

Turning from research to the area of tuition support, one finds that the federal government, in conditioning the acceptance of federal funds for student loans and other aid, requires educational institutions to follow several burdensome regulations. Vocational schools must keep attendance records, and many other types of institutions must conduct inquiries to determine what their graduates are doing professionally. Federal regulations also tell the institutions how to write their admissions bulletins and how to describe the nature of the educational program. Such descriptions must indicate how the program prepares a student for a particular career and must offer data on the success of graduates in finding jobs.[14] Institutions whose students obtain assistance through a GI bill and the Veterans Administration must struggle with the 85-15 rule, a regulation disqualifying courses of study for federally aided veterans where 85 percent or more of the students receive aid from a federal agency. The same statute disqualifies courses for veterans if they have been offered by institutions covered by the act for less than two years. The United States Supreme Court earlier this year reversed a lower court decision that had invalidated such federal rules as discriminatory.[15]

In the early 1970s Congress passed legislation barring colleges and universities from distributing federal financial assistance through the National Science Foundation or the National Aeronautics and Space Administration to students convicted of serious acts of disruption of educational activities on campus. Most observers feel these acts were passed to punish content of antiwar activities as much as the violence and disruptiveness involved.[16]

Complaints about federally enforced secrecy regarding research continue to appear in educational journals. A June 1978 report in the *Chronicle of Higher Education* told of a federal order to a University of Wisconsin associate professor who had done computer science research and applied for a patent on a device for enciphering and deciphering computer information. It ordered him "in no wise to publish or disclose the invention or any material information with respect thereto, including hitherto unpublished details of the subject matter . . . in any way to any person not cognizant of the invention prior to the date of the order." The professor was further ordered to advise persons already so "cognizant" they were also subject to the secrecy order and to prison terms of two years and fines of $10,000 if they violated it.[17] Protests by the university chancellor ultimately caused the order to be withdrawn. Other scientists working in the area of computer data enciphering were subjected to less formal means of harassment when threats by representatives of the National Security Agency indicated that presentation of research findings at professional meetings would be viewed by the agency as violations of law.

Indirect Interference through the Spending Power

An obvious indirect impact of the flow of federal largess on institutions of higher education is that the very availability of funds for certain areas of research or certain special education programs strongly influences decision making by faculty and administration. The professor is clearly influenced in deciding what research projects to undertake by the availability of federal money. So is the administrator, who must consider the availability of funds when deciding whether to establish a new department or hire a new employee. For example, post-Sputnik federal intervention through the grant process has assuredly increased the size of the faculty concerned with hard sciences as well as the amount of research work in these areas. On the other hand, the percentage of funds going to the humanities and social sciences has declined in comparison.

After the general decision has been made to emphasize a particular area for research or teaching, the grant system still affects the details of the program in spite of the fact that, in some instances, neither the act of Congress providing for the grant nor the federal regulations implementing that act directly specify the precise manner in which the study or class shall be pursued. The indirect control exists because the funds authorized by Congress are limited (and the federal supply seldom meets the institutional demand) and because necessary human factors are involved when a large number of applications for grant funds must be rejected and only a few accepted. The federal officer responsible for deciding who gets the limited funds—and those working with him in the agency—will of course have some personal views as to what type of research or instructional program will best implement the federal policy behind the grant legislation. Such officials may also conceive of the grant process as a vehicle for advancing other, unrelated federal policies (such as affirmative action hiring for blacks, an important federal policy but not one related to the congressional motive in implementing funds to promote, for example, Russian studies).

There are at least two means through which educational institutions learn about the unofficial and unpublished views that will have considerable effect on the likelihood of favorable review for a particular grant application. First, the applicant institution can rely on the experiences of other institutions and thus determine which types of programs have obtained funding under the legislation at issue. In many cases data concerning the rejected programs may be obtained through a cooperative effort. In addition, if the institution's own application is initially rejected, commentary explaining that rejection can be examined under the Freedom of Information Act (and is apparently presently supplied by some federal agencies without the applicant having to invoke the procedures of the FOIA).

The second method of gathering information pertaining to the unofficial federal preference in research or instruction is through the "peer review system." In the case of science research grants, a peer review committee, made up of several well-known scientists involved in the area covered by the grant legislation, is assembled by the administering federal agency (e.g., NIH or NSF). These committee scientists work for the agency by carrying out the committee's task of visiting the institution applying for federal funds,[18] inspecting its facilities, and interviewing its personnel. Discussions between these peer review committee members and the university professors or administrators will be a rich source of information as to just what details or emphasis in the project will appeal to the agency chief or personnel making the who-gets-the-grant-money decision.[19] It hardly needs to be noted that the information so received is likely to be acted on by the institution in designing the program.

Direct Interference through "Direct" Powers of Congress

Some parts of the civil rights act legislation, such as provisions against racial and sex discrimination in hiring, are binding on educational institutions not only because they receive federal funds but also because of what I have called the direct powers of Congress to legislate.[20] The federal government is empowered to compel compliance because of its power to regulate interstate commerce, its power to assure the defense of the nation, or its power to implement the equal protection clause of the Fourteenth Amendment, for example. Where the regulated institution is not receiving federal funds, regulatory legislation based on these direct powers must be supported by some sanction other than cutting off the federal money in order to be effective. Such sanction could be a criminal fine or subjecting a violating party to an injunctive order.

The commerce power of Congress is very broad. The practice of an institution of higher education in hiring faculty and staff, fixing their pay, giving them promotions, and discharging them almost certainly will be found by the courts in any given case to have the necessary impact on interstate commerce to authorize federal regulation of the "business" aspects of the education "industry."

Because the acts constitute "state action," it is possible that public institutions receiving no federal aid can also be regulated by Congress with respect to discrimination on the basis of race, gender, age, etc., under the Fourteenth Amendment. Some constitutional law scholars suggest that under section 5, the implementation clause of the Fourteenth Amendment, Congress may be able to regulate those activities in which the courts could not themselves find the state action necessary to support a judicially declared violation of the amendment. That is, Congress may perhaps constitutionally declare the educational process to be so historically related to the functions of state and local government (since education is traditionally a state activity) that the acts of purely private schools not accepting federal funds are subject to federal control under section 5.

This brings up a point to keep in mind when assessing the contention that conditions on federal grants are abuses of the federal spending power. In some instances when Congress has sought to rest its authority on the spending power (i.e., "if you take our money you must do the following things. . . ."), the federal legislation could also be upheld under one or more of the "direct" powers of Congress. It is not only the "power of the purse" which allows Congress to regulate.

Federal regulations enacted under the commerce power or other direct powers which expressly limit the discretion of an institution of higher education in such areas as whom to hire for a faculty position are examples of regulatory-direct and impact-direct federal intrusions into the broad area of academic freedom. The civil rights provision involved in the *Bakke* case, section 601 of Title VI of the Civil Rights Act of 1964 requiring all institutions receiving federal aid to refrain from racial discrimination in the admissions process, is an example of a federal rule purportedly based on the spending power which could also be upheld, most likely, under section 5 of the Fourteenth Amendment.

Indirect Interference through "Direct" Powers of Congress

To many educators who complain about federal interference in the higher education process, the primary displeasure lies in the great deal of paperwork cast on the institutions by a series of acts of Congress directed not just to higher education but to business generally. The source of federal power to enact these provisions is primarily the commerce power. An editorial in *Change* magazine—decrying a "bureaucratic disease . . . in which the country's educational institutions are perhaps one of its most dramatic victims"—listed twelve federally controlled areas of bureaucracy as constituting the bulk of this form of federal interference. They included the Social Security Act and its various amendments, the Occupational Safety and Health Act (OSHA), the Fair Labor Standards Act, the Equal Pay Act, the Employee Retirement Income Security Act (ERISA), the Health Maintenance Organizations (HMOs) Act, and unemployment insurance legislation.[21]

According to this editorial (written in 1976), compliance with this "series of mindless enforcement and regulatory proceedings that could have come out of *Alice in Wonderland*" costs higher education $2 billion a year. Such a sum, together with time wasted by teachers and administrators shuffling papers and filling out forms, could have been devoted to research, instruction, or basic administration. Another study estimated the cost at 5 to 10 percent of tuition, while a third found that complying with the "federally mandated social programs" alone consumed 1 to 4 percent of the institution's operating budget.

University of Michigan President Robben W. Fleming, writing in 1978, stated:

> [U]niversity personnel find themselves spending an inordinate amount of time completing endless forms and reports, many of which are known to go unread because there is no one at the other end with time enough to read them. The reporting requirement, moreover, imposes additional administrative costs on the university and additional burdens on faculty.[22]

The Effect of Governmental Interference: How Serious Is the Problem?

Regulatory-Direct Interference

The federal legislation enacted under the commerce power and other "direct" powers, which some educators have objected to as drowning higher education in a senseless tidal wave of paperwork, operatively treats higher education like any other American industry. For example, colleges subject to ERISA have to file with federal agencies (and employees) the same mass of forms concerning pension plans that large private commercial employers have to file. Similarly, colleges are subject to the same irksome OSHA inspections and regulations imposed on privately owned industrial plants. Both must defend charges of discrimination in hiring under the same civil rights act principles. In other words, higher education has become one more regulated industry, with virtually no exemption from the red tape and paperwork extended to it in its capacity as the repository of academic freedom.[23]

Commentators' opinions vary greatly on the issue of whether burdensome paperwork and excessive red tape is unfair to higher education and threat to academic freedom. Russell Kirk is particularly disturbed by the degree of interference resulting from the mass of paperwork and bureaucratic detail thrust on educational institutions by regulatory-direct federal schemes such as OSHA.[24] The general counsel of Johns Hopkins University, Estelle A. Fishbein, echoes this view in describing the red tape maze as no mere wave but a "tidal wave."[25]

On the other hand, Professor Stephen Bailey of the Harvard Graduate School of Education considers the academic response to such federal regulatory activity an overreaction.[26] He sees no basis for academia to seek any exemption from regulatory schemes directed at racial and sex-based discrimination. Gellhorn and Boyer[27] agree: "Universities are too important a force in society to escape the contemporary demands for fairness, openness, equality of opportunity, and accountability that are being pressed upon all large and powerful institutions. . . . By increasing the accountability of the universities, administrative procedures can help higher education to maintain the confidence of its constituencies and of the general public."[28] Rather than complaining, suggest Gellhorn and Boyer, academics should learn how to live as a regulated industry. Administrators should negotiate compromises with the federal agencies and learn how to apply pressure at appropriate times in key points in the administrative process.[29] Finally, these writers recommend that higher education infiltrate the regulatory agencies and if possible take control of them.[30]

In the main it appears that the criticism one may have against the wave of red tape engulfing academia is criticism that can appropriately be directed at government regulatory programs generally, not at any particular impact on institutions of higher education. That is, what is an unreasonable "reporting" requirement for a college is similarly unreasonable for a private commercial company.

Three arguments for singling out the impact of bureaucratic regulation on education have been put forward—the first two have little merit and the third is at most debatable. First, the contention that government ought to trust institutions of higher education to carry out federal social reform policies without being subject to close government scrutiny through the regulatory process seems unfounded. For whatever reason, higher education, at least until recently, has from a statistical standpoint done poorly in the hiring of women and minorities as faculty members. The statistics give rise to suspicion rather than trust. Although recent records indicate that positive steps have been taken in the area of hiring, the response of colleges and universities to federal efforts to obtain a fairer, if not gender-equal, allocation of resources between men's and women's physical education and intercollegiate athletics programs has frequently been hostile rather than cooperative.

Secondly, the point that institutions of higher education are the cradle of academic freedom is a non sequitur when the issue is whether colleges should be subject to regulatory schemes such as OSHA, ERISA, etc. Some aspects of academic freedom are, as has been discussed, protected by the First Amendment against government interference, just as are some aspects of operating a newspaper or a church. But the First Amendment provides a shield only against that government action which interferes with the practice of or assertion of the protected right. Just as a church cannot conceivably claim immunity from building code regulations designed to make its hall of worship earthquake proof, universities can find no basis in the First Amendment for evading safety regulations, minimum wage rules, and antidiscrimination guidelines. This is especially true when the major thrust of objection is not to the substantive rule but rather the amount of paperwork and red tape it involves, for in such instances the relationship of academic freedom to the First Amendment seems irrelevant.

The third argument, made by all of the educators who object to existing form-filing and red tape procedures, is that higher education stands in a different posture than private industry because it cannot pass along the cost of compliance to the consumer, students, or the public in general, by increasing the cost of the product. With respect to public colleges and universities, this is true only to the extent that there may be political difficulties in obtaining from the legislature or other governing body increased appropriations sufficient to offset the growing costs of complying with government regulatory schemes. Certainly the cost *can* be passed on to the public in general through the taxing process. Tuition or student fee increases are also possible. For private institutions, however, the method of passing on the cost is limited to the tuition increase, and it is urged that this places a hardship on students from low- and moderate-income families. True enough, but these students are also eligible for federal assistance in paying their tuition through low-interest loans and to some extent federal grants. A shift from student assistance to a subsidy for private schools to defray the paperwork cost of regulatory compliance would mute the criticism that institutions incapable of passing on such costs should not be treated in the same regulatory manner as businesses that can. In the final analysis, however, the overall impact on higher education would remain the same.

Constitutional Attacks on Regulatory-Direct Interference

Even if there is merit to the argument that it is unfair to subject institutions of higher education to the same regulatory schemes imposed on private industries capable of passing on the costs of compliance to consumers, it does not provide grounds for a constitutional attack on the federal legislation.[31] It has never been, to my knowledge, suggested by the courts that the Fifth Amendment precludes application of a regulatory scheme otherwise valid to entities who will find difficulty in absorbing the cost. Indeed, equal protection aspects of Fifth Amendment due process seem more clearly satisfied by legislation that requires compliance by all parties than with a scheme that tries to divide the regulated into two groups, one of which (e.g., academia) is subjected to less rigorous enforcement procedures.

Arbitrary and capricious operation of a regulatory-direct statute, excluding for no reasonable bases certain classes of parties from the impact of the statute, would be a basis for finding it unconstitutional. Higher education also has two other bases for constitutional objection. First, there is the contention that the basis of constitutionally granted power relied on by Congress is unavailable in light of the particular matter sought to be regulated. For example, an attempt by Congress to rely on the commerce power to force institutions of higher education to increase the enrollment of students pursuing specified professions (such as medicine) might be held unconstitutional under an analysis revealing that such programs would have no measurable impact on interstate commerce. This lack of commercial impact could arise in a situation where needs for American doctors were being met by citizens studying in Mexico and elsewhere rather than within the United States.[32]

The second basis for constitutional attack is available only to state-operated institutions and rests on the contention that the direct regulation of the state's educational system has such impact as to interfere with the state's sovereignty. *National League of Cities v. Usery*, 1976, [33] involved an attempt by Congress to utilize the federal commerce power to impose a minimum wage scheme for various classes of state employees. A prior decision, *Maryland v. Wirtz*, 1968,[34] had upheld a federal minimum wage for state teachers, but it was overruled in *National League of Cities*. A reading of the latter case suggests that the Supreme Court is using a reasonableness test to determine when otherwise proper federal implementation of constitutionally granted powers (e.g., the commerce power) will be held invalid as applied to state agencies and employees because of interference in the carrying on of state "governmental functions." One can reasonably suspect that the interference must be rather extreme or at least the federal rule must appear somewhat silly, as it did in *National League of Cities*, where costly overtime pay scales severely restricted state flexibility in fixing employee time schedules. The Supreme Court seems to have felt that Congress was unreasonably forcing the state, as employer, into a rigid and somewhat awkward scheme in spite of the availability of numerous other programs designed to achieve the same ends. Also, it was undoubtedly important in *National League of Cities* that the federal interest asserted was the power to regulate commerce rather than the power to protect against state abridgment of basic human rights.[35]

Any future congressional attempt to tamper with the college curriculum (e.g., by making certain courses mandatory) through use of the commerce power should fail under the rationale of *National League of Cities*. Similarly, Congress may not invoke the commerce power in order to regulate the hiring, firing, and tenure policies (other, perhaps, than to protect against discrimination against minorities and women, etc.) of state academic institutions. However, where congressional regulation relies on a different source of power, *National League of Cities* will be of little benefit to state institutions seeking to avoid federal regulation.[36]

The foregoing discussion of the unconstitutionality of certain regulatory-direct federal schemes, although it seems to be outside the scope of government interference in education through the grant process, is pertinent to the major inquiry because frequently the conditions on grants consist of regulations which have been alternately imposed through direct regulation. For example, conditions requiring that the recipient institution be in compliance with the civil rights acts may rest on the commerce power and/or section 5 of the Fourteenth Amendment. (Executive Order No. 11246 has, by use of the spending power, this effect with respect to certain classes of government contracts.) If the condition is unconstitutional as a regulatory-direct burden on higher education, under the doctrine of unconstitutional conditions discussed below, the same condition is likely to be unconstitutional in grant legislation. On the other hand, if the condition is constitutional as a regulatory-direct measure, it is difficult to imagine prevailing on an argument that the same condition is unconstitutionally irrational when attached to a grant provision, although by subjecting only those persons and institutions which have accepted federal funds to the regulation, the program is left open to attack on grounds of arbitrary line drawing. One would expect the courts, however, to hold that Congress can attack a regulatory problem part by part and thereby reasonably decide that initially the controls should be placed on recipients of federal funds, notwithstanding the constitutional power to include others within the scope of the rule. Such a decision may be based upon the conclusion that it would be morally wrong or internationally indelicate for the national government to be spending federal monies in support of the activity now to be regulated.

Interference through the Spending Power

Most educators agree that at least until recent years the interference with academic freedom caused by regulatory-direct federal legislation enacted under the spending power (e.g., grant legislation detailing the required curriculum) has been slight. Stanford's Rosenzweig recently said he considered it "remarkabl[e]" that "the hand of government has been largely absent from the classroom, the laboratory, and even the admissions committee—despite the enormous sums of federal money spent on teaching, research, and student assistance." But Rosenzweig was worried about an increasing tide of impact-direct interference— citing the original "Guadalajara Amendment" and the DNA research bill as prime examples. He fears that Congress will increasingly utilize the spending power to interject federal control into higher education— that at least increased control of the health professions schools, which have become heavily dependent on federal grants, is to be expected.

Of course the ability of Congress to purchase obedience turns on the degree of dependence of the college or university on federal funds. Even if alternative sources exist—such as private foundations or state government—the type of condition and restriction objected to in the federal scheme may be attached. In addition, recent practice indicates that institutions of higher education have seldom said "no thanks" to federal money, despite the annoying, costly, and time-consuming conditions and procedures that come hand in hand with the funds. As University of Michigan President Fleming has said: "[N]o matter how true it may be that government funds can be freely declined, in practice few institutions can survive without complying with the conditions that qualify for them for public money."[37] This is particularly true in the physical sciences area, where some research projects are so expensive that only the federal government is really capable of subsidizing them. It will be recalled that despite considerable uproar from academia over the original Guadalajara Amendment, less than 20 percent of American medical schools indicated they would refuse capitation grants rather than discard their admissions standards to abide by the federal model.

Russell Kirk has written about some of the effects of higher education's dependence on federal subsidies. One result is that the government rather than the institution decides the areas of scientific research that will receive emphasis. Administrators often become uneasy about criticism of the government from the faculty and tend to mute their own criticism. It is also significant to note that many faculty members are hired, advanced, and tenured in large measure because they can attract grants (and because they are not feuding with the federal government). Finally, the curriculum is directly affected by a dependency on federal funding because certain professors are forced to move into research and certain departments are reduced in size as a direct result of their failure to attract grants. In a similar manner, utilitarian and immediate objectives are favored in research projects over pure science and basic research, and researchers fear to publish theories or conclusions that the grant-givers may find controversial or displeasing.[38]

Kidd, in his article *The Implications of Research Funds for Academic Freedom*,[39] lists other effects. When the grant is made to an individual scientist, it tends to make him or her independent of the university and to shift his or her loyalties. Where the grant gives a dean or department head control over expenditures, the dean's power increases. On the other hand, Kidd notes that the receipt of grants, even for strictly limited purposes, increases the institution's freedom in several respects by opening up areas of study that would otherwise be untouched by it. Moreover, if state and private institutions of higher education will not participate in national defense efforts through grants and government contracts, the federal government will increasingly set up its own "think tanks" and research agencies, drawing more and more top scientists (and a few other academicians) away from the colleges and universities.

Kidd's thoughtful article—which I consider the most useful writing on the topic and highly recommend—after a detailed analysis of the benefits and detriments of the university's accepting *typical* government grants for specific research (and the same would follow of *typical* grants for specific instruction projects), concludes that these funds should ordinarily be accepted and that the institution has little basis to object to regulatory conditions that assure the government that the monies are spent as intended. These conditions may require the institution to file reports, authorize governmental inspections and audits of the university, and even give the government control of the use made of research data by limiting publication. As long as the country has defense needs, classified research must be done, and faculty members who are experts in their field may be the best qualified men and women in the country to do the work. If there is need for secrecy, the institution has no basis for complaining about conditions placed on fund use and operation of the project, for without such safeguards it would be difficult to protect the country's national security interests.

What Kidd, writing in 1963, was speaking of when he concluded that higher education had little basis for objection to the existence of the federal grant process was the ordinary take-it-or-leave-it, restricted-use grant. For example, suppose that $1 million is offered to a qualified university laboratory to do certain studies on nuclear particles. If X University declines to become involved in the experimentation, the "harm" to it is that its physicists may not be able to pursue such research due to budget problems. The university is not, however, penalized for refusing to become a partner with the government in the research project. Similarly, if it applies for and receives a grant, failure to abide by the conditions may result in forfeiture of the authorization and an obligation to repay federal funds misapplied.[40] Additional "punishment" to the institution for noncooperation was not provided for in the grant (although, of course, researchers who violated lawful secrecy orders could be criminally prosecuted).

Without doubt these types of grant programs can in practice put considerable pressure on higher education to alter research and instruction practices in order to qualify the institution for assistance. For example, the aid to clinical legal education programs described above would strongly encourage law schools to switch from trial practice instruction based on simulated cases to instruction through the assisted trial of "real" cases, in order to satisfy the federal notion of what constitutes a clinical course. As a law school faculty member I find this unfortunate, but I cannot assert that Congress, charged by the Constitution to spend money collected from taxpayers for the general welfare, should not attempt to place some controls on the use of funds it allocates to education. It would be irresponsible to the taxpayers simply to turn money over to higher education with the invitation to spend it as each institution deems advisable. Under such a setup there would be no assurance that the money was being used to help meet current national needs. True, education in general might be advanced, but the taxpaying electorate demands more accountability of its representatives in Washington than that sums were spent "for education." Congress is being accountable if it conditions grant programs so that there is assurance that the funds achieve particular ends, such as increasing the number of family-practice physicians, improving the litigation skills of lawyers who will represent the poor, etc. Even a grant "to legal education" is arguably too broad to assure congressional accountability. In all probability, most of the money would be wisely expended by the various recipient law schools on projects offering direct and immediate benefits to the public—the type of "general welfare" spending the electorate expects of its representatives. It seems unreasonable, however, not to expect Congress to demand some assurance that sums will not be diverted to esoteric research of historical interest but not of direct and immediate benefit to the public.

In summary, then, a reasoned reaction to the federal clinical education grant program is that Congress should not be faulted for attempting to limit the type of instruction it was willing to fund; it simply made a foolish value judgment in excluding simulated trial clinical courses. The response of law schools wishing to continue simulated trial instruction is to forego asking for federal money for these programs and to lobby for a change in the restrictions on the aid program. It is clearly a political problem. Even though there are First Amendment overtones to academic freedom, it could not be reasonably argued that the enacted spending program was unconstitutional. The decision that simulated-trial clinical instruction does not sufficiently advance the general welfare and thus warrant federal monetary support will not be second-guessed by the courts. Similarly, no true penalty is legislatively imposed on educators who, exercising their academic freedom, decide not to follow the federal model in teaching the legal clinic course.

Very different from the "typical" grant program described above—and deserving of concern and criticism—is the twisting of the granting process to achieve some benefits other than those to be purchased with the federal money, coupled by such a heavy threatened "punishment" for institutions that do not toe the line that agreement becomes almost coerced rather than the product of a reasoned analysis of the benefits and detriments of becoming involved in a particular program.

One example of this newly emerging type of federal power play utilizing the spending power is the Buckley Amendment, formally known as the Family Educational Rights and Privacy Act.[41] It requires educational institutions to make available for inspection by students and parents many types of records previously held in closed or confidential files. The cost of setting up an inspection system that satisfies the act is probably no more than a few thousand dollars a year at each college and university.[42] Whatever the costs, the penalty provision for a university that does not set up procedures following the Buckley Amendment is undeniably severe. The act begins as follows: "No funds shall be made available under any applicable program to any educational agency or institution" which does not comply.[43] Other statutes disclose that the applicable programs, funds of which are forfeited by noncompliance, are all the grant programs administered by the Office of Education.[44] Thus, if the university administrators disagree with the Buckley Amendment, the cost of asserting that academic freedom right will be staggering. Hundreds of thousands of federal dollars for research apparently can be lost, even though the projects have nothing at all to do with maintenance of the disciplinary records which the university prefers the student not see.

The various conditions to the capitation grants for health professions graduate schools—requiring altering the admissions process and adding federally designed courses to the curriculum—are further examples of the coercive use of the spending power. Noncompliance with a condition relating only to admissions or curriculum forfeits hundreds of thousands of dollars of aid employed for various educational purposes, many of which have nothing to do with the aspect of the educational process in which the breach of condition occurred.

Constitutional Attacks on Abuse of the Spending Power in the Educational Grant Process

As president of Yale University, Kingman Brewster warned that "use of the leverage of the government dollar to accomplish objectives which have nothing to do with the purpose for which the dollar is given, has become dangerously fashionable." As quoted in O'Neil, *God and Government at Yale: The Limits of Federal Regulation of Higher Education,*[45] Brewster challenged legal scholars to fashion a constitutional theory so that this "coercive power of government is made subject to a rule of law."

Professor O'Neil responded to this challenge with a thoughtful and scholarly article, on which I draw heavily in the following brief survey of the various grounds of constitutional attack that have been suggested.

The First Amendment. Numerous United States Supreme Court decisions could be marshalled to support the statement in *Griswold v. Connecticut,* 1964,[46] that the First Amendment "right of Freedom of Speech and Press includes not only the right to utter or to print but . . . indeed the freedom of the entire university community." But what is protected against is actual punishment for exercising rights of academic freedom. The prohibited punishment may be criminal prosecution (see *Meyer v. Nebraska*[47] [teaching a language other than English cannot be made a crime]; *Epperson v. Arkansas*[48] [teaching evolution cannot be made a crime]), or discharge of a teacher for expressing unpopular political views or refusing to take a vaguely worded anticommunist loyalty oath.

Even where the faculty member has no contractual or other "entitlement" to keep his job, a decision not to rehire made to penalize him for expressing unpopular views on such matters as politics or the role of education may raise a constitutional basis for relief.[49]

But in other contexts the Supreme Court has held that denial of governmental largess sought by a party who wishes to exercise a constitutional right but cannot otherwise afford it is not an unconstitutional governmental interference with the right. Thus the Constitution protects against interference by government in a woman's private decision whether or not to have an abortion, but the Court has also held that an act of Congress terminating federal funding of abortions for the poor was not an unconstitutional interference with the right. There is a constitutional right to travel, but it would be ludicrous to translate that into an obligation on the part of government to provide a poor person with airline tickets.

So, even if it is assumed that the First Amendment may protect from discharge a faculty member who teaches a course in a manner not consistent with the federal model that must be followed to qualify for federal money,[50] the consequent loss of funding decreed by Congress is, based on these facts, constitutionally unobjectionable.

The doctrine of unconstitutional conditions. Some years ago a litigant objecting on constitutional grounds to nonreceipt of some form of federal largess such as grant money would have been answered by the courts that he had no basis for complaint because what was denied him was a mere privilege or gratuity, not a right. This doctrine has been squarely repudiated (see, e.g., *Elrod v. Burns*, 1976).[51] Relief will be granted today against federal rules that restrict disbursements by requiring the recipient to act unconstitutionally or give up a constitutional right.[52] Thus, a state unemployment compensation scheme must accommodate a worker whose religion forbids her or him to work on Saturday, and it may not, constitutionally, summarily deny such welfare benefits to one who practices the First Amendment-protected belief.[53]

If the Congress conditioned a grant on the doing of an act prohibited by the Constitution—e.g., if institutions of higher education receiving federal funds were required to periodically conduct random strip searches of students in an effort to uncover illegal drugs—relief in court could be had under this doctrine (although, as noted below, what the remedy would be is a separate issue). But this will seldom be the case. It has been said by some that the doctrine of unconstitutional conditions prohibits Congress from doing indirectly what it cannot do directly. This could be misleading. I would assume that no grant of federal power would authorize Congress to directly compel educational institutions— particularly private colleges and universities—to follow the Buckley Amendment procedures. A statute simply ordering them to do so would be unconstitutional under the Tenth Amendment and the principle that the federal government exercises only the specific powers granted it by the states in the Constitution. Yet is is clear that for a state to do what the Buckley Amendment demands and open up records for examination by students and parents is not prohibited by the Constitution. As it has been applied to date, then, the doctrine of unconstitutional conditions offers no basis for relief in this situation.

A theory of "impermissible consideration." Delgado and Millen, in *God, Galileo, and Government: Toward Constitutional Protection for Scientific Inquiry,*[54] invite the courts to grant researchers relief when the federal government cuts off or denies them funds for what the authors call "impermissible considerations." Exactly what this means is unclear to me, but they illustrate the theory by proposing the case where the government declines to grant funds to study the relationship between intelligence and race. Apparently the idea is that if the grant decision turns on a political or moral judgment (such as that black people would be offended by a study that might return data showing a genetic basis for blacks not doing as well as whites on some intelligence tests), the decision is unconstitutional. The authors do not discuss the question of remedy, such as how much money the courts are supposed to order the government to pay to the aggrieved researchers.

I must reject the proposed theory as unworkable. Each time funding is requested for a particular project, the Constitution itself demands that the government inquire whether the proposed expenditure would promote the general welfare more than competing applications for funds. While all studies arguably advance knowledge to some degree, there are certain areas of knowledge where present needs are greater. Solar energy is a present problem. We are getting along just fine, however, without knowing whether there is a genetic relationship between race and intelligence. It seems entirely permissible and proper for government to make that judgment in determining how funds are to be spent.[55] The First Amendment presently protects against interjection of some "impermissible considerations" into the grant-giving process, for I would assume it would entitle a researcher or instructor to relief if it could be shown his program or study that met all the statutory and regulatory criteria had been denied funding because of some political or sociological views that the applicant had expressed. (For example, a geneticist who expressed the view that study of the relationship between race and intelligence should be undertaken could not for this reason be turned down on his or her grant application for a quite different project.)

An "entitlement theory." Delgado and Millen also have proffered the bizarre theory that academics can obtain a property right or entitlement to federal funds for research. The argument rests on the theory that the government possesses a research funding monopoly so that a rejected applicant has nowhere else to go for money.

> Arguably, the heavy governmental incursion into the area of scientific research has reversed this situation [of a free marketplace in ideas and research], however, with the result that ideas and proposals of which the government disapproves stand little chance of being developed. To the extent that this is so, there is a danger that investigations of which governmental grant-givers disapprove will never be carried out. The effect is thus the same as if the ideas were directly prohibited. This argument, of course, rests on the assumption that government should not be permitted to do indirectly what it cannot do directly.[56]

I cannot accept the conclusion that for the government to cut off funding to a researcher who seeks to show marijuana may heighten sexual arousal is constitutionally the equivalent to prohibiting the advancement of this theory, as the First Amendment would assure the researcher the right to do. Moreover, the very nature of this "entitlement" theory based on federal monopoly power eliminates any mechanism for screening silly studies that will do little to promote the general welfare. Nor does the theory provide any means for allocating scarce resource funds among the various proposed projects, none of which the government could give a flat "no" to.

A "relevant conditions" theory. Kingman Brewster's own theory, which he proposed for study by scholars of constitutional law, was that grant conditions would have to be relevant, in the sense of tending to promote or implement the purpose of the study or instructional project. As Professor O'Neil points out, there are no Supreme Court decisions directly on point. He suggests there may be some support for the idea in lower court cases addressing the question as to when action of a nominally private college is state action to be tested as such under the Fourteenth Amendment and implementing statutes. Suppose one department of a university has allegedly denied the due process of law owed a student or faculty member by government institutions. Can state and federal funding and involvement of other departments of the college be relied on to find state action in the incident complained of? O'Neil found a split of authority in the lower court decisions, with the most recent holdings looking to university-wide involvement of the government, not just its involvement in the department allegedly denying due process. Such decisions by analogy cut against Brewster's "relevance" argument.

An additional problem is presented by Brewster's own argument, in that he sought to have his "relevance" criterion applied to conditions on grants where the government was seeking to achieve through the spending power what it could have perhaps ordered directly. For example, he argued that a private university should not lose federal money for physics research because some other department is not recruiting minority admissions. It is unclear whether Congress could under the Fourteenth and/or Thirteenth amendments directly order private universities to undertake such affirmative action programs. Almost certainly public institutions could be so directly regulated; with respect to them the condition thus *is* relevant to achieving a distinct goal which the federal government is constitutionally entitled to pursue without twisting the spending power. The problem would not seem to be relevance at all but discrimination in the scope of the regulation (only grant-taking institutions bound) and possible unreasonable severity of punishment for noncompliance.

Turning to an example where Congress could not directly regulate to achieve the goal of the allegedly irrelevant condition—e.g., cutting off research grants to schools not abiding by Buckley Amendment procedures—there remain problems with Brewster's relevance theory. Under the Constitution, Congress is charged with seeing that such grants are spent on the public welfare. It must be clear to all that just about every grant gives some financial support to the recipient institution as a whole. Money for physics research may enable the university to revise its budget by cutting back on laboratory equipment and on internal funds used to compensate the faculty and staff in the physics department, thus releasing money for other departments and general administration. Cannot Congress determine that it is not spending for the general welfare when it so bolsters an institution which, in Congress' eyes, treats its students unfairly by preventing them from locating potentially career-damaging false accusations of wrongdoing in institutional files—files into which those writing recommendation letters for the student can peek but not the student himself?

Brewster's proposal of a "relevance" test to determine the constitutionality of alleged abuses of the federal spending power is provocative and certainly cannot be rejected out of hand. It merits study; it seems unlikely to be adopted in full flower by the United States Supreme Court at an early date, however.

Testing for rationality and discrimination. In dispensing governmental largess, the Congress may not under the Fifth Amendment act capriciously.[57] Generally, a condition restricting receipt of social security benefits must satisfy in the courts only the any-rational-basis test.[58] In *Cleland v. National College of Business*, 1978,[59] an educational institution contended that certain provisions of the GI bills providing tuition support for student-veterans discriminated against it because of the nature of its student body. The statute cut off federal aid for enrollment in courses where more than 85 percent of the students were receiving federal assistance.[60] Apparently finding no problem in the standing of the college to present the constitutional contention, the Court held there was good reason for the restriction: to protect veterans from enrolling in educationally unsound and inefficient schools that are unable to attract a reasonable number of students who are paying their own way.[61]

The irrationality inquiry is not the same as the previously discussed relevance test, for I would assume that many conditions that Brewster would find irrelevant are still rational when the secondary goal, different from that of the appropriation itself, is considered. Thus, compelling compliance with the Buckley Amendment is a rational way to achieve a goal of assuring a system of recordkeeping at educational institutions that is fair to students, although making compliance a condition for receipt of research money for the physics department means the proposed relevance test is not satisfied.

The any-rational-basis limitation on Congress' power to restrict spending in the general welfare is a well-established doctrine of constitutional law. Unfortunately, the test is so easily satisfied that it will seldom be available as the vehicle for validating federal use of the spending power to coerce state action.

Testing the severity of punishment on noncompliance. Closely related to the proposed "relevance" test for constitutionality, yet distinct, would be a standard that required the penalty in loss of funding resulting from failing to meet a grant condition to be commensurate with the nature of that failure. To return to the hypothetical multi-million-dollar physics study grant conditioned on the recordkeeping office obeying the Buckley Amendment procedures, this approach would not authorize a holding that the *condition* was unconstitutional; rather, the penalty of loss of all such funding would fall. Congress would be told by the courts to fashion a less severe sanction. Professor O'Neil's article found that such a reasonableness-of-penalty provision weakened any constitutional attack on the manner in which some of the civil rights acts provisions are applied to higher education.[62] For example, where sex discrimination by an aided educational institution is found, 20 U.S.C. sec. 1682 limits the cutting off of funds to those used by "the particular education program or activity or part thereof in which noncompliance has been found."

The notion that the government's penalty ought to fit the crime may underlie an interesting recent administrative law judge's decision against HEW.[63] The ruling was that HEW could not terminate all federal support for student aid programs used at Hillsdale College even though the college refused to certify compliance with the anti-sex discrimination provisions of Title IX of the Education Amendments of 1972. This decision was not based on constitutional principles, for an applicable regulation said HEW "may" refuse financial assistance in such a case, not that the termination was mandatory. The severe impact of the proposed punishment on the college apparently was a major factor leading to the conclusion that discretion had been abused.

So far as I know, the proposed inquiry into severity of penalty as a basis for constitutionally safeguarding against abuse of the spending power has no greater support in the reported cases than Brewster's relevance formula. One case where the restrained penalty may have precluded a court holding of unconstitutional abuse is *Oklahoma v. Civil Service Comm'n.*, 1947.[64] Congress had attempted to apply to state employees through the spending power the federal system's Hatch Act ban on active involvement in partisan politics of certain classes of government employees. A member of the Oklahoma State Highway Commission had been caught raising money for a Democratic party "victory dinner," a prohibited activity because he was employed by a state agency that received and disbursed federal funds. In the year in question, over $2 million in federal grants for highway use went through the department. Under the act of Congress the penalty to be imposed on Oklahoma was not loss of the full $2 million but a sum equal to double the salary of the offending employee.

The opinion of the Court is less than clear as to whether it was considering the grant condition (that employees not engage in partisan politics) under a relevance test of the type Brewster advocates. The Court did say that "the end sought by Congress through the Hatch Act is better public service by requiring those who administer funds for national needs to abstain from political partisanship." I would suggest this is a separate goal from purpose of the grant, fostering a network of interstate highways; unless the relevance test is extremely weak it seems not satisfied here.[65] Some passages of the opinion suggest there is no relevance requirement at all:

> While the United States is not concerned with, and has no power to regulate, local political activities as such of state officials, it does have power to fix the terms upon which its money allotments to states shall be disbursed. ... The offer of benefits to a state by the United States dependent upon cooperation by the state with federal plans, assumedly for the general welfare, is not unusual.[66]

The state of Oklahoma was told that its "remedy" if it did not want to discharge the partisan highway commissioner was to accept the loss of funding. Although the relation of the penalty to the violation was not discussed, I suggest that coercive effect of the federal act would have raised further constitutional problems if Congress had sought to forfeit millions of dollars of grants to the state.

State sovereignty as a limitation on the spending power. In *League of Cities*, the Supreme Court specifically left open the question of whether conditions attached to federal grants to states would be invalid if their purpose was to achieve the same interference with state control of state governmental functions as did the regulatory-direct minimum wage laws involved there. For example, Congress could stipulate that no federal funds for education would be provided to a state that did not meet specified minimum wage standards for its teachers. Or the act might go farther and attempt to penalize the failure to pay state teachers according to federal standards of fairness by terminating not only aid to education but *all* federal grants, for highways, air pollution control, rapid transit, etc.

Where the penalty is the cessation of funding only for the activity not being run according to federal notions of fairness, *Oklahoma v. Civil Service Comm'n.* strongly suggests that restrictions not allowed under direct regulations may be placed as conditions on grants. Indeed, for the United States to attempt to tell Oklahoma it must fire an employee because of his involvement in a partisan victory dinner seems every bit as much an interference with the sovereign's power to hire the agents of its choice as was the minimum wage law in *League of Cities*.

If, on the other hand, the penalty is loss of hundreds of millions of dollars in federal funds, the coercive effect in a practical sense is to force the states to agree to an invasion of sovereignty by Congress under the spending power. Whatever *League of Cities* held could not be done in regulatory-direct fashion could at once be achieved through the spending power.[67] It seems likely, therefore, that at least public colleges and universities, being able to invoke state sovereignty as a limitation on federal intervention in education, should be able to make a convincing argument that the Constitution prohibits an unreasonable penalty for failure to abide by some types of grant conditions.

Severability of an unconstitutional grant condition. Even if a university or other recipient successfully argues in court that a congressionally enacted grant condition (or, for that matter, one imposed in regulations or practice by a federal agency) is unconstitutional, it does not necessarily mean the court will hold the recipient entitled to receive funds while disregarding the invalid condition. The federal government may urge that the condition is not a severable part of the grant legislation; that is, the condition alone cannot be stricken by the court—the entire statute must be valid or invalid.

When such an argument is made, and the legislation has no provision addressed to the severability issue, the court tries to guess what the unexpressed will of Congress would be. Would it prefer the entire act invalidated (so that no grant money is available)? Would it prefer grants to be made without the intended use condition?[68]

The courts have generally assumed that Congress wants its programs of spending for the general welfare to continue to operate with unconstitutional provisions stricken rather than to be completely scuttled. Thus, some restrictions in social security and military benefits schemes that were found to be unconstitutional because of sex discrimination have in recent years been excised from these spending programs without much serious consideration of the alternative of invalidating the entire scheme.

But Congress could in the future eliminate uncertainty as to its intent by including a nonseverance clause in the grant legislation. This may be politically feasible. Congress seems a bit petulant following the verbal attacks by Brewster and other academic leaders and the angry response to the original Guadalajara Amendment. The House report recommending revision of the amendment contains a lightly veiled threat to higher education to hush its complaints:

> The announcement by some schools that they would forego capitation support unless the conditions for receipt were altered raises a significant question as to the need for continuation of this type of support. One of the principal bases for the committee's insistence that capitation support be included in the 1976 legislation was its belief, based upon assertions during hearings, that such support was necessary to insure the financial stability of medical schools. Such assertions clearly are inconsistent with announcements that schools were considering declining capitation support. It may well be that Federal funds would be better spent through special project grants such as the direct funding of residency programs in the primary care specialties and increased support of area health education centers. The committee intends to closely examine this issue during 1978.[69]

The examination has begun with a federal GAO audit of eleven medical schools, including four that had announced they would reject capitation grants rather than accept the original Guadalajara Amendment.

HEW Secretary Califano in a recent speech warned that the long-standing congressional tradition against interference in matters of academic freedom could not now be taken for granted: "Mere tradition may not be strong enough to protect these state and local prerogatives at a time when the federal role is changing and expanding."

It is thus possible that Congress may begin adding antiseverance clauses to grant legislation in an attempt to head off court attacks contending that a particular use condition or penalty provision is unconstitutional. That would not deny a party standing to raise the claim of unconstitutionality.[70] After all, it could be contended that the nonseverance provision was also invalid because of its coercive effect.

Nevertheless, since there is little precedent on which to base an argument that Congress cannot constitutionally cause termination of an entire program if any part of it is found invalid, educational institutions that need the federal funding but object to the allegedly unconstitutional conditions will certainly be discouraged from bringing suit. On the other hand, a wealthy institution seeking to increase its competitive advantage over other institutions by causing termination of the program is encouraged by the nonseverance provision to bring suit. I would not expect the courts to rule that the ulterior motive undercuts its standing to sue.

Conclusion

Article I, sec. 8, of the U.S. Constitution specifically authorizes the federal government to collect taxes and to "provide for the . . . general Welfare of the United States." It is well established that this general welfare includes grants for education and research by state and private institutions.[71] Within these broad areas, education and research, it is undeniable that general welfare will be more helpfully advanced by certain types of instruction and studies. Congress thus cannot be expected to turn over large sums of federal money to be dealt with as educators please. And when Congress does restrict the use of the funds to projects it has determined to be especially beneficial at the time of the appropriation, it is reasonable for it to demand that the education institution account for how the funds were spent. Reasonable procedures to prevent abuse or even fraudulent diversion of funds are constitutionally unobjectionable and politically imperative if the representatives are to be accountable to the taxpaying electorate.

In the delicate line-drawing between the permissible and prohibited expenditure, Congress may make errors at times (as I feel it did with the program for aid to legal clinical instruction); Congress would usually be best advised to state in broad terms the goals it wishes to implement by the grants and leave details of implementation to educators at the benefited institution. Yet Congress certainly has the constitutional right, if it does not unreasonably discriminate, to draw tight lines in reaching its conclusions as to what will and will not best provide for the general welfare.

When Congress makes an allegedly irrelevant grant condition, there is little basis for objection when the matter is one subject to direct federal regulation (as are antidiscrimination conditions) unless the penalty of loss of all funding is too severe a sanction for violation of the condition.

On the other hand, if what Kingman Brewster would call an irrelevant condition is not a matter the federal government could directly regulate,[72] it can be cogently argued that Congress is abusing the spending power, particularly if the sanction for violating the condition is extreme. Whether the U.S. Supreme Court will adopt any form of relevance test to prevent abuse of the spending power is dubious. Likewise there is little basis for predicting that a due process argument based on unreasonableness of the sanction will prevail.

Not every bad law is unconstitutional. Civil libertarians concerned over interference with academic freedom through abuse of the grant process may find the best course to pursue is lobbying Congress to quit using the clumsy technique of trying to coerce changes in education by grant restrictions. Outcry from higher education did get the original Guadalajara Amendment promptly changed (and educators also got Congress to make changes in the Buckley Amendment so it was less of an interference with confidential records).

Some members of Congress, however, defend using the spending power to work changes in higher education. For example, Senator Edward Kennedy (backer of a bill to federally control recombinant DNA research), quoted in the March 1978 issue of *Change,* concedes that with respect to health-professions schools, "the federal government has begun to use its ever increasing investments . . . to exert some leverage for reform and innovation." It did so, he says, because it found a crisis in health care. The senator also concedes that such use of the federal spending "lever" can "tyrannize the academic community." He nevertheless defends its use:

> But the option of not using the lever at all is just as dangerous. It would be a violation of the public trust. It would allow you [medical schools] to set your own course exclusively on your own terms . . . and to neglect the problems that now seem peripheral to your mission.

In other words, Congress is viewed as the appropriate body to determine the true boundaries of the "mission" of medical education—the administrators at the school cannot be trusted to do so.

This type of attitude—the we-in-Washington-know-how-to-do-it-better syndrome—will lead to further seizing on the spending power to apply pressure on higher education. It may force the Supreme Court to find some mechanism for preventing spending-power abuse.

Such use of the spending power is obviously destructive of federalism. Indeed, the altering of power in the area of education in favor of the federal government is the openly stated intent of Senator Kennedy. Also destructive of federalism, although in a more subtle way, is the wave of forms, red tape, and paperwork that accompanies federal intrusion. It can stifle the states (and their allies, private institutions) and prevent them from moving ahead to meet social needs through local action. It is the view of most civil libertarians, including, one suspects, Justice Douglas,[73] that a mechanism must be found for preventing this suffocating effect and enabling federalism to flourish.

Notes

1. HEW Secretary Califano recently noted that the number of pages of federal legislation dealing with such matters as restrictions on expenditures—and that would not include agency regulations—concerning education in 1976 was 360, up from 80 in 1964.

2. The dependency that concerned Califano—risking potential loss of institutional control over such areas as admissions, curriculum, teaching assignments, grading, etc.—could conceivably arise upon an institution's accepting grants from large private foundations and from a private college or university's receiving funds from state or even local governments.

Interference with the operation of a state-created and state-financed institution of higher education by the legislature or a state agency not directly responsible for overseeing the education process can also be a problem causing considerable distress to educators. But this raises an issue primarily of distribution of power within the entity—the state—necessarily in ultimate control of the institution and the appropriate entity to be funding it. Such problems are of a partly different nature than those discussed herein.

Except where control over such matters as curriculum choice is shielded from legislative tinkering by imposition of an autonomous governing body created by the state constitution (see Beckham, *Reasonable Independence for Public Higher Education: Legal Implications of Constitutionally Autonomous Status,* 7 J. of Law and Ed. 177 [1978]), there is little basis for invalidating a state providing a list of required courses even at the college level in public schools. At its last session, the North Carolina general assembly served up to state secondary schools an act requiring courses in "the free enterprise system," "harmful or illegal drugs," and "Americanism." (N.C. Gen Stat. secs. 115-198.) Similarly, a state university faculty could, subject to constitutional attack, be presented with something like the incredible North Carolina rule for secondary schools ordering teachers "in connection with" the instruction on harmful drugs "to screen and observe all pupils in order to detect signs and symptoms of deviation from normal and to record and report the results of their findings. . . ."

3. See Fuchs, *Academic Freedom—Its Basic Philosophy, Function, and History*, 28 Law and Contemp. Prob. 431 (1963).

4. 360 U.S. 109, 112 (1959).

5. 354 U.S. 234, 250 (1957).

6. Regents of University of California v. Bakke (1978).

7. The new provision also excuses the enrollment increase if the institution can establish that such admissions would cost it its accreditation or would prevent it from providing high-quality clinical training for its third-year students.

8. In operation, the revised "Guadalajara Amendment" will in all probability bring the foreign transfers to the least prestigious domestic medical schools. (I.e., four-star-quality medical schools will take their required transfers from each other or three-star schools; the latter will choose transfers from slightly less competitive schools, and so forth, until the Americans in foreign schools, who could not previously get admitted anywhere in the United States are absorbed at the least competitive schools [which probably are those least able to forego the capitation grants to uphold admissions standards].)

9. 42 U.S.C. sec. 295f-1(d).

10. 42 U.S.C. sec. 295f-1(e).

11. At my law school, Duke, and at several others, the faculty has determined, after experience with several types of clinics, that for most students the simulated-trial basis for instruction is far more rewarding educationally to the student than the trial of a "real case." The professors can assure the trial is on a debatable legal point and that the witnesses will be furnished facts that raise interesting, as well as tactical, evidence law problems. Trial of the "real" case may be cut and dried—perhaps there will be a default. Certainly there are likely to be delays, making it impossible to assure the trial will be held during the period of the clinical course. And limiting the instruction to trials of "real" cases can only put pressure on the supervising attorney-instructor to litigate some matters that could readily be settled. In sum, the federal conclusion as to what the best clinical education at law school consists of is at the very least debatable and in my view foolish.

12. Similar NIH guidelines are addressed to grant-receiving institutions doing research involving tests on human subjects. They have generated controversy. For example, a March 1976 news story concerned a guideline which indicated that consent of the subject for a drug treatment study is not enough. Under this rule a close relative must also consent. The unfortunate result is that this rule effectively disqualifies all subjects who wish to invoke a right of privacy in the matter and to keep their participation confidential.

13. These and other rather startling proposals to restrict freedom of inquiry are collected in Delgado and Millen, *God, Galileo, and Government: Toward Constitutional Protection for Scientific Inquiry*, 53 Wash. L. Rev. 349 (1978).

14. See Jenkins, *Regulation of Colleges and Universities Under the Guaranteed Student Loan Program*, 4 J.C. and U.L. 13 (1976).

15. Cleland v. National College of Business (1978).

16. Similarly it is widely believed that the California legislature took action—by excluding faculty of the University of California from a salary increase following campus reaction to the Cambodia incursion—so as to punish professors, almost 50 percent of whom had in some manner lent support to student protests by "reconstituting" courses into Southeast Asia policy seminars, excusing student protestors from taking an examination, or giving all students an A.

17. It is unclear from the report whether the basis of federal power to impose the order was the war and defense power (direct regulation) or a right obtained under the spending power when the university accepted federal funds to promote research by the professor's department.

18. Frequently the application is for a renewal of grant approval, in which case the peer review committee will want to observe how the institution or professor is presently conducting the project and expending the funds.

19. As observed earlier, the "suggestions" to the university could relate to the method of scientific inquiry itself or to such tangential matters of federal interest as whether women and minorities are well represented in high-ranking positions on the staff handling the project.

20. See Larson, 1 Employment Discrimination sec. 5.20 (1975).

21. Private colleges and universities are not exempted from any of these acts. ERISA does not bind public institutions, and some university faculties are not participating in the basic social security program. Additionally, National League of Cities v. Usery, 426 U.S. 833 (1976) exempts employees of public colleges from the minimum wage provisions of the Fair Labor Standards Act.

22. Some state statutes add to the red tape maze. For example, in Washington State an open-meeting law has been held applicable to meetings of the law school faculty. Cathcart v. Anderson, 85 Wash. 2d 102, 530 P. 2d 313 (1975).

23. The same is true under some regulatory-indirect federal schemes not directed just at education. An example is Executive Order 11246, requiring entities that wish to make major contracts with the U.S. government to institute affirmative action employment programs to benefit minorities and women. The burden on a college or university to establish that it is operating such a program is functionally the same burden placed on private industrial entities that contract with the federal government.

24. *Central Political Power and Academic Freedom*, 29 J. Gen. Educ. 255 (1977).

25. See W. Hobbs, ed., Government Regulation of Higher Education 58 (1978).

26. Id. at 106.

27. *Government and Education: The University as a Regulated Industry*, 1977 Ariz. St. L.J. 569.

28. Id. at 572, 573.

29. "Much of the hostile reaction among academicians to the process of administrative regulation seems to be directed toward the formal model, which is perceived as a system of inflexible rules imposed by rigid, unresponsive bureaucracies, and backed by devastating sanctions. Such a limited view of the regulatory process may be not only distorted, but also self-defeating. Most

regulatory bureaucracies can be moved, but only by those who push hard and in the right places. Knowing where and how to 'push' requires an appreciation of both the formal and the informal procedural tools that are available to the university as a regulated industry." 1977 Ariz. St. L.J. at 587.

30. "There are already some signs that higher education is following the patterns set by the regulated industries in their dealing with government agencies. ACE and the more specialized professional and academic associations are becoming more effective participants in the regulatory process.... Moreover, the 'capture' of administrative agencies by the regulated industry seems to be well advanced in the field of higher education. Two university chancellors were appointed recently to the ranking positions dealing with higher education in the federal bureaucracy." Id. at 594, n. 70.

31. This is not to say that the argument is without force politically.

32. There are, of course, other possible constitutional problems, such as a taking of property in violation of due process, that the hypothetical statute might raise.

33. 426 U.S. 833 (1976).

34. 392 U.S. 183 (1968).

35. National League of Cities actually cautions in footnote 3 of the majority opinion that the decision does not express any views of the Court as to the degree to which Congress can interfere in state government operations "by exercising authority granted it under other sections of the Constitution such as the spending power, Art. I, sec. 8, cl. 1, sec. 5 of the Fourteenth Amendment."

36. For a provocative view of where National League of Cities may actually be leading the development of constitutional law principles see Tribe, Unraveling National League of Cities: The New Federalism and Affirmative Rights to Essential Government Services, 90 Harv. L. Rev. 1065 (1977).

37. W. Hobbs, ed., Government Regulation of Higher Education 17 (1978).

38. Kirk, Massive Subsidies and Academic Freedom, 28 Law and Contemp. Prob. 607 (1963).

39. 28 Law and Contemp. Prob. 613 (1963).

40. The educators' media report, for example, that in the spring of 1976 Stanford University was asked by the government to refund some research grant funds on the ground that the professors involved had spent too much time on outside consulting projects rather than doing the work the federal government contracted for when it picked up part of their salaries.

41. 20 U.S.C. sec. 2132g.

42. Although Change magazine includes the Buckley Amendment in its list of senselessly costly federal programs that constitute the mass of red tape that "threatens to kill the university," Gellhorn and Boyer cite studies which have determined that the compliance costs are not nearly as great as academia complained they would be. 1977 Ariz. State L.J. at 584.

43. 20 U.S.C. sec. 1232g.

44. 20 U.S.C. sec. 1221 b and c.

45. 44 U. Cin. L. Rev. 525 (1978).

46. 381 U.S. 479, 483 (1964).

47. 262 U.S. 390 (1923).

48. 393 U.S. 97 (1968).

49. See discussion in Board of Regents v. Roth, 408 U.S. 564 (1972).

50. If the instructor has disobeyed an order of a superior who has decided that the institution wishes to qualify for the federal funds, it is hard to imagine how the First Amendment protects the former from discipline.

51. 98 S.Ct. 2673 (1976).

52. The right-privilege distinction may not be entirely dead. At least in federal district court, former federal (CIA) employee Frank Snepp, author of *Decent Interval*, failed to have excised from his federal employment contract as an unconstitutional condition a provision that he offer to the CIA for prepublication censorship any writings to be published that dealt with his employment for the CIA. I should think the First Amendment would likely bar a prepublication censorship order imposed on a writer who had not agreed to it as a condition of receiving government benefits (in Snepp's case, employment).

53. Sherbert v. Werner, 374 U.S. sec. 398 (1963).

54. 53 Wash. L. Rev. 349 (1978).

55. It follows I can see no constitutional objection to the appropriations bill proviso that no federal funds be spent on research into the effect of marijuana on sexual desires, although equal protection would be denied if the bar were limited to studies undertaken at Southern Illinois University (where they have been under way), as one media report of the appropriations bill indicated.

56. 153 Wash. L. Rev. at 397 n. 272.

57. See Fleming v. Nestor, 363 U.S. 603 (1960).

58. Where suspect classifications such as race are involved, a much stricter standard is used. Such is the case also when the benefit not extended is specifically guaranteed by the Constitution. But the decision in San Antonio Ind. School Dist. v. Rodriguez, 411 U.S. 1 (1974), seems to establish for the present that education as such is not guaranteed by the Constitution. Moreover, even if *Rodriguez* were overturned on this point, one would expect the Supreme Court to place the burden of providing necessary funds on state governments, not the federal government. Additionally, it is very unlikely the Court would find a directly granted constitutional right to education beyond the secondary level.

59. 98 S.Ct. 1024 (1978).

60. Another provision, also upheld, disqualified at certain types of schools courses which had not been taught for at least two years.

61. It is interesting to note that this analysis meets Kingman Brewster's "relevance" test. The federal goal was to obtain top-quality education for veterans generally, not to support a particular business college. Forcing the college to appeal to and attract nonveteran students was protective of the GI bill students themselves, thought the Court.

62. 44 U. Cin. L. Rev. at 530-531.

63. Higher Education 34 at 6.

64. 330 U.S. 127 (1947).

65. Of course it could be argued that the appropriate roads might not be built if funds were dispensed with an eye to currying political favor by an employee involved in partisan politics. I would hope the proposed relevance requires a

more convincing argument than that.

66. 330 U.S. at 143, 144.

67. The courts could no more rely on the self-interest of the states' elected senators and representatives to prevent such coercive abuse of the spending power than it could trust such self-interest to vote down the regulatory-direct intervention in *League of Cities*. One case where spending-power abuse was found is United States v. Butler, 297 U.S. 1 (1936). In indicating the federal government was not under its commerce power entitled to run an agricultural support program, *Butler* is probably no longer good law. What is interesting is that the *Butler* dissent, which would have the use made of the spending power there, was careful to state that this power "may not be used to coerce action left to state control." 297 U.S. at 87.

68. See Atkins v. United States, 556 F. 2d 1028 (Ct. Cl. 1977).

69. H.R. No. 95-707, at p. 5 (1977), on H.R. 9418, by the Committee on Interstate and Foreign Commerce.

70. See United States v. Raines, 362 U.S. 17, 23 (1960).

71. See, e.g., Tilton v. Richardson, 403 U.S. 672, 679 (1971).

72. I have found no existing statute with such a condition, although the Buckley Amendment approaches it. There would have been such a statute if the congressional reaction to the announcements of fifteen or nineteen medical schools that they would decline capitation grants rather than abide by the original Guadalajara Amendment had been different. What Congress did was to water down that provision, but it could have tried to increase the coercive pressure on universities to accept the amendment by making adherence to it a condition of eligibility for other grant programs affecting other schools and departments of the university, such as physics research grants, student loans for undergraduates, etc.

73. See Linde, *Justice Douglas on Freedom in the Welfare State: Constitutional Rights in the Public Sector,* 39 Wash. L. Rev. 4, 28 (1964).

EIGHT

RIGHTS OF GOVERNMENT EMPLOYEES

Steven B. Duke

Nearly three million people are employed by the federal government (not counting the military). Twelve million work for state and local governments. Thus, almost a sixth of the labor force is employed by government.

The importance of the subject is not fully demonstrated by the numbers. As jobs become more and more specialized and government agencies take on new tasks, more of us become dependent upon government for our livelihood. If we can't work for the government, many of us can't work at all, because the private sector has no need for our skills and training.

As government moves in the direction of monopolizing jobs at the same time it expands its share of the work force, the dangers inherent in stifling the freedom of government workers are magnified. Moreover, government employees have exclusive control over crucial information about how the government is run. Democracy cannot function if this information is regularly withheld—and it can be if the employee can be forced by his superior to withhold, distort, or falsify facts about government conduct.

On the other hand, the citizenry has a vital interest in the efficient, competent performance of its servants, an interest which will also increase as the bureaucracy grows. This interest will often be disserved by insubordination, external attacks on superiors, and intemperate or bizarre behavior. Defining the rights of government employees would also be much simpler if we could ignore another complicating, troublesome, but incontestable fact: for the effective operation of some aspects of government, and the protection of legitimate privacy interests, some secrecy is essential.

We have come a long way since 1892, when Justice Holmes pithily disposed of the problem by observing that a policeman who complained of his discharge for political activities "may have a constitutional right

---

Steven B. Duke is professor of law at Yale University.

to talk politics, but he has no constitutional right to be a policeman."
Great strides have been made in protecting public employees from
discrimination on the grounds of religion, race, and sex; some
protections for the handicapped and the elderly have been recognized;
and the individual's freedom to conduct his life off the job in the way he
prefers has grown. However, only in the last decade, indeed largely since
Watergate, has the freedom of employees to criticize their agencies, to
reveal or decline to engage in wrongdoing, surfaced as a fit subject for
court concern. Procedural rights of public workers have also been
recognized, albeit grudgingly and in many cases inadequately. The
recipients of government largess have fared much better on the
procedural front.

Justice Holmes' dictum has been replaced by another sweeping
judicial generalization: "public employment . . . may not be
conditioned upon the surrender of constitutional rights which could not
be abridged by direct government action." This too is oversimplified
and hard to give concrete meaning, yet as a starting point for analysis it
surely better reflects today's realities than its nineteenth-century
predecessor.

Loyalty Qualifications

Loyalty oaths which require an employee to forswear membership in
political organizations or adherence to proscribed political beliefs have
played a persistent and prominent part in our history, from the
Revolutionary War to the post–World War II, McCarthy era. The
application of constitutional principles to invalidate such oaths has
been one of the bright chapters in the recent record of the Supreme
Court. It has struck down oaths such as Washington's, requiring the
applicant for employment to swear that he "will by precept and example
promote respect for the flag and [government] institutions, reverence for
law and order and undivided allegiance to the Government," and
Arizona's, requiring disavowal of membership in the Communist party.
It now seems clear that little more than an oath of allegiance can
constitutionally be required, i.e., a promise to perform one's duties
lawfully.

Until recently, however, an applicant could be, and often was,
required to disclose his past and present memberships in political
organizations as a condition of employment. Courts have recently held
that this may not be done, consistent with the First Amendment, for
ordinary civil service positions. In 1976, the Civil Service Commission
dropped all political loyalty questions from its standard application
forms.

Policymaking employees, their confidential assistants, and those in security-sensitive positions, may still be required to prove their loyalty, and their political affiliations may certainly be inquired into. In most aspects of government, however, reliance upon elaborate oaths and periodic inquisitions has fallen into disuse. As practices of this type are determined to be illegal at the rank and file level, they gradually become abhorrent to policymakers, many of whom are selected from lower levels of government and have grown accustomed to their dignity and freedom. Even if lawful, such practices at the policymaking level are often inexpedient and costly. Thus, protections of the rank and file tend over time to redound to the benefit of all. One may hope and even expect, therefore, that routine oaths and inquisitions into political associations and sympathies will soon be relegated permanently to the history books.

Rights of Privacy and Association

The legal rights of government employees to live their own lives are more substantial than those of their counterparts in much of the private sector. The fact that the government is bound by the Constitution makes a difference. Yet government agencies often regulate, usually in an ad hoc fashion, the private lives of their employees. Membership in a nudist colony has been used as a reason to fire policemen. Several policemen and at least one FBI agent were fired for living with women out of wedlock. Reputed or suspected homosexuals have been fired or refused employment in hordes. Recently, white southern public school teachers have been dismissed for sending their children to segregated private schools. Twenty years ago, they might have been fired for *not* doing so. Government employees are often forbidden to associate with "undesirables," on pain of dismissal. Restaurants and bars are sometimes declared "off limits" to off-duty law enforcement personnel.

The trend seems clearly toward curbing such practices. Federal courts recently held that an applicant for a position as a policeman cannot constitutionally be denied a job because of his lawful activities as a nudist, nor a schoolteacher applicant rejected for living in an interracial religious commune. A California court also ruled that a schoolteacher's license could not be revoked for private noncriminal homosexual acts with another adult.

The freedom of association guaranteed by the First Amendment is violated when a government employee is punished for living, loving, or associating lawfully with others while off duty. Efforts to regulate such associations are subject to "close scrutiny" and are unconstitutional unless there is "a real and substantial relation between the employee's conduct and the operation by the employee of the public service." It is virtually impossible to show such a relation in most government jobs. Nor is it a panacea that the off-duty activity is unlawful. Criminal laws concerning consensual private sexual conduct are rarely enforced. Those against adultery, fornication, or cohabitation virtually never are. Such conduct, even though in many places still technically criminal, bears almost no relation to a worker's fitness for the job, and most recent decisions so hold.

Yet there are limits. A married junior college teacher, caught by a policeman engaging in sex with a female student in his car on a public street near the campus, who then ran over the policeman and fled at 100 miles per hour, was held to have exceeded them, as was a schoolteacher who belonged to a "swinger's" club, was observed there engaging in semipublic sex with several men, and bragged about it on a television program. In both cases, the courts emphasized the notoriety of the conduct, the fact that it was not private, that it was felonious, and that the employees were schoolteachers who served as role models for their students. The decisions would have been wrong if the employees had been firemen, mechanics, carpenters, or custodians.

Dismissal of employees for their off-duty conduct is often accomplished under statutes or regulations authorizing discharge for "moral turpitude," "unfitness," "conduct unbecoming," or "behavior inimical to the service." Courts are beginning to recognize that such standards are too vague to warrant dismissals for marginal misconduct. Thus, where the FBI fired a clerk for permitting a woman to spend the night with him on two occasions, the court of appeals reversed. The government had the temerity to contend that the FBI was entitled to impose moral standards for all its employees—clerks as well as agents—that would "satisfy the little old lady from Dubuque." Passing the question whether the bureau had any right to impose such a standard, the court said that it could not be done without clear prior notice to FBI employees "that they must meet not only the general standards of their own community, but also the special standards of the lady from Dubuque."

Occasionally, more specific prohibitions are invalidated as overboard. A disciplinary rule which prohibited policemen from "engaging in any activity, conversation, deliberation or discussion which is derogatory to the Department or any member or policy of the Department" was declared unconstitutional on its face.

The courts should move more forthrightly in these directions. Employees should not be required to live in fear that their off-duty conduct might violate some vague standard. If off-duty behavior is to be the basis for adverse personnel actions, rules and regulations should attempt to specify what that conduct is. Employees would then have a chance to conform, if they so chose, to seek employment elsewhere, or to challenge the rule or regulation in court prior to being stigmatized by dismissal. There is still too much room for arbitrary action concerning off-duty behavior.

Inquiries

Until the past decade, government employers were free to ask virtually any questions of an applicant for employment. Paralleling developments concerning the criteria for hiring or firing, however, courts have imposed restrictions. While an employer may ask questions to which an affirmative answer would disqualify the applicant, there must be a rational relationship between the question asked and fitness for the job.

The rational relationship will vary with the nature of the job. If it is a position involving great temptations and opportunities to engage in dishonesty, questions designed to turn up prior dishonesty may be warranted. An applicant for the foreign service or the FBI may be required to submit to more intrusive inquiries than an agricultural inspector.

Among other factors which may justify questions of a personal nature are whether the agency has some information about or reason to suspect that the particular applicant has something relevant to hide, and whether the agency communicates to the applicant a plausible purpose for the questions.

In most cases, inquiries about private sexual activities or inclinations may not be asked. Some courts have held that the First Amendment is a shield against such inquiries. Questions about past criminal behavior are less clear. Prior felony convictions may be inquired into for most jobs, especially if not too remote in time. But this does not provide carte blanche to ask a barrage of questions about prior activities and associations that did not result in criminal charges. For many positions, prior arrests on serious charges are arguably relevant, even though some states prohibit such questions by statute. This creates a serious dilemma for many applicants whose prior records have been erased under state statutes. The judgment reflected in such statutes is that the individual should not bear the stigma of an erased arrest or conviction for any purpose, even an investigative one. The law should act as if the event never occurred. Yet if the applicant is asked about the prior offense, how can he respond? Apparently, he cannot provide a negative answer, unless a statute expressly authorizes him to do so. It is doubtful even in that case that he may lawfully provide a negative answer on an application to the federal government or another state which does not prohibit the inquiry.

A federal-state conflict is also inherent in the odious practice of polygraphy in employment screening. More than a dozen states prohibit it by statute, yet it is commonly employed by many federal agencies. Some states, strangely, prohibit its use by private employers but permit public agencies to use it. The constitutionality of compulsory use of polygraphs is still unsettled. Test cases are rarely brought by applicants, for obvious reasons. Moreover, except for sensitive positions, the routine use of polygraphs in employment screening is precluded by its cost. When an agency suspects an employee of having engaged in improper conduct, however, it often resorts to the machine. Employees have frequently been discharged for refusing to submit to polygraph examination.

All but a few courts hold that findings by a polygraph examiner are inadmissible in court, in part because of their unreliability. They are inadmissible in criminal cases, in civil cases, and in administrative proceedings. Nor is a party's willingness or unwillingness to submit to a polygraph admissible. A criminal defendant, on trial for his life, cannot even get a court to order the prosecution witness to submit to a polygraph. The reason: it is not calculated to lead to admissible evidence. Thus, even though an employee could probably not be fired for flunking a polygraph question concerning his embezzlement of public funds, he can, in the opinion of some courts, be fired for refusing to take the test. The more they explain it, the less I understand it. One court explained its order upholding discharge of a policeman on the ground that he had a "sworn duty to aid in the investigation of crime," he was under investigation, and the test has "some value in investigation." Another reached the same conclusion because the tests may "guide police investigators in their hypotheses." These decisions disregard entirely the competing interests. To many, a polygraph examination is a fearsome experience, producing powerful fantasies of execution by electric chair, which the device resembles. A compulsory examination is, in any event, a massive assault on the dignity of the taker. It is exacerbated by the fact that the employee cannot choose the examiner, and it is agreed by even the most ardent advocates of polygraphy that the training, experience, and bias of the examiner are crucial components in assessing the validity of his conclusions.

Another reason the courts assign for excluding polygraph evidence in court is their fear that the jury will attach excessive weight to the results. But they forget this when they fail to consider the dilemma of the employee who "fails" or produces an "inconclusive" test. How does he erase the stigma of such conclusions, especially when the results are released to the public, which they can be and often are? It is a common investigative technique for an examiner, or another interrogator, to lie about the results; to tell a suspect he flunked, even if he passed. (This sometimes produces a confession.) Such lies can easily be leaked to the public. How can they be answered?

The courts who put their imprimatur on compulsory polygraphs also fail to realize that an examination for a specific, narrow *purpose*, e.g., to determine if the employee stole some money or leaked security information, cannot be confined to such a specific narrow *inquiry*. Examiners ask "test" or "control" questions which often delve deeply into the subject's personal life. Typical test questions are "Have you ever used marijuana?," "Have you ever stolen anything in your life?". There is no way that a polygraph examination can even be useful in "guiding hypotheses" without such test questions. If they cannot be asked on an employment application, how can they be asked under a polygraph? Compulsory polygraphs should be held to violate due process.

Political Activities

Perhaps the most controversial—certainly the most persistent—issue involving government employees is their right to participate in political activities. The Hatch Act, enacted in 1940, prohibits all but certain policymaking federal employees from taking "any active part in political management or political campaigns." Another less controversial but equally vague section of the act forbids the use of "official authority or influence for the purpose of interfering with an election or affecting the result thereof." State employees are also forbidden to seek elective office, use official influence over elections, or encourage political contributions. The constitutionality of the law has twice been upheld by the Supreme Court.

There is much to be said against such restrictions, apart from the fact that they seem to conflict directly with the First Amendment, not only as read by Justices Douglas and Black, but as any schoolchild might be expected to read it. Such restrictions deprive government of the services of many of our most talented, public-spirited, articulate citizens. Surrendering the right to participate in politics is too high a price for many to pay for a government job. Those who do pay the price and enter government service are in possession of facts and expertise which would be invaluable to the electorate, yet the law denies the electorate access to much of their information and virtually all of their political services. As construed by the Civil Service Commission, the act forbids a federal employee from holding office in even a local subdivision of a national political organization. Nor may he solicit funds for a "partisan" political cause, publicly endorse or oppose a political candidate, make a speech at political gatherings, nor circulate a nominating petition. What rights are not taken away? Beyond retaining the right to vote, the rest is unclear. He may display a political poster in his home, wear a political badge or button, or attend a political gathering if he displays no partisanship. He may also express his opinions to friends and coworkers and even be "politically active" on an issue which is "not specifically identified with a political party," if there is one.

The principal justification for the Hatch Act is a powerful one—to protect employees, and hence the government, from the spoils system; to free them from pressures by the party in power to help maintain the status quo. Such restrictions, it is argued, are essential to the preservation of a two-party system. The critics contend, however, that the act's provisions are overboard. As Justice Douglas said, if "the interests of the employees in the exercise of cherished constitutional rights . . . are to be qualified by the larger requirements of modern democratic government, the restrictions should be narrowly and selectively drawn 'to define and punish the specific conduct which constitutes a clear and present danger to the operations of government."

In 1976, Congress voted to sharply restrict the prohibitions in the Hatch Act, but President Ford vetoed the bill and the veto was upheld. The House passed a similar bill in the summer of 1977, and the Committee on Post Office and Civil Service tacked it onto the Civil Service Reform Act, which has passed both houses of Congress and is in conference committee. It seems likely that the reforms will be enacted and doubtless will be signed by the president.

The preamble sounds good: "It is the policy of the Congress that employees should be encouraged to fully exercise, freely and without fear of penalty or reprisal, and to the extent not expressly prohibited by law . . . their rights to participate or to refrain from participating in the political processes of our Nation and . . . to form, join . . . or refrain from . . . joining . . . any organization, political party, committee, association, or other group. . . ." The Hatch Act's vague prohibition against official influence on elections is essentially retained, but "use of official authority or influence" is defined to comprehend only offers or threats to take official action. There is little danger that an employee who engages in political activity will fall afoul of the law merely because he identifies himself as a federal employee or official.

The bill contains specific prohibitions against buying and selling votes, making political contributions to superiors, soliciting such contributions from fellow employees or in government buildings, and against giving such contributions to or receiving them from persons having business with the employee's agency. The bill also prohibits "political activity" while on duty, in a government office, or in uniform. It does not define "political activity," a concept only slightly less vague than "obscenity."

The bill leaves intact the existing prohibitions against state or local employees using their official influence over elections or advising other employees to make political contributions. It repeals the prohibition against such an employee seeking elective office. A federal employee is permitted by the bill to run for elective office and is permitted, but not required, to obtain leave without pay or with accrued vacation pay while doing so.

The Hatch Act's prohibition against employee political activity off duty is not gone, but it is confined to persons occupying "restricted positions," a label to be attached by the Office of Personnel Management, by regulation, upon a determination that the job involves foreign intelligence activities, the *"enforcement of any civil or criminal law,"* or the awarding of government contracts, licenses, *"subsidies or other benefits"* having "a substantial monetary value." It is hard to imagine an employee of the federal government whose job could not qualify for restriction. One whose job does not involve enforcement of civil or criminal law or government contracts or benefits arguably has nothing to do. Yet, one may hope that excessively broad interpretations of these categories will not be indulged in. Moreover, even though an employee's job otherwise qualifies, the Office of Personnel Management cannot restrict it unless it determines that the restrictions on political activity are required "to insure the integrity of the Government or the public's confidence in the integrity of the Government." One may doubt that these provisions are as "narrowly and selectively drawn" as Justice Douglas would require, but they are surely a substantial improvement over the Hatch Act.

Disclosure of Information ("Whistle Blowing")

The scandals that rocked the nation in the 1970s, involving the White House, the CIA and the FBI, the General Services Administration, the Pentagon, the Congress, and mayors' and governors' offices too numerous to recount, often resulted from "unauthorized" disclosures by present or former employees. This has led to a powerful consensus that government must be more open to public scrutiny and that "whistle-blowers" should receive legal protection. Such protection has not yet been legislated and the courts have found little comfort for the whistle-blower in the Constitution.

Underlying judicial resistance to protecting whistle-blowers from reprisals may be more than the customary conservatism of courts. It may appear to some that the public is so grateful to those who have disclosed criminal wrongdoing in the White House, the intelligence agencies, and the state houses of America that however perilous the employee's position may be with his agency, he really has little to fear. Quick fame and juicy book or lecture contracts await him. His dismissal or demotion may merely fatten his royalties. But this will soon pass. As more and more employees seek to cash in, or to cover up their own inadequacies with postures of exposing wrongdoing, the public will tune out the din of whistles; the Fitzgeralds, if not the Ellsbergs, will be lost in the chorus.

Reasonable people, of whom there are several in the judiciary, may also fear that things have already gotten out of hand. With minutes of Cabinet meetings being leaked to the press, it sometimes seems as if there is nothing newsworthy in government which can transpire free from exposure to the public spotlight. Such fears can have a serious chilling effect on the free expression of our most important policymakers. A condition which burdens free expression also curbs thought, and that is dangerous.

Judges may also have longer memories than the public. They remember the loudest whistle-blower of the century, Senator Joseph McCarthy and some of his federal employee followers, who found "spies" and "traitors" at every level of government and in the process created crippling fear and suspicion from which the country may not yet have recovered. Many are reluctant to construe the Constitution or federal statutes to protect such behavior.

Defining protected behavior is also enormously difficult. Employees may disclose agency information from a multitude of motives. The purpose may be vindictive, to embarrass a disliked superior or coworker, or to enhance the discloser's own position in the agency. The disclosure may stem from a policy disagreement with a superior and constitute an ad hoc form of appeal over the head of the superior. The employee's job may be in peril for other reasons, and the disclosure may be a cloak to disguise his real problem and to divert or stave off the predicted course of events. The employee may be under pressure to engage in illegal conduct, the disclosure designed to relieve the pressure. His motive may be greed or disloyalty. He may be bribed or blackmailed. He may be setting the stage for employment in the private sector, seeking to ingratiate himself with a prospective employer. One can argue that the employee's motivation is irrelevant, but courts have held otherwise.

Among other factors which courts consider relevant in determining whether an employee may be sanctioned for an unauthorized disclosure are:

Form and forum. The form of the disclosure may vary greatly. The employee may register an intra-agency grievance over his superior's head, which becomes public only when the employee resists his ouster.

The disclosure may be in response to a subpoena from a legislative committee, a court, or an agency, and in answer to questions which the employee may or may not have triggered clandestinely. The employee may go directly to the press, openly or covertly. Again, courts have held that the forum in which the disclosure occurs is relevant in determining if it is protected.

Style and tone. Disclosures of alleged misfeasance or incompetence are often clothed in unwarranted characterizations of criminality or other hyperbole. Rarely is a whistle-blower's statement confined to objective facts. Allegations of mismanagement are now so common that one cannot expect to have his claims recognized as a whistle without mentioning "cover-up," "fraud," "corruption," or a similar epithet. Yet such characterizations threaten far greater damage to the morale and efficiency of the agency than a simple statement of fact.

Truth. An obviously significant variable is the truth or falsity of the charges. Often they will be a mixture of both. And disagreements about policy decisions, or about the legality of agency practices, cannot comfortably be labelled as either.

Malice with respect to truth. Courts have held, in limited contexts, that the First Amendment protects employee statements which, even though false, were not made with knowledge of falsity or a reckless disregard of that risk. In other words, the limit of liability for libelous statements about public figures, established in *New York Times v. Sullivan*, may be applicable.

Relation to job. The more remote a criticism, revelation, or public comment is from the speaker's ordinary duties the more likely it is to be protected. Thus, a policeman who complains publicly about his job assignments is more vulnerable than if he complains about "crime-coddling courts" or "disrespect for law and order." He is even less vulnerable if he announces that welfare recipients should be forced to work or that abortions should be outlawed. In commenting on such matters, he is speaking as a "citizen" rather than as a policeman. Policemen have a constitutional right to talk politics as long as the subject isn't police politics. Then there is trouble.

Nature of the job. Significant differences in protection may also vary with the nature of the job. Policemen and FBI agents, for example, are confined in their freedom to criticize superiors on the theory that the nature of the job requires tight discipline; external criticism threatens that discipline. A schoolteacher, on the other hand, requires and normally possesses far more independence on the job. Regimentation concerning educational policies and practices is neither customary nor desirable. The courts also recognize a dichotomy between policymaking and nonpolicymaking employees, intimating and sometimes holding that policymakers have no constitutional rights publicly (or privately) to differ with their superiors. The theory is that the elected official is presumptively authorized by the electorate to implement his own policies, and to permit a subordinate to criticize them (or disclose the decision process underlying them) would thwart those policies, undermining the will of the electorate. Similar strictures, for essentially the same reasons, may be placed upon the constitutional rights of persons in a close confidential relationship to a policymaker.

Privacy interests of citizens. Government, particularly the federal government, has awesome power to compel citizens to disclose private details of their personal lives, to collect such information from diverse sources, and to make it easily accessible to a bureaucrat. Precious privacy interests are at stake when such information is disclosed to the public, and they must be balanced against the public's need to know how government is working.

Need for secrecy. The necessity of secrecy or confidentiality to the effective operation of an agency ranges widely, both among and within agencies. However appalled we may be at the illegal, sometimes criminal, misbehavior of the CIA and the FBI, few can deny that the normal intelligence-gathering activities of those agencies must be shielded from the media.* Nor can courts or adjudicating agencies function if employees are free to divulge their deliberative processes.

The secrecy norm violated. Also relevant is the substantiality of the violation of the statute, rule, custom, or expectation concerning secrecy: how *clearly* was the norm departed from? Related to that, and equally important, is the question by what process and with what authority was the secrecy norm established? A norm of wide application, established by the governing legislative body, may be entitled to greater deference than one established by regulation of the agency whose norm was violated; the latter may be given greater weight than an unpublished but well-established custom of the agency, which itself may weigh more than an ad hoc order of a superior. At or near the lower end of this hierarchy is the idea of contract. May a superior insulate himself or his agency from disclosure by requiring a new employee to agree not to divulge information? That is the position of the Justice Department in its efforts to enjoin publication of a book by former CIA agent Frank Snepp.

This list of relevant variables—there are many more—should suffice

---

*Which is not to say that they should be immune from independent scrutiny. See *Control of Intelligence Agencies.*

to illustrate the complexity of the problem. About the only generalization one can safely make about the court decisions is that the employee usually loses. Among prominent exceptions is *Swaaley v. United States,* where the Court of Claims held that an employee of a naval shipyard who wrote to the secretary of the navy alleging favoritism in promotions could not be dismissed for failure to prove the truth of his claims. An employee who confines his complaint to his ultimate superior, the court said, is protected by the First Amendment to the same extent as a newspaper which defames a public figure. He is safe from reprisal, even for false statements, as long as he meets the tests of *New York Times v. Sullivan,* i.e., unless he lies.

The Supreme Court also applied the *Times* test to a schoolteacher in *Pickering v. Board of Education.* There, the teacher had written a letter to a local newspaper criticizing the Board of Education's budgeting practices and certain actions of the superintendent. The Court did not hold the *Times* test generally applicable, however. Among factors the Court found to warrant its decision was the fact that the statements were not "directed towards any person with whom appellant would normally be in contact in the course of his daily work as a teacher," the targets of the criticism did not have a relationship with the teacher requiring "personal loyalty and confidence," there was no evidence that the publication of the letter "damaged the professional reputations of the Board and the superintendent" or that it fomented "conflict." Rather, the letter was apparently regarded by everyone but the Board "with massive apathy and total disbelief." Nor was there any evidence that the letter was "detrimental to the interest of the school," and its subject was clearly a matter of public interest. Furthermore, the Court said, Pickering's claims about the athletic budget "were matters of public record on which his position as a teacher did not qualify him to speak with any greater authority than any other taxpayer." The *Pickering* decision, therefore, offers little comfort to any employee who criticizes his superiors on a subject of his expertise or who is otherwise effective. *Pickering* suggests that the full protection of the First Amendment may be reserved for patent fools. If the Board had dismissed Pickering not for defaming it but for demonstrating poor judgment, the result might have been different. In *Turner v. Kennedy,* the Court of Appeals for the District of Columbia upheld the dismissal of an FBI agent who wrote letters to a senator and a congressman. He was dismissed not for writing the letters per se, but for demonstrating, by sending them, his "unsuitability."

The strongest case for protection is that of an employee of the executive branch who provides information to Congress (or his counterpart at the state level). Congress has inherent power to investigate the executive branch and to protect those who supply information. Retaliation against an employee who responds to a legitimate congressional inquiry should be precluded on separation-of-powers principles, as well as the First Amendment. The United States Code goes even further:

> The right of employees, individually or collectively, to petition Congress or a member of Congress, or to furnish information to either House of Congress, or to a committee or member thereof, may not be interfered with or denied.

The statutory right to petition Congress has been held to protect an employee who takes a grievance directly to Congress, provided it is not maliciously false, but not to protect one who launches "a broad public appeal to induce [his] friends and sympathizers to write to their Congressman." Another significant limitation of the right is that a protected petition to Congress does not create a "mantle of immunity" over other statements, e.g., to the press on the same subject, even, apparently, if the "petition to Congress" generated the press inquiries. So construed, the provision may be as much a trap as it is a protection.

The Code also makes it a crime to "influence, intimidate, or impede any witness in . . . connection with any inquiry or investigation being held by either House, or any committee of either House," or to injure any witness "in his person or property on account of his attending such proceeding, inquiry, or investigation or . . . testifying. . . ." Another provision defines as a crime efforts to "prevent the communication of information relating to the violation of any criminal statute of the United States . . . to a criminal investigator." These criminal prohibitions have never been invoked against one who discharged or threatened to discharge a federal employee. They can only be invoked by the attorney general, a political appointee. Legislation is plainly required.

H.R. 11280, the House version of the Civil Service Reform Act, attempts to meet the problem by prohibiting, with respect to covered employees, any "personnel action" affecting any employee or applicant for employment "as a reprisal for" a "disclosure of information . . . which the employee or applicant reasonably believes evidences . . . a violation of any law, rule, or regulation, or . . . mismanagement, a waste of funds, an abuse of authority, or a substantial and specific danger to public health or safety," provided disclosure is not "specifically prohibited by law" or required to be kept secret by executive order "in the interest of national defense or the conduct of foreign affairs." In some respects, this seems to go beyond existing constitutional protections. I have several problems with it, however.

Swaaley and *Pickering* held that under some circumstances the employee cannot be sanctioned unless his statements were knowingly or recklessly false. There is no comparable provision in H.R. 11280. The focus in the bill is not on the truth or falsity of the revelation but upon the employee's reasonable belief concerning its character or quality, that is, whether it evidences a violation of law, mismanagement, a waste of funds, an abuse of authority, a danger to health or safety. One whose revelations failed the *Times* test could surely not have such a belief concerning the "information" he was "disclosing." To that extent, therefore, the *Times* test and H.R. 11280 are compatible. But what of the employee whose belief concerning the truth of his disclosure is unreasonable but not reckless? Or even the employee who reasonably but erroneously believes he is disclosing truth? Both, it can be argued, are outside the bill because they have "disclosed" no "information," merely falsehood. If they do not lose on this ground, the employee who reasonably believed in the truth of what he said will be protected, provided he *also* reasonably believes that the revelation evidences violation of the law, etc.; but the employee who was unreasonable in *either* respect (assessment of truth or the implications of the facts) is abandoned by the bill. He must try to plant his exposure on the treacherous territory of *Swaaley* or *Pickering*.

There is also a serious omission in the bill. Literally, it applies only to employees who "disclose information." The position of the employee who comments on facts which are available to but not yet disseminated to the public is unclear; one who merely criticizes or comments upon the conduct of a superior or his agency is not covered. Perhaps such an employee is not a "whistle-blower," but is he not entitled to some protection? Should he be required to leak information, along with his criticism, in order to gain protected status? I don't think so, and I would substitute "communication" for "disclosure of information."

A crucial phrase in H.R. 11280 is "as a reprisal for." This suggests that if the adverse personnel action is not punitive, it is not prohibited. The way seems open to cloak punitive actions with the garb of "unsuitability," "instability," "insubordination," "uncooperativeness," "disloyalty," "immaturity," "irresponsibility," "erraticness," "poor judgment," and so forth. Even more troublesome than the possibility of easy circumvention by word play is the fundamental issue avoided by the bill: may an unauthorized but not illegal disclosure of information—or criticism outside established channels—constitute evidence upon which an employee may be adversely treated in his job? Is it, like the exercise of the privilege against self-incrimination, an act as to which no adverse inference may lawfully be drawn? The bill certainly does not say so, and I doubt that it would be so construed. Suppose, for example, an employee has clear evidence that a superior has violated the law, either in his official capacity or in his private life. He sells or gives the information to another whom he knows wants to blackmail the superior. It seems doubtful that the disclosure is "specifically prohibited by law," even if the discloser is an accessory to blackmail. Can it be doubted, however, that the employee should be fired? Or imagine a clerk in the FBI who overhears and collects gossip about extramarital sex in the office and sells it to a scandal sheet. He has disclosed information about a "violation of law," yet he should surely be fired. And what of the oddball who writes critical but otherwise barely comprehensible letters to the press, *daily*, about the incompetence or dishonesty of his boss? Even if the criticism is substantially true, isn't it grounds for denying a promotion? Unauthorized disclosures of information or employer criticism are often powerful evidence of character or the lack thereof; of maturity, judgment, intelligence, and other qualities highly relevant to personnel decisions. Should they be ignored? *Can* they be ignored? This issue should be faced by legislation.

The bill in the foregoing respects seems too narrow; in others, it seems too broad. Virtually any action of any agency can arguably be said to constitute "mismanagement, a waste of funds, [or] an abuse of authority." Prominent practitioners of the "Chicago school" of economics, some of whom it has been alleged are "reasonable" persons, have contended that most federal and state agencies are a "waste of funds," an "abuse of authority," or both. Moreover, there are few actions of few agencies or federal employees which cannot plausibly be called a "violation of any law, rule, or regulation."

The bill apparently regards the employee's motivation as irrelevant. It does not matter whether he discloses the "mismanagement" or "violation of law" out of greed, vindictiveness, submission to blackmail, or a refined and mature sense of injustice.

The most serious problem, however, is that the bill may be an empty shell. It protects only disclosures which are not "specifically prohibited by law." Does this mean by statute, by regulation, by court decision, or perhaps, even, by contract?

Two federal district courts held recently, at the urging of the Justice Department, that a criminal statute punishing one who "without authority" conveys any "thing of value of the United States" applies to unauthorized disclosures of information by a federal employee. As Anthony Lewis observed, "For advocates of secrecy, the beauty of that legal theory is that it applies no matter what kind of government information is involved. The price of food in the White House mess, the Amtrak deficit—any fact that leaked could be the subject of criminal prosecution." If these decisions are not overturned, and the criminal provision is considered a "specific prohibition," the provisions of the bill are completely hollow. Any disclosure which is not "authorized" would be "specifically prohibited by law." Yet if the criminal statute is not a "specific prohibition," we may find our country in the absurd position that an employee who discloses unclassified information may not be sanctioned in his job for doing so but may be sent to prison. Can he be fired for failure to show up for work because he is in prison?

These quandaries are reminiscent of the "catch 22" position in which a GSA investigator recently found himself. Unable to get his superiors to pay attention to evidence of irregularities in contracting procedures, he went to the press. He cited a code of ethics approved by Congress which says it is a government worker's duty to "expose corruption where discovered." He was told, however, that the code of ethics was not the law, because Congress had approved it as a resolution rather than a statute. Moreover, the code also told him to obey agency regulations, and one GSA regulation forbade him to disclose information.

With uncertainties like "as a reprisal for" and "specifically prohibited by law," it is unlikely that the whistle-blower provisions in H.R. 11280 will cause the dike of government secrecy to collapse. But a system which has rested so long on employee intimidation to maintain confidentiality of government information is in some peril unless there is a quick but comprehensive review of the need for secrecy and appropriate rules enacted to fill in gaps and uncertainties created by whistle-blower legislation.

Procedural Due Process

The right of a government employee to "due process" before dismissal—a hearing before an impartial decision maker, a statement of charges, an opportunity to confront and test the evidence against him and to offer evidence in his defense, and a statement of reasons—is in a state of confusion. In a recent foray, no majority of the Supreme Court was able to agree on anything except the result: no hearing.

Patronage dismissals. The essence of a patronage dismissal is that no process is needed, other than a notice of discharge. Until recently, whether a job was subject to patronage was determined by a combination of custom, ordinance or statute, agency regulation, and collective bargaining agreements. During the Bicentennial, the Court discovered that the Constitution is implicated.

In England, during the prerevolutionary period and into the nineteenth century, public offices were treated as the property of the occupant. Over much of that period, offices were bought, sold, and inherited. Some of these practices continued in the colonies. The Constitution is silent on the subject. In 1789, however, Congress, in establishing the office of secretary for the Department of Foreign Affairs, acknowledged the removal power of the president. Jefferson, the first president to displace the administration of a different party, removed employees for purely partisan reasons. Jackson did it in grand style. Thus, it is substantially accurate to say, as did Justice Powell recently, that the practice is as "old as the Republic."

In a 1976 decision *Elrod v. Burns*, the Supreme Court held that a newly elected sheriff of Cook County, Illinois, could not dismiss patronage employees appointed by his predecessor merely because they were members of the Republican party. The Court was unable to agree on the reasons. Justice Brennan, in the plurality opinion, said that patronage dismissals of employees who are neither "policymakers" nor in a confidential relationship to them violates their constitutional rights to freedom of belief and association.

This issue will produce a flood of litigation as dismissed state and federal employees seek shelter as nonpolicymakers. Instead of inflating the power and importance of their jobs, employees, for the first time in history, will try to minimize them. We may even hear United States attorneys or their assistants describing their jobs as "routine," requiring only "the application of facts to law," and similar nonsense.

The practice of patronage dismissals at the higher levels of federal, state, and local government is not in jeopardy, however. As even Justice Brennan recognized, democracy itself would be threatened if an elected official could not freely hire and fire confidential and policymaking subordinates, for he would then lack the tools with which to implement the policies for which he was elected. This countervailing consideration suggests a tangle of problems beyond that inherent in the vagueness of "policymaker." Suppose an official is elected largely on a single issue: that employees of the governmental unit over which he seeks authority have become lazy, incompetent, indifferent, inefficient, out of touch, corrupt. He promises to "clean house." Does this affect the constitutional rights of the employees? Can he dig deeper into public employment in his initial takeover than if he had promised all his supporters jobs and dismisses employees in order to create vacancies? May his campaign promises warrant his presuming middle level "insubordination," which would otherwise be arbitrary? If not, can he circumvent *Elrod v. Burns* by "reorganizing"—eliminating departments and jobs, creating new departments and new jobs subject to his appointing power? The courts will be occupied with these questions for a long time.

Apart from these uncertainties, *Elrod v. Burns* implies that the practice of wholesale replacement of middle-level, non–civil service employees solely because of their political affiliation is on its way out. As Justice Brennan noted, "as government employment, state or Federal, becomes more pervasive, the greater the dependence on it becomes, and therefore the greater becomes the power to starve political opposition. . . ."

It is unrealistic, in most cases, to presume on a wholesale basis that lower- or middle-level employees will subvert the policies of a newly elected official. And even though protected against patronage dismissals, they may be fired, on an individual basis, for "insubordination." Whether this is a viable alternative to the patronage dismissal, however, depends on the procedural barriers imposed.

Nonpolicymakers. Due process is slow, costly, and cumbersome. If granted to an employee, it makes it difficult not only to fire him but to keep him in line. It protects against grossly improper dismissals, such as those grounded on race or sex, but it also interferes with firings for incompetence or dishonesty. It should come as no surprise, therefore, that the constitutional imperatives are still murky.

The greatest contributor to confusion in recent times is a 1974 decision, *Arnett v. Kennedy*. In that case, an OEO civil service employee was dismissed for allegedly making false statements accusing a superior of taking a bribe. This was pursuant to a statute authorizing removal or suspension "for such cause as will promote the efficiency of the service." He claimed, among other things, that the Constitution required, prior to dismissal, a trial-type hearing before an unbiased decider. The Supreme Court held otherwise. There were five opinions in the case, none for a majority. Justice Rehnquist, who wrote for three, echoed the nineteenth-century views of Justice Holmes. Kennedy had accepted the job under a statute that gave him only limited procedural rights. He could therefore have had no legitimate expectancy beyond those rights. "One may not retain the benefits of an Act while attacking the constitutionality of one of its conditions." Kennedy "must take the bitter with the sweet." As Justice Marshall noted in dissent, this approach reflects the view, many times rejected by the Court, that government can condition a job on any termination procedure, no matter how arbitrary. Six members of the Court disagreed, being of the view that Kennedy had a constitutionally protected interest, and that the Constitution imposes restrictions on how that interest can be taken away. Three members of the Court thought, however, that the process Kennedy received was no more than was "due" under the Constitution.*

Too much has been read into this decision by lower courts. It is nothing short of bizarre that, as the Court has held, a due process hearing is required by the Constitution before a welfare or unemployment compensation recipient may be taken off the rolls, a state college student expelled or his tenured teacher fired, a driver's license revoked, or a stereo sold on credit may be repossessed, but that a nonprobationary government employee may be dismissed for alleged misconduct without such a hearing. *Kennedy* is a legal derelict.

A government employee who, by reason of statute, regulation, custom, contract, or having performed satisfactorily for a lengthy period of time, has a reasonable expectation that he will not be terminated without cause, has a constitutional right to a fair evidentiary hearing, where that cause must be established before he may be fired. Whether his job is "property" or "liberty"—a question which has consumed enormous judicial energy—is not important. It would seem to be both. In any event, the government acts unconstitutionally if it denies him a fair hearing, and he plainly has interests which give him standing to complain.

A probationary, provisional, or temporary employee has no such right, unless it is found in a statute, regulation, or contract. Yet if such an employee can produce evidence—or even a plausible claim—that he is about to be fired for constitutionally impermissible reasons, e.g., making a speech, blowing a whistle, race, or patronage, he can usually get a temporary restraining order from a federal court and obtain the hearing administratively denied him. A federal employee may resort to the same remedy if he claims that he is about to be fired in violation of the Constitution, a statute, a regulation, or a contract. In court, the employee will be able to take the testimony of his superiors, examine agency files, have a trial and an appeal. Yet if the agency which employs him, or another with jurisdiction, has a fair hearing procedure, he cannot go into court unless he first "exhausts" that procedure. If that procedure affords him due process and the determination is still against him, it is very difficult, if not impossible, to get a court trial on the same issues.** Thus, it seems absurd for government employers to deny fair

---

*He was entitled to a hearing some time *after* discharge.

**There are exceptions to these propositions, most notably where the employee claims discrimination on the ground of race, religion, or sex in violation of Title VII of the Civil Rights Act. A state employee can go directly to court (a federal employee cannot). If either goes through the agency first, he can apparently still have a full trial, rather than a review of the record. These results, however, are the products of statutory interpretation.

administrative hearings to employees who want them. It is far more cumbersome, and more costly to the employee, the agency, and the courts to litigate the causes of dismissals in court than in fair administrative hearings. *Arnett v. Kennedy* notwithstanding, the courts can surely find some help in the Constitution to relieve them of the necessity of acting as a super civil service commission. Due process is the answer.

PART FOUR

FREEDOM AND THE DUTY
OF THE GOVERNMENT
TO CONTROL PRIVATE POWER

NINE

PRIVATE DISCRIMINATION
ON THE BASIS OF RACE,
SEX, AGE, AND DISABILITY
Vern Countryman

A society which imposes, assists others in imposing, or permits others to impose unjustifiable discriminatory treatment on some of its members, solely because they do not conform to the physical or mental characteristics of the dominant group in that society, is imposing, assisting, or permitting substantial restrictions on the freedom of the victims of that discrimination. Presumably, a society like ours, committed through the Bill of Rights and other provisions of our Constitution to a maximization of individual freedom and to equal treatment before the law should not only refrain from imposing or assisting unjustifiable discrimination but should exercise its governing powers to protect against such discrimination.

I have spoken of "unjustifiable discrimination" because of physical or mental characteristics. Sometimes there may be justifiable discrimination because there is a rational relationship between the physical or mental characteristic which is the occasion for the discrimination and a legitimate interest to be served by the discriminator. In the present state of our knowledge, at least, I suppose most would agree that a concern for the well-being of the young justifies child labor laws and that the same would be true in the absence of such laws if a private employer were to decide not to hire employees below a certain age, although we would probably differ about just what that age might be. Similarly, in the present state of our knowledge we would probably agree that commercial airlines should not be required to employ as pilots persons of limited vision.

Our concern here is with unjustifiable private discrimination and the duty and the efforts of government to protect against it and eliminate its consequences. We will be concerned with the extent to which the Constitution protects against unjustifiable discrimination by government only as that bears on the power of government to protect against

Vern Countryman is professor of law at Harvard University and chairman of the Board of Review of The Douglas Inquiry.

private discrimination. Because of limitations of time and space, our inquiry will be confined to discrimination on the basis of race, sex, age, and disability.

Race

For most of the history of our country, blacks and less numerous minorities—American Indians, Orientals on the West Coast, Chicanos in the Southwest, and Puerto Ricans in the East—have suffered from discrimination, both governmental and private. For a long time there was no legal obstacle to such discrimination. Our Constitution, proclaiming in its Preamble the rights of "We the People," also contained a provision ensuring that the slave trade would be legal at least until 1808. Earlier, the Declaration of Independence had proclaimed as "self-evident" that "all men are created equal" and endowed "with certain inalienable rights," but that proclamation was not intended to reach to blacks. An earlier draft submitted by Jefferson to the Continental Congress had included among the charges against the King one that he had engaged in the slave trade. Colonists implicated in that trade succeeded in having this charge deleted.

Ostensibly, a change was wrought by the Civil War amendments to the Constitution. The Thirteenth Amendment abolished slavery and involuntary servitude. The Fourteenth forbade the states to deny any person the equal protection of the laws, and the Fifteenth forbade abridgement of the right to vote on account of race, color, or previous condition of servitude. But in the *Civil Rights Cases*[1] the Supreme Court soon held that, despite express provision in the Fourteenth Amendment authorizing Congress to enact legislation to enforce its provisions, Congress could not enact legislation forbidding private discrimination—only state action was within the reach of that amendment. And in *Plessy v. Ferguson*[2] the Court also held that the equal protection clause was satisfied by state Jim Crow laws which provided "separate but equal" accommodations for blacks and whites. These laws, which covered everything from railroad cars and schools to houses of prostitution,[3] required, as Justice Brennan recently commented, a "status before the law . . . always separate but seldom equal."[4]

Only since 1954 has there been significant change in racial minorities' "status before the law." Although our concern here is with private discrimination, that change began with challenges to government discrimination against blacks. And we must consider, at least briefly, the origin of that change, because in its genesis there arguably lurk some limitations on the ability of government to offer protection against private discrimination.

Brown v. Board of Education[5] held that separate was not equal in public school education, and later decisions have expanded that ruling to government-imposed or government-assisted racial segregation with respect to such facilities as transportation systems, restaurants, public auditoriums, public parks, public golf courses, public beaches, courtrooms, and prison systems. Segregation in private facilities has also been held unconstitutional, even though not state imposed or assisted, where the state leases the facilities to a private segregationist.[6]

Now, almost twenty-five years later, substantial progress has been made in desegregating southern school systems, and other public facilities, despite some massive resistance. The same cannot be said for school systems in the North and West. It was only in the fall of 1978 that a federal district court lifted a receivership it had imposed upon South Boston High School four years ago, and events may yet demonstrate that that action was premature. At least in the large cities of the North and West, residential segregation, whether de jure or de facto, poses a substantial obstacle to school desegregation.[7]

Now, also, it seems clear, despite some gains in educational opportunity and in voting rights as a consequence of the Voting Rights Act of 1965,[8] that blacks and other racial minorities still suffer from unequal opportunities with respect to even more fundamental, if not unrelated, matters: employment and housing conditions.

Although blacks now constitute 11.5 percent of our population, they are only 1.29 percent of the lawyers and judges, 2 percent of the doctors, 2.3 percent of the dentists, 1.1 percent of the engineers, and 2.6 percent of the college professors. For black adults, the unemployment rate is twice that of whites; for black teenagers it is nearly three times that for white teenagers. A black male college graduate can expect a median annual income of only $110 more than a white male who has not gone beyond high school. The median income of the black family is only 60 percent of the median of a white family.[9]

The 1970 Census revealed that 23 percent of all nonwhites live in substandard housing. Last year, the median value of black homes was $10,800; only 8 percent were worth $15,000 or more. Blacks were four times more likely than whites to live in substandard houses, and three times more likely to be overcrowded.[10]

Those who do not subscribe to some of the unorthodox genetic theories described by Leonard Boudin in chapter 3 will have little hesitation in concluding that these gloomy figures are directly attributable to centuries of bigotry.

Difficult though it may be, it is easier to integrate a school than a neighborhood or a labor force. This is true not only because children, regardless of race, are more nearly fungible and thus susceptible to exchange than are families of disparate means or workers of disparate qualifications; it is true also because much of the racial discrimination in housing and employment is private rather than governmental discrimination.

There is no doubt about the power of the states to legislate against private discrimination in housing and employment,[11] and many of them have done so. But the decision in the *Civil Rights Cases*[12]—that the Fourteenth Amendment's provision authorizing Congress to enforce that amendment by "appropriate legislation" (there are similar provisions in the Thirteenth and Fifteenth amendments) did not authorize legislation against private discrimination—was raised as an obstacle to federal legislation. Hence, the provisions against private racial discrimination in public accommodations and in employment in our most comprehensive federal legislation in those areas, the Civil Rights Act of 1964, were enacted and upheld as an exercise of the commerce power.[13] As Justice Douglas pointed out in concurring opinions which would have found the power in the "appropriate legislation" provision of the Fourteenth Amendment, the commerce clause justification leaves open to inquiry in every case whether the discriminatory conduct sought to be subjected to the Civil Rights Act affects interstate commerce.

However that may be, the provisions against racial discrimination in Title VII of the 1964 act impose more restraints on governmental and private employers than the Constitution imposes on the government as employer. Title VII is violated by employment practices which have a discriminatory effect, regardless of the employer's intent, unless he can show that the practice is necessary to the safe and efficient operation of his business.[14] As the Supreme Court has recently announced, neither the equal protection clause of the Fourteenth Amendment, applicable to the states, nor the "equal protection component" of the due process clause of the Fifth Amendment,[15] applicable to the federal government, is violated unless a "purpose to discriminate" is shown.[16]

In two cases decided in 1966, the Court ruled that the "appropriate legislation" provisions of the Fourteenth Amendment empowered Congress in the Voting Rights Act of 1965 to forbid the states to require voters who were literate in another language to be literate in English before they could vote,[17] and that the "appropriate legislation" provisions of the Fourteenth and Fifteenth amendment empowered Congress by that act to forbid literacy tests entirely in both state and federal elections.[18]

Two years later, the Court held that the ancient Civil Rights Act of 1866 forbade all racial discrimination, private as well as public, in the sale or rental of property, and was an exercise of the "appropriate legislation" provision of the Thirteenth Amendment since such discrimination constituted "badges and incidents" of slavery which the Thirteenth Amendment abolished.[19] Then, in 1976, it also held that another provision of the 1866 act forbidding racial discrimination in the making and enforcing of contracts was a valid prohibition against racial discrimination in the admission of blacks to private schools.[20]

But, in the companion case, the Court decided that the same 1866 provision, as well as the provision against racial discrimination in the Civil Rights Act of 1964, would prohibit an employer from imposing harsher penalties for theft on white employees than on black employees. Both provisions were meant to protect whites as well as blacks against racial discrimination.[21] Some saw in this decision an obstacle to the latest development in governmental action against private discrimination. For it had become apparent that a law against racial discrimination which provided a remedy for those who could prove that they had been discriminated against—usually no easy task[22]—was a drop-in-the-bucket solution to a massive problem. Although the Civil Rights Act of 1968 charged the Department of Housing and Urban Development to act against private racial discrimination in housing, there has been little progress for nonwhites.[23] Similarly, Title VII of the Civil Rights Act of 1964, forbidding racial discrimination in employment, even as amended by the Equal Employment Opportunity Act of 1972, has not much improved the general lot of nonwhites.[24]

Hence, a more recent trend has been to a concept of "affirmative action"—known to its opponents as "reverse discrimination"—which requires preferential treatment for racial minorities. A 1965 executive order[25] requires those who contract with the government to pursue such affirmative action programs, and a provision in the Equal Employment Opportunity Act of 1972 exempts such contractors' programs from penalty.[26] Many private employers follow similar policies without government compulsion. Recent Supreme Court decisions have also required that preferences be given to racial minorities by those found to have violated the antidiscriminatory provisions of Title VII of the Civil Rights Act of 1964, and so have many decisions of the lower federal courts.[27] Moreover, some of the lower court decisions have approved racial quotas for violators[28] of Title VII or Title VI of the Civil Rights Act of 1954, the latter forbidding racial discrimination under any program receiving federal financial assistance.

The Department of Health, Education and Welfare, which provides much of federal assistance to educational institutions, has adopted regulations requiring affirmative action by recipients who have previously discriminated and permitting affirmative action by those who have not.[29] In the Public Works Employment Act of 1977, Congress

forbade federal grants for any local public works project unless
the applicant for federal assistance gave adequate assurance that at least
10 percent of the amount of each grant would go to minority business
enterprises—as explicit a quota as can be imagined.[30] Without statutory
requirement, the Department of Transportation has adopted a similar
but larger—15 percent—minority quota for work to improve the
Northeast Rail Corridor. The Department of the Interior is contem-
plating a 20 percent quota for its spending with minority firms. And
President Carter has called for a tripling by the end of fiscal 1979 of the
$1.2 billion of federal procurements from minority firms next year.

   Then came the Supreme Court's decision in June 1978 in the *Bakke*
case.[31] That case involved neither private discrimination nor private
affirmative action. It involved instead affirmative action in its
admissions program by the medical school of the University of
California at Davis. In simple terms, that program set aside sixteen
places out of each entering class of one hundred for blacks, Chicanos,
Asians, and American Indians. This quota was a floor but not a ceiling.
The designated minorities could also compete for the remaining eighty-
four places in the class, but whites could not compete for the sixteen
places reserved for the designated racial minorities.

   It takes some special Supreme Court arithmetic to describe the result
reached by the Supreme Court. The California program was challenged
under both the Fourteenth Amendment and Title VI of the Civil Rights
Act of 1964, forbidding racial discrimination under any program
receiving federal assistance. (The California Medical School, like all
medical schools, receives federal assistance.) Five Justices—Powell,
Brennan, White, Marshall, and Blackmun—concluded that Title VI
forbids no more discrimination than does the Fourteenth Amendment
and hence decided the case on constitutional grounds. The four
remaining Justices—Burger, Stewart, Rehnquist, and Stevens—concluded that the California quota system violated Title VI and did not
reach the constitutional question. Of the majority of five, four
Justices—Brennan, White, Marshall, and Blackmun—were prepared to
hold that neither a system which took race into account nor the
California quota system violated the Constitution. But, since Justice
Powell believed that the Constitution forbade the kind of discrimination
against whites embodied in the California quota system but did not
forbid an admissions system which "considers race only as one factor,"
along with such others as geographic origin and rural background, in
any effort to achieve diversity in the class, that was the judgment of the
Court.

   Although this case was decided after Justice Douglas left the Court, we
have a better than usual indication of how he would have voted had he

been there. Four years before *Bakke* was decided, another case reached
the Court in which the admissions policy of the University of
Washington Law School was challenged by a white applicant who had
not been admitted.[32] That policy was similar to the one involved in
Bakke in that black, Chicano, American Indian, and Filipino applicants
were considered as a separate group and were never compared directly
with white applicants, but it differed from the *Bakke* program in that no
specific quota of places in the entering class was assigned to minority
applicants. But, because the complaining white applicant in this case
had been ordered admitted by the trial court and was in his final term in
the law school by the time his case was argued in the Supreme Court, and
the school assured the Court that he would be allowed to finish
regardless of the outcome of the case, the Court concluded that the case
was moot and declined to decide it. Justice Douglas joined dissenters
who believed the case was not moot. Proceeding alone to the merits, he
concluded that the Washington admissions policy violated the
Fourteenth Amendment. While he did not believe that the amendment
forbade the school to consider factors other than grades, such as the
overcoming of disadvantage, he read it to forbid the basing of
admissions decisions on race rather than on the individual attributes of
each applicant. "The key to the problem is the consideration of each
application *in a racially neutral way*." Thus, I believe we may fairly
conclude that, if Justice Douglas had participated in the *Bakke* decision,
he would have been with the dissenters as Justice Stevens was, and the
case would have been decided the same way.

Since governments, federal or state, cannot require private discrimination which the Constitution forbids, the *Bakke* case has serious
implications for affirmative action programs required by government.
Certainly, *Bakke* raises serious questions about any quota system, such
as the one required by the Public Works Act of 1977.[33] Certainly, also,
more decisions will be required to fix the bounds within which race may
be considered as "one factor" in affirmative action programs which fall
short of employing a quota.[34]

Justice Douglas has never required me to agree with him, even when I
was his employee. With deference to him and other Justices, I feel
compelled to say that there is one aspect of this problem that seems never
to have been argued to or considered by the Court. When the Court in the
Brown case[35] in 1954 decided that separate was not equal in public
education, it set the case down for further argument on what must be
done to correct this unconstitutional condition in the segregated
schools. One year later, in *Brown II*,[36] it ordered that there be "a prompt
and reasonable start" toward desegregation, and that defendant school
officials move toward admission on a nondiscriminatory basis "with all

deliberate speed." Ten years after *Brown I* was decided—ten years of massive resistance and delaying tactics—the Court ruled that "the time for mere 'deliberate speed' has run out,"[37] which did not, of course, mean that dual school systems were immediately eliminated even then—the Court was still insisting, in cases decided some fifteen years after *Brown I,* that they be eliminated "at once."[38]

What the Court did in these cases, in recognition of the administrative problems involved in desegregating a school system, was to allow the continuation, for at least fifteen years, of school systems which were in violation of the Constitution. Is not the affirmative action program the reverse side of the coin? Even though racial quotas, or even any special consideration of race, are regarded as unconstitutional, shouldn't those who are attempting in good faith to correct the results of centuries of racial discrimination be allowed at least as much constitutional license[39] as those who strove to perpetuate that discrimination despite the ruling in *Brown I?*

Sex

By head count, women are not a minority in this country; they are more than 51 percent of our population.[40] But they have always been victimized by a stereotype that was accepted until recently by most men and women. The conventional view was only slightly overstated by Justice Bradley in an 1873 case allowing a state to refuse a woman a license to practice law solely because she was a woman:[41]

> Man is, or should be, woman's protector and defender. The natural and proper timidity and delicacy which belongs to the female sex evidently unfits it for many of the occupations of civil life. The constitution of the family organization, which is founded in the divine ordinance, as well as in the nature of things, indicates the domestic sphere as that which properly belongs to the domain and functions of womanhood. The harmony, not to say identity, of interests and views which belong or should belong to the family institution, is repugnant to the idea of a woman adopting a distinct and independent career from her husband. . . .
>
> It is true that many women are unmarried and not affected by any of the duties, complications, and incapacities arising out of the married state, but these are exceptions to the general rule. The paramount destiny and mission of women is to fulfill the noble and benign office of wife and mother. This is the law of the Creator, and the rules of civil society must be adapted to the general constitution of things, and cannot be based upon exceptional cases.

Similar views pervade later Supreme Court decisions finding no constitutional violation when the states confined the right to vote to men alone[42] (a decision overruled only in 1920 by the adoption of the Nineteenth Amendment), or limited the number of hours a woman was permitted to work,[43] or denied women licenses to work as bartenders unless they were wives or daughters of a male owner of the bar.[44] As recently as 1961 the Court upheld a state statute excluding women from jury service unless they voluntarily registered for it, with an opinion that professed to recognize the modern "enlightened emancipation of women" but which observed that "woman is still regarded as the center of family life."[45]

But the times are changing. Many (most?) women now reject the stereotype and some men try to do so. Nearly half of all adult women are in the labor force (holding or looking for jobs), and they account for more than one-third of that force. About one-fifth of those working women are married to working husbands. The working women constitute more than 58 percent of women with school-age children, and over 41 percent of the mothers of preschool children.

This is not to say that women are yet extended equal opportunities with men. They earn, on the average, about $6 for every $10 earned by men. They constitute only 12 percent of the doctors, and 10 percent of the lawyers. Save for Katherine Graham of the *Washington Post,* no woman is the chief executive officer of either the first or second group of *Fortune*'s 500 companies. There are only 50 women among the 37,000 pilots and engineers on certified U.S. airline carriers. The mean salary for male Ph.D.s in 1975 was almost $18,000; for women it was almost $15,500. In 1976, in "professional-technical" jobs, women received 73 percent of men's pay, in "clerical" jobs, they received 64 percent, and in "sales" only 45 percent.

The Catholic Church has recently reiterated its ban on women priests, and the Episcopalians are currently riven on the same issue. Only eighteen women were in Congress in 1977, and women accounted for only about 9 percent of state legislators, less than 2 percent of state judges, less than 3 percent of county commissioners, and hold less than 8 percent of local elective offices. We are still three (or seven, if rescissions of earlier ratifications are effective) states short of ratifying a proposed Twenty-Seventh Amendment which would proclaim, "Equality of rights under the law shall not be denied or abridged . . . on account of sex." And we may be further away than that if Congress cannot extend the time for ratification beyond the seven years it originally fixed on March 22, 1972.[46]

But there is a growing indication that the Supreme Court reads more than the election returns. Beginning in 1971 the Court has struck down under the equal protection clause state statutes giving a preference to men over women among persons otherwise "equally entitled" to administer a decedent's estate,[47] or requiring divorced parents to support unmarried male children until age twenty-one but unmarried female children only until age eighteen.[48] In the last instance, the Court rejected a justification for the distinction in child support based on "old notions" that the man's primary responsibility is to provide a home, so that he should receive a good education, whereas women tend to mature and marry earlier, announcing "no longer is the female destined solely for the home and the rearing of the family, and only the male for the marketplace and the world of ideas."[49]

The Court has also held the due process clause of the Fifth Amendment to be violated by a federal statute providing that wives of male members of the armed forces are dependents for purposes of obtaining increased quarters allowances and medical benefits, but that husbands of female members are not dependents unless they are in fact dependent for over one-half of their support. Such a statute was held to deprive servicewomen of some of the protections for their families which servicemen receive.[50] For the same reason, the Court invalidated provisions in the federal Social Security Act providing "mother benefits" to widows of employees who have children in their care but no similar benefits to widowers left in the same position,[51] and other provisions in the same act giving benefits to widows without regard to dependency but limiting benefits to widowers who were receiving one-half of their support from their wives.[52]

But the new constitutional law against discrimination on the basis of sex cuts both ways. It also reaches to discrimination against men. Thus, a state cannot permit the sale of beer to women of age eighteen while forbidding its sale to men until they reach twenty-one.[53] But, in cases where males were the complainants, the Court seems to have shown some tendency to sanction what might be described as affirmative action programs. A state tax exemption for widows was sustained in 1974 because, the Court explained in an opinion by Justice Douglas, 1970-72 statistics showed that in the majority of families where both spouses were present the woman was not employed, and that when women were employed they earned less than men. "Whether from overt discrimination or from the socialization process of a male-dominated culture, the job market is inhospitable to the woman seeking any but the lowest-paid jobs," so that the tax exemption for widows would cushion the "financial impact of spousal loss upon the sex for which that loss imposes a disproportionately heavy burden."[54] Later in the same year, the Court sustained federal statutes which required discharge of male navy line officers who had been twice passed over for promotions regardless of length of service, but which gave female line officers a minimum of thirteen years of tenure before discharge for want of promotion. Since other statutes forbade the women officers to serve on aircraft engaged in combat or on naval vessels other than hospital ships or transports, the Court concluded, over the dissents of Justices Brennan, Douglas, Marshall, and White, that the tenure guaranty was justified because women would not generally have compiled service records comparable to men's records.[55] Ironically, Federal District Judge Sirica in July 1978 held unconstitutional the statute limiting women's service on naval ships.[56]

The cases invalidating on constitutional grounds governmental discrimination on the basis of sex would also require invalidation of government-required or government-assisted private discrimination, including affirmative action programs. But the Supreme Court's treatment of discrimination on the basis of sex under the Constitution may leave more leeway both for discrimination and for affirmative action. Distinction on the ground of race, national origin, or alienage, the Court has said, is "inherently suspect" and will be subjected to "strict" judicial scrutiny[57]—a scrutiny which usually proves fatal.[58] Distinctions on grounds not inherently suspect, on the other hand, require only a minimally rational connection between the distinction and some legitimate governmental objective.[59] Thus far, the Court has refused, over the protests of Justices Brennan, Douglas, Marshall, and White, to categorize distinctions on the basis of sex as inherently suspect and therefore subject to strict scrutiny.[60]

However that may be, Title VII of the Civil Rights Act of 1964 forbids discrimination by governmental or private employers on the ground of sex, as do the laws of most states, and so does the executive order applicable to government contractors,[61] which also requires affirmative action.

Most of the Supreme Court's concern with sex discrimination under Title VII has been with the employer's treatment of an employee's pregnancy.[62] But the Court's consideration of this matter began with a constitutional decision. In the *La Fleur* case[63] the Court struck down under the due process clause of the Fourteenth Amendment school board rules requiring pregnant teachers to terminate their employment at the end of, in one case, the fourth, and in the other case, the fifth month of pregnancy, and making them ineligible to return to work until three months after giving birth. Because these rules in effect created an unrebuttable presumption of physical incompetence which would be contrary to fact in many cases, they were held unconstitutionally arbitrary.

Thereafter, over the dissents of Justices Douglas, Brennan, and Marshall, the Court found no discriminatory treatment of women under

Title VII in a state's contributory unemployment disability program for private employees which excluded from coverage disabilities resulting from normal pregnancy, dipsomania, drug addiction, or being a sexual psychopath. Although it did acknowledge that "only women can become pregnant," the Court found no sexual discrimination involved in a plan that distinguished between employees who were pregnant and those who were not. "There is no risk from which men are protected and women are not. Likewise, there is no risk from which women are protected and men are not."[64] That decision was followed by a similar ruling with respect to a private employer's disability plan for non-work related illness and accidents which also excluded disabilities resulting from pregnancy. Such disabilities constituted "an *additional* risk, unique to women and the failure to compensate them for this risk does not destroy the presumed benefits, accruing to men and women alike, which result from the facially even-handed *inclusion* of risks."[65] Last year the Court once more reaffirmed that ruling, but found sex discrimination in a plan which also provided that employees disabled by pregnancy would forfeit all seniority while employees disabled for any other reason would not. It also suggested that this discriminatory feature of the disability plan might be treated as evidence that the exclusion of pregnancy benefits was a mere pretext designed to discriminate against women.[66]

One other aspect of employment conditions is not unique to women, though it is probably most frequently encountered by them—sexual harassment of employees by supervisors. At least when the employee is female and the supervisor is male, the lower federal courts have concluded that where the employee is discharged or otherwise adversely treated for resisting her supervisor's advances, and where the employer knew or should have known of the supervisor's proclivities, a violation of Title VII is established.[67]

One factual difference between men and women probably is not immutable, although it seems to be increasing. On the average, women live longer than men.[68] The Supreme Court has held, however, that Title VII is violated where a city for that reason requires its female employees to make larger contributions than male employees to a pension fund. Averages won't do. Many women will not live as long as the average man, and Title VII makes it unlawful to discriminate against "any *individual*" on grounds of sex:

> Myths and purely habitual assumptions about a woman's inability to perform certain kinds of work are no longer acceptable reasons for refusing to employ qualified individuals or for paying them less. . . . [But even] a true generalization about the class is an insufficient reason for disqualifying an individual to whom the generalization does not apply.[69]

Another substantial factual difference between men and women probably is also not immutable, and indeed seems to be decreasing slightly. The overwhelming majority of veterans of military service are men.[70] The federal government, most states, and many municipalities grant some sort of a preference to veterans seeking public employment. But the veterans' lobby is strong as well as predominantly male, and there is an exception in Title VII for veterans' preference systems. Recently a lower federal court held that the discriminatory effect of a Massachusetts veterans' preference system (only 2 percent of Massachusetts veterans were women) violated the equal protection clause of the Fourteenth Amendment. But the Supreme Court only two months later decided that the Constitution forbade only purposeful racial discrimination.[71] Accordingly, when the veterans' preference case reached it last year, it vacated the judgment and remanded to the court below for reconsideration in light of its ruling on unconstitutional race discrimination.[72] One state supreme court has already viewed this action as removing all question about the constitutionality of veterans' preference systems.[73]

As in racial discrimination cases under Title VII, if a complainant establishes that employment practices have a discriminatory effect against one sex, even though not so intended by the employer, a violation is shown unless the employer can show that the practice is necessary to safe and efficient operation. Thus Alabama failed to persuade the Supreme Court that its requirement that its prison guards be at least five feet two inches tall and weigh at least 120 pounds, which had a discriminatory effect on women, was necessary to obtain guards of sufficient strength—a quality which could be tested directly. But the same decision sustained another Alabama rule which excluded women entirely from prison guard positions involving close physical contact with male prisoners. This rule was found to establish a justifiable work-related qualification for a variety of reasons.[74] Conditions in the Alabama prisons were so unsafe and otherwise intolerable that a federal district court had held a year earlier that incarceration in them constituted "cruel and unusual punishment" in violation of the Eighth Amendment and had enjoined Alabama to bring its system up to constitutional standards.[75] Like most prisons in this country, Alabama's are segregated on the basis of sex, and that created "a real risk that inmates deprived of a normal heterosexual environment would assault women guards because they were women." And that risk was aggravated by the fact that a substantial portion of the inmates were sex offenders.[76]

There is some overlap between Title VII and the earlier Equal Pay Act of 1963 in matters of sex discrimination. That act forbids discrimination on the basis of sex by paying wages "of a rate less than the rate [paid] to

employees of the opposite sex" for "equal work" on jobs requiring
"equal skill, effort, and responsibility" performed under similar
working conditions. There are similar statutes in most of the states. The
lower federal courts have held that discrimination can be shown even
when the male and female employees are not simultaneously employed,
when the man is hired at a higher wage to replace the woman.[77] They
have also held that the jobs need not be identical but only substantively
equal.[78]

This act contains exceptions for differentials based on seniority,
merit, or productivity systems, or "on any other factor other than sex."
The Supreme Court has held that a pension plan requiring women to
make larger contributions than men because, on the average, women
live longer will not qualify under the quoted language.[79] The act also
contains a provision which forbids the employer to correct a violation by
reducing the wages of any employee. The Supreme Court has quite
reasonably interpreted this provision as meaning that the employer can
bring himself into compliance only by raising the wage of the lower-
paid employee.[80]

Another prohibition against sex discrimination of apparently broader
scope is Title IX of the federal Education Amendments of 1972, which
applies to public or private study at all levels. Title IX provides that no
person shall, "on the basis of sex, be denied the benefits of, or be
subjected to discrimination under any education program or activity
receiving financial assistance," with numerous exceptions, including
some for schools which are converting from all-male or all-female to
coeducational status (affirmative action?), for schools which "traditionally and continually" admit only students of one sex and are not
converting, and for scholarships awarded to winners of beauty contests.

Yale University is currently involved in litigation to determine
whether there was sexual harassment of women students by faculty
members and, if so, whether such harassment violates this provision. In
other respects, Title IX may not be as broad as it appears. An argument
has been made that it does not apply to athletic programs which receive
no federal assistance, even though in other respects a particular school
does receive such assistance.[81] But HEW disputed that interpretation,
and fixed July 25, 1978, as the deadline for female equality in athletic
programs of colleges and universities—a deadline which has quite
obviously been massively ignored. Three federal district courts have also
read Title IX as reaching only to sex discrimination against students,
who are the beneficiaries of the federal funding, and not to
discrimination against employees of the educational institution, at least
where the discrimination against employees does not result in
discrimination against students.[82]

Finally, women get some protection against discrimination in the granting of credit. Title VIII of the Civil Rights Act of 1968 forbids private commercial real estate lenders and private real estate brokers to discriminate on the basis of sex as well as of race. And the Equal Credit Opportunity Act of 1974, as originally enacted, forbade all credit grantors, governmental as well as private, to discriminate on the basis of sex or marital status; discrimination on the basis of race was added in 1976.[83]

All of these congressional actions against sex discrimination will doubtless contribute in some measure to women's battle to overcome the stereotype, but that battle is by no means won. The chief obstacle to full equality is still the disadvantage women suffer with respect to professional and employment opportunities. As with racial discrimination, the individual remedies provided by Title VII of the Civil Rights Act of 1964 are not likely to make rapid changes in this area. Hence, the courts finding sex-based violations of Title VII have on occasion required affirmative action, including quotas, just as they have in cases of race-based discrimination.[84] The executive order applicable to government contracts requires affirmative action programs for sex as well as race. Title IX of the Education Amendments of 1972, forbidding sex-based discrimination in educational institutions receiving federal assistance, seems to permit affirmative action and even quotas by single-sex schools which are converted to coeducational institutions. HEW regulations under Title IX condition federal assistance on assurances that the schools will "take affirmative action to overcome the effects of conditions which resulted in limited participation [in a program or activity] by persons of a particular sex."[85] If, as suggested earlier, there is more leeway for affirmative action with respect to sex than with respect to race, the *Bakke* decision may have a lesser impact on those efforts on behalf of women than on affirmative action to overcome the effects of racial discrimination.

Age

Almost twenty-three million of our population, nearly 11 percent, are age sixty-five or older.[86] This group is also one of the fastest-growing segments of the population. On an assumption of zero population growth by the year 2000, it is estimated that those over sixty-five will number more than 31 million, or about 11.5 percent of the population.[87]

Until quite recently it was generally assumed that employees should terminate their employment—and many employers required them to do so—at age sixty-five, or sixty, or even earlier. Only in 1976, in the *Murgia* case, did the Supreme Court consider whether such a requirement, when imposed by the state, violated the equal protection clause of the Fourteenth Amendment.[88] The Court concluded that it did not. The case involved a Massachusetts requirement that its state police officers retire at age 50, applied to an officer who had just passed his annual physical examination and who was conceded to be in excellent physical and mental health. While the evidence indicated that many over age 50 could safely perform the functions of police officers, it also established that the risks of physical failure, particularly in the cardiovascular system, increase with age, and that was enough. Classifications based on age, like those based on sex, were not inherently suspect, strict judicial scrutiny was not required, and the age classification bore a minimally rational relation to the state's legitimate objective of maintaining a physically able police force. Since that decision, one federal court of appeals has held that a high school biology teacher required by the state to retire at age sixty-five was entitled to reinstatement if, after a hearing, a court concluded that there was no rational relationship between that age and her ability to teach.[89] But another court of appeals has disagreed and found no substantial constitutional question presented by a state's requirement that kindergarten teachers, judges, or state tax lawyers retire at age seventy.[90] The Supreme Court now has before it for review another lower court decision holding that mandatory retirement at age sixty for those in our federal foreign service violates the due process clause of the Fifth Amendment.[91]

In 1967 Congress enacted the Age Discrimination in Employment Act forbidding employers engaged in industries affecting interstate or foreign commerce to discriminate on the basis of age against employees between forty and sixty-five years of age. Just last April that law was amended to extend its protection to age seventy, although the extension does not apply to tenured college and university professors until 1982. Most states have similar laws against age-based discrimination in employment.

The federal act, like Title VII of the Civil Rights Act of 1964 dealing with discrimination on grounds of race, imposes a more rigid standard than the Supreme Court found in the Constitution in the *Murgia* case. Once discriminatory though unintentional effect is shown, the employer must establish that his employment practice is related to the safe and efficient operation of his business.[92] But the act does allow employers to act on the basis not only of bona fide occupational qualification but also on bona fide cause for discharge or discipline, or on "reasonable factors other than age." Originally, the act also allowed compulsory retirement pursuant to any bona fide seniority or retirement system,[93] but that exception is eliminated by the 1978 amendments.

Under this act, as under Title VII, the forbidden discrimination is frequently difficult to prove, particularly because there are physical and mental disabilities that often come with advanced age. Some of the same sort of problem is encountered in attempting to prove a violation of the federal Age Discrimination Act of 1975, forbidding age discrimination under any program or activity receiving federal financial assistance.

Eventually, age does bring job disqualification, and then the plight of many of the elderly rapidly worsens. HEW Secretary Califano reports that one in seven persons over age sixty-five are below the poverty line and that one in four are not far above it. The 1974 amendment to the Equal Credit Opportunity Act forbidding discrimination in credit extension on the basis of age will not help them, although federal hot lunch and part-time job programs may do so.

Beginning in 1956 with a series of federal housing acts, the federal government has allowed the elderly certain preferences in public housing and has provided low-interest loans for private housing for the elderly and for public housing units for them. In addition, the Senior Citizens Housing Act of 1962 provides rental supplements for the elderly. By 1973 a total of 452,414 units for the elderly had been built with federal assistance, of which some 348,730 were publicly owned. But even those who are able, with or without a federal rent supplement, to live in these housing units are reported to be turning increasingly to drugs and alcohol to combat loneliness and despair.

Moreover, more than one million of our elderly are now incarcerated in nursing homes. It was recently reported that a survey found 58 percent of them to be "senile," a term most of us use to cover everything from organic brain disease—which is what the medical profession regards as senility—to mental depression. But that report may be exaggerated, since the nurses who filled out the forms were not supplied with a precise definition of senility. In any event, most of those whose families put them in nursing homes will remain there for the rest of their days, sedated if necessary. Meanwhile, scientists are just beginning to search for some relief from or prevention of senility.[94]

For a very sizable part of our aged population, then, the later years of life are grim. Those still willing and able to perform in gainful occupations who are denied the opportunity to do so are the victims of conventional stereotypes about age-connected disabilities. Those no longer able to provide for themselves are too often the victims of neglect. That they have received what attention they have from their government is attributable to a number of factors. There is some genuine concern about discrimination against them. There is also some concern about the economic stability of the Social Security system, which would be somewhat eased if older workers continued working. Some legislators are themselves approaching or have passed an age that brings them within the conventional stereotype. Finally, all of the aged are old enough to vote, and as they organize their voting strength their views become matters for concern by those who seek elective office.

Disability

How many Americans suffer from physical or mental disability? We have no precise figures. The first White House Conference on Handicapped Individuals in 1977 reported there were more than 35 million but gave no details.[95] The 1970 U.S. Census, the first to ask about disabilities, reported 40 million, not including those in institutions. The National Arts and the Handicapped Information Service believes that there are some 37.5 million persons, or over 17 percent of our population, permanently handicapped in roughly the following categories (some fall into several): 11.7 million physically disabled (including 500,000 in wheelchairs and 3 million who depend on crutches, canes, braces, or walkers); 2.4 million deaf and 11 million with impaired hearing; 1.3 million blind and 8.2 million visually handicapped; 6.8 million mentally disabled; 1.7 million homebound; and 2.1 million institutionalized. And these numbers are increasing as medical science has reduced the mortality rate for accidents and diseases. The handicapped, like women and the aged, have only recently begun to organize. Many of the 490,000 disabled Vietnam veterans have been active in the organizing effort.[96]

Many of the handicapped, though not institutionalized, are largely isolated in a society dominated by the able-bodied. Many of them have no access to public or private buildings, to voting booths, to buses or subways, to restrooms, or even to public drinking fountains. Even street curbs may constitute an obstacle to their mobility. While the airlines accommodate some passengers in wheelchairs, a Federal Aviation Administration regulation requires the blind to surrender their canes during takeoff and landing, precisely when they are most anxious to have them. The handicapped have been unable to attend schools of their choice. Some estimates place employment at 40 percent of those considered employable. Many of the disabled who are working are stuck in sheltered workshops where they work at minor tasks for low wages. According to the 1970 Census, the proportion of the disabled living at the poverty level is almost twice as high as that for the general population, and the conditions in many of our institutions for the physically and mentally disabled make the nursing homes for the elderly look very good by comparison.

But perhaps worse, from the viewpoint of many of the disabled, is our attitude toward them. We are uncomfortable in their presence because they are different; hence we tend to avoid them when we can. This is perhaps the worst neglect of all.

The Supreme Court has not yet had occasion to consider whether the Constitution offers any protection against discrimination on the basis of disability.[97] One lower federal court has held that a city rule excluding a blind secondary English teacher from teaching sighted students, without giving her an opportunity to demonstrate her competence to do so, violated the due process clause of the Fourteenth Amendment,[98] just as the Supreme Court held in the *La Fleur* case[99] that mandatory pregnancy leaves violated that clause by creating an unrebuttable presumption of incompetence to teach. Others have recognized that mentally retarded children raise substantial constitutional claims under both due process and equal protection clauses when they challenge state action that excludes them from public schools without an opportunity to demonstrate that they can function there, while providing them with no alternative education;[100] and that mentally retarded inmates of state institutions, although not entitled to treatment because nontreatable, are entitled under the due process and equal protection clauses to minimally adequate "habilitation, i.e., education, training, and care."[101] Thus, the law to date provides little basis for attempting to determine whether classification on the basis of disability, or of some disabilities, will be viewed as inherently suspect and thus subject to strict judicial scrutiny, with a possible impairment of government's ability either to impose or assist private discrimination or to require or encourage affirmative action programs.[102]

But the recent organized activity by the handicapped has led to a flood of legislation at both federal and state levels. Thus, the federal Architectural Barriers Act of 1968 requires government buildings thereafter constructed, altered, or leased by the government, and other buildings financed by federal funds the intended use for which will require that they be accessible to the public or will result in employment or residence therein of physically handicapped persons, to be designed "to insure whenever possible that physically handicapped persons will have ready access to and use of such buildings." By 1970 and 1973 amendments to the Urban Mass Transportation Act of 1964, the secretary of transportation is authorized to provide financial assistance to state and local governments and private nonprofit institutions to provide mass transportation which "elderly and handicapped persons" can effectively use. Title IX of the federal Education Amendments of 1972, forbidding discrimination on the basis of sex in any educational program receiving federal assistance, also forbids denial of admission on the basis of blindness or impaired vision to any educational institution receiving federal assistance for any program or activity, although it expressly does not require the educational institution to provide any special services to the blind or sight-impaired student. The 1975 Education for All Handicapped Children Act goes further by providing federal funds to states that by 1978 implemented a policy "that assures all handicapped children" aged three to eighteen (and, by 1980, three to twenty) "the right to a free public education," including transportation services and "other supportive services . . . as may be required to assist a handicapped child to benefit from special education." Most recently, a provision in the Tax Reduction and Simplification Act of 1977 offers a subsidy of a different sort by providing a tax credit of 10 percent of the unemployment insurance wages paid to employees with physical or mental disabilities.

But perhaps the most comprehensive of the federal laws in this area is the Rehabilitation Act of 1973, which not only amends existing law providing federal financial assistance for state vocational rehabilitation programs but also contains three substantive provisions. The executive branch of the federal government is required to pursue affirmative action programs for the employment of the physically and mentally handicapped. So are all federal contractors whose contracts exceed $2,500. And no otherwise qualified handicapped person is to be subjected to discrimination solely because of his handicap in any program or activity receiving federal financial assistance. Implementing regulations from HEW were needed under the Rehabilitation Act, but it took almost three and one-half years, and a twenty-five-day sit-in by nearly 100 handicapped people in the San Francisco regional office of HEW to produce them. In the next four months HEW received 377 complaints of discrimination against the disabled, far more than the complaints received about race- and sex-based discrimination together.

Implementation of many of these new federal programs, and of some similar state programs, will of course cost huge sums of money—the price of 200 years of ignoring the disabled in the construction and operation of many facilities, including schools. HEW estimates that compliance with its regulations alone in this area will cost $2.8 billion a year. School officials estimate that it will cost $2,800 a year to educate each handicapped child—double the cost for other students. A special new bus, designed with wheelchair lifts, costs $80 million to develop. At a time when government officials are sensitive to a "taxpayer's revolt," some foot-dragging may be expected. This, the handicapped say, is putting a price tag on their justifiable claims for equal opportunity.

Clearly the plight of the disabled is a product of our tendency to regard those different from ourselves as not quite human. Many of the disabled say that some of their severest deprivations are the "attitudinal barriers" erected by the able-bodied who are uneasy in their presence and choose to avoid and ignore them. For a long time we also chose to ignore their needs for mobility and other physical requirements, for education, and for career and employment opportunities. It will take a massive effort to overcome the effects of two centuries of mistreatment and neglect.

Conclusion

I have variously attributed the discrimination with which we are here concerned to bigotry, prejudice, and conventional stereotypes. One word probably covers it all: ignorance—to which must be added a measure of selfishness. Unfortunately, these characteristics are not confined to the dominant group. When some government agencies tended to expand their programs for minorities to include persons "socially or economically disadvantaged" rather than merely those of certain races, some black and Hispanic leaders complained that their piece of the pie was being invaded.[103] A black columnist for the *Washington Post* praises mandatory retirement laws for the aged to make more jobs for the young and suggests that perhaps such laws should be amended to retire the aged "automatically to retirement homes."[104] Because government effort to protect against discrimination must combat such ingrained ignorance and selfishness, progress has not been rapid.

But some progress has been made, and it is, I believe, a twofold kind of progress. To the extent that we are required to cease our discriminatory treatment we perforce expand our association with those we have been discriminating against. Through that association will come some education for most of us that will eliminate the ignorance which led us to discriminate in the first place.

Notes

1. 109 U.S. 3 (1883).

2. 163 U.S. 537 (1896).

3. See the separate opinion of Justice Marshall in Regents of California v. Bakke, 98 S.Ct. 2733, 2801 (1978).

4. Regents of California v. Bakke, note 3, supra, at 2767.

5. 347 U.S. 483 (1954). At the same time that the equal protection clause of the Fourteenth Amendment was held to forbid state segregated schools, the due process clause of the Fifth Amendment was held to forbid federally segregated schools in the District of Columbia. Bolling v. Sharpe, 347 U.S. 497 (1954).

6. Burton v. Wilmington Parking Authority, 364 U.S. 715 (1961); Turner v. Memphis, 369 U.S. 350 (1962).

7. See Zashin, *The Progress of Black Americans in Civil Rights: The Past*

Two Decades Assessed, 107 Daedalus 239, 242-247 (1978).

8. See Zashin, note 7, supra, at 247-250.

9. See the separate opinion of Justice Marshall, note 3, supra, at 2802. See also Freeman, *Black Economic Progress Since 1964,* The Public Interest, Summer 1978, 52; National Urban League, *The State of Black America 1977,* 9 Black Scholar 2 (1977).

10. See Zashin, note 7, supra at 255.

11. See District of Columbia v. John B. Thompson Co., 346 U.S. 100 (1953); Colorado Anti-Discrimination Commission v. Continental Air Lines, 373 U.S. 714 (1963); Railway Mail Association v. Corsi, 326 U.S. 88 (1945).

12. Note 1, supra.

13. Heart of Atlanta Motel, Inc., v. United States, 379 U.S. 241 (1964); Katzenbach v. McClung, 379 U.S. 294 (1964); Hamm v. Rock Hill, 379 U.S. 306 (1964); Daniel v. Paul, 395 U.S. 298 (1969).

14. Griggs v. Duke River Co., 401 U.S. 424 (1975).

15. See note 5, supra.

16. Washington v. Davis, 426 U.S. 229 (1976).

17. Katzenbach v. Morgan, 384 U.S. 641 (1966).

18. South Carolina v. Katzenbach, 383 U.S. 301 (1966).

19. Jones v. Mayer Co., 392 U.S. 409 (1968). Title VIII of the Civil Rights Act of 1968 now forbids private commercial real estate lenders and private real estate brokers to discriminate on the basis of race, and the Equal Credit Opportunity Act of 1974, as amended in 1976, forbids such discrimination by all credit granters, governmental as well as private.

20. Runyon v. McCrary, 427 U.S. 160 (1976).

21. McDonald v. Santa Fe Trail Transportation Co., 427 U.S. 273 (1976).

22. See Lopatka, *A 1977 Primer of the Federal Regulation of Employment Discrimination,* 1977 U. Ill. L. Forum 69; International Brotherhood of Teamsters v. United States, 431 U.S. 324 (1977); Furnco Construction Corp. v. United States, 98 S.Ct. 2493 (1975).

23. Zashin, note 7, supra, at 255-258.

24. Ibid, at 250-255; Freeman, note 9, supra.

25. Executive Order 11,236 (1965) as amended by Executive Order 11,735 (1967), reprinted following 42 U.S.C. sec. 2000e.

26. 42 U.S.C. sec. 2000e-17.

27. See the opinion of Justice Brennan in Regents of California v. Bakke, note 3, supra, at 2781.

28. See Lopatka, note 22, supra, at 135-144.

29. 45 Code of Fed. Reg. secs. 80.3(b)(6)(i)(ii), 80.5(i).

30. 42 U.S.C. sec. 6705(f)(2).

31. Regents of University of California v. Bakke, note 3, supra.

32. De Funis v. Odegaard, 416 U.S. 312, 334 (1974).

33. After *Bakke,* in three other pending cases involving the validity of that act, the Supreme Court vacated the judgments and remanded for the courts below to consider the question of mootness. Los Angles County v. Associated General Contractors of California, 98 S.Ct. 3132 (1978); Associated General Contractors of California v. Kreps, 98 S.Ct. 3132 (1978); Kreps v. Associated General

Contractors of California, 98 S.Ct. 3133 (1978).

34. After *Bakke* also, the Court declined to review a case challenging the provisions of an affirmative action consent decree entered against an employer under the Equal Employment Opportunity Act (Communications Unions of America v. Equal Employment Opportunity Commission, 98 S.Ct. 3145 [1978]), vacated a judgment fixing racial quotas for student governmental bodies in a state university, and remanded for reconsideration in light of *Bakke*. Friday v. Uzzell, 98 S.Ct. 3139 (1978).

35. Note 5, supra.

36. Brown v. Board of Education, 349 U.S. 294, 300-301 (1955).

37. Griffith v. School Board, 377 U.S. 218, 234 (1964).

38. Alexander v. Holmes County Board of Education, 396 U.S. 19, 20 (1969); Carter v. West Feliciana School Board, 396 U.S. 290, 291 (1970); Northcross v. Board of Education of Memphis, 397 U.S. 232, 235 (1970).

39. Justice Blackmun in *Bakke*, note 3, supra, expressed the hope that if affirmative action programs were followed they might eliminate the problem in a decade, but admitted that "that hope is a slim one." 98 S.Ct. at 2806.

40. Bureau of the Census, *Statistical Abstract of the United States* 25 (1977).

41. Bradwell v. Illinois, 16 Wall. 130, 141-142 (1873) (concurring opinion). The applicant did not invoke the equal protection clause of the Fourteenth Amendment, but another provision of that amendment forbidding the state to make or enforce any law abridging privileges or immunities of U.S. citizenship. As the subsequent discussion will show, there is no reason to believe that invocation of the equal protection clause would have made any difference.

42. Minor v. Happersett, 21 Wall. 162 (1875).

43. Muller v. Oregon, 208 U.S. 412 (1908).

44. Goesaert v. Cleary, 335 U.S. 464 (1948).

45. Hoyt v. Florida, 368 U.S. 57, 61-62 (1961).

46. Information in this and the preceding paragraphs is taken from Robertson, *The Top Women in Business*, 98 Fortune 58 (1978); Ferber and Kordick, *Sex Differentials in the Earnings of Ph.D.s*, 31 Ind. and Lab. Rel. Rev. 227 (1978); Parker, *Women at Work and in School*, 106 Intellect 310 (1978); Abuhoff, *Title VII and the Appointment of Women Clergy: A Statutory and Constitutional Quagmire*, 13 Col. J. of Law and Soc. Probs. 257 (1977); Wall St. J., July 19, 1978, p. 1; id., August 28, 1978, p. 1; id., September 8, 1978, p. 1; Boston Globe, July 27, 1978, p. 3; id., June 5, 1978, p. 12; Time, September 4, 1978, p. 41.

47. Reed v. Reed, 404 U.S. 71 (1971).

48. Stanton v. Stanton, 421 U.S. 7 (1975).

49. 421 U.S. at 14.

50. Frontiero v. Richardson, 411 U.S. 677 (1973).

51. Weinberger v. Weisenfeld, 420 U.S. 636 (1975).

52. Califano v. Goldfarb, 430 U.S. 199 (1977).

53. Craig v. Boren, 429 U.S. 190 (1976).

54. Kahn v. Shevin, 416 U.S. 351, 353, 355 (1974).

55. Schlesinger v. Ballard, 419 U.S. 498 (1974).

56. New York Times, July 28, 1978, p. 1.

57. L. Tribe, American Constitutional Law, sec. 16-6 (1978).

58. Gunther, *In Search of Evolving Doctrine on a Changing Court: A Model for a Newer Equal Protection*, 86 Harv. L. Rev. 1, 8 (1972).

59. Tribe, note 57, supra, sec. 16-2.

60. Stanton v. Stanton, note 58, supra; Schlesinger v. Ballard, note 55, supra; Frontiero v. Richardson, note 50, supra.

61. Note 25, supra.

62. Phillips v. Martin Marietta Corp., 400 U.S. 542 (1971), did find a violation of Title VII where an employer refused to hire mothers of preschool children but imposed no similar ban on the employment of fathers of such children, and where the employer did not prove that conflicting family obligations were more relevant to the job performance of a woman than a man.

63. Cleveland Board of Education v. La Fleur, 414 U.S. 632 (1974).

64. Gedelug v. Aiello, 417 U.S. 484, 496-497 (1974).

65. General Electric Co. v Gilbert, 429 U.S. 125 (1976).

66. Nashville Gas Co. v. Satto, 98 S.Ct. 237 (1974). Congressional reaction to this decision was the passage in both houses in summer 1978 of bills (H.R. 6075 and S. 995, 95th Congress) which would amend Title VII to require that women disabled by "pregnancy, childbirth, or related medical conditions" be treated the same for "all employment-related purposes" as employees disabled for other reasons. But the right-to-life lobby obtained a rider on the House bill excluding disability due to abortions save when the life of the mother would be endangered, although permitting employers to provide abortion benefits voluntarily or as a consequence of collective bargaining. Hence, the bills are still tied up in Conference Committee.

67. Tomkins v. Public Service Electric and Gas Co., 568 F.2d 1044 (3d Cir. 1977); Barnes v. Costle, 561 F.2d 983 (D.C. Cir. 1977); Garber v. Saxon Business Prods., 552 F.2d 1032 (4th Cir. 1977); Heelan v. Johns-Manville Corp., 451 F. Supp. 1382 (D. Colo. 1978), and cases cited.

68. The life expectancy of persons born in 1920 was 54.4 for white men, 55.6 for white women, 45.5 for nonwhite men, and 45.2 for nonwhite women. For those born in 1975, life expectancy was 68.7 for white men, 76.5 for white women, 63.6 for nonwhite men, and 72.3 for nonwhite women. Bureau of the Census, *Statistical Abstract of the United States* 65 (1977).

69. City of Los Angeles v. Manhart, 98 S.Ct. 1370, 1375 (1978).

70. Department of Defense statistics reveal that the percentage of women in the armed services, which never exceeded 2.19 percent during World War II, was slightly more than 5 percent in 1976. Fleming and Shanor, *Veterans' Preferences in Public Employment: Unconstitutional Gender Discrimination?*, 26 Emory L. Rev. 13 (1977).

71. Washington v. Davis, note 16, supra.

72. Massachusetts v. Feeney, 98 S.Ct. 252 (1977).

73. Ballou v. State Department of Civil Service, 382 A.2d 118 (N.J. 1978). See also Bannerman v. Department of Youth Authority, 436 F. Supp. 1273 (N.D. Calif. 1977).

74. Dothard v. Rawlinson, 433 U.S. 321, 335 (1977). Cf. Boyd v. Ozark Airlines, Inc., 568 F.2d 50 (8th Cir. 1977), finding that an airline's height

requirement of five feet seven inches for pilots effected discrimination against women and was not job-related, but that a five-foot five-inch height requirement was justifiable in order to enable the pilot to reach all of the instruments in the cockpit; and Batyko v. Penn. Liquor Control Board, 450 F. Supp. 32 (W.D. Pa. 1978), finding no violation of Title VII where the court was persuaded that a fifty-six-year-old woman liquor store clerk, who was five feet tall and weighed one hundred and eighteen pounds, was discharged because she could not carry and stack cartons of liquor.

75. James v. Wallace, 406 F. Supp. 318 (M.D. Ala. 1976). The decision was later affirmed, with some modifications in the injunction. Newalan v. Alabama, 559 F.2d 283 (5th Cir. 1977), cert. denied 98 S.Ct. 3144 (1978).

76. All of this seems to come very close to saying that two or more wrongs make a right. See also the cases holding that there was no discrimination against women in an airline's refusal to hire married women as stewardesses as long as the airline was in violation of Title VII in refusing to hire any male stewards. Equal Employment Opportunity Commission v. Delta Air Lines, Inc., 578 F.2d 115 (1978); Stroud v. Delta Air Lines, Inc., 544 F.2d 892 (5th Cir.), cert. denied 434 U.S. 844 (1977).

77. Di Salvo v. Chamber of Commerce, 568 F.2d 593 (8th Cir. 1978).

78. Schultz v. Wheaton Glass Co., 421 F.2d 259 (3d Cir.), cert. denied 398 U.S. 905 (1970); Brennan v. Owensboro-Davis County Hospital, 538 F.2d 859 (6th Cir. 1975); Wetzel v. Liberty Mutual Ins. Co., 449 F. Supp. 397 (W.D. Pa. 1978); Usery v. Johnson, 436 F. Supp. 35 (D.C.N.D. 1977); Huckeby v. Frozen Food Express, 427 F. Supp. 967 (N.D. Tex.), app. dismissed 555 F.2d 542 (5th Cir. 1977).

79. City of Los Angeles v. Manhart, note 69, supra.

80. Corning Glass Works v. Brennan, 417 U.S. 188 (1974).

81. Kuhn, *Title IX: Employment and Athletics Are Outside HEW's Jurisdiction*, 65 Geo. L. J. 49 (1976). A number of state and lower federal courts have found state and federal constitutional objections to sex discrimination in school athletic programs. See Yellow Springs Exempted Village School District v. Ohio High School Athletic Association, 443 F. Supp. 753 (S.D. Ohio 1978); *Opinion of the Justices*, 371 N.E.2d 426 (Mass. 1977), and cases cited. Cf. Leffel v. Wisconsin Interscholastic Athletic Association, 444 F. Supp. 1117 (E.D. Wis. 1978).

82. Brunswick School Board v. Califano, 449 F. Supp. 866 (D. Me. 1978), and cases cited.

83. See Comment, 22 St. Louis U. L. J. 326 (1978).

84. See Lopatka, note 22, supra, at 134-144; United States v. City of Philadelphia, 573 F.2d 802 (3rd Cir. 1978).

85. 45 C.F.R. secs. 86.3, 86.4.

86. Bureau of the Census, *Statistical Abstract of the United States* 28 (1977).

87. C. Edelman and I. Siegler, *Federal Age Discrimination in Employment Law* 12 (1978).

88. Massachusetts Board of Retirement v. Murgia, 427 U.S. 307 (1976). Earlier, the court had dismissed an appeal from a Pennsylvania supreme court decision upholding that state's mandatory retirement of state police officers at age sixty as not presenting a substantial constitutional question (McIlvaine v. Pennsyl-

vania, 415 U.S. 986 [1974]) and had summarily affirmed a decision sustaining a statute requiring federal employees in the executive branch to retire at age seventy (Weisbrod v. Lynn, 420 U.S. 940 [1975].)

89. Gault v. Garrison, 569 F.2d 993 (7th Cir. 1977).

90. Palmer v. Ticcione, 576 F.2d 459 (2d Cir. 1978); Johnson v. Lefkowitz, 566 F.2d 866 (2d Cir. 1977); Rubino v. Ghezzi, 512 F.2d 431 (2d Cir.), cert. denied 423 U.S. 891 (1975).

91. Vance v. Bradley, 98 S.Ct. 2230 (1978).

92. Edelman and Siegler, note 87, supra, at 91-134; Lopatka, note 22, supra, at 154-161; Houghton v. McDonnell Douglas Corp., 553 F.2d 561 (8th Cir. 1977), cert. denied 98 S.Ct. 506 (1977).

93. See United Air Lines, Inc., v. McMann, 98 S.Ct. 444 (1977).

94. Information contained in this and the preceding two paragraphs was obtained from New York Times, July 18, 1978, p. B-10; id., July 5, 1978, p. D-15; id., July 26, 1978, p. A-4; Boston Globe, June 29, 1978, p. 23; Melman, *Housing for the Aged—The Government Response*, 8 Urban Lawyer 123, 126-129 (1976).

95. Final Report, Part A, p. 1.

96. Kleinfield, *The Handicapped: Hidden No Longer*, Atlantic Monthly, December, 1977, p. 86; *Symposium on the Rights of the Handicapped*, 50 Temple L. Q. 941 (1977).

97. The Court did hold in Robinson v. California, 370 U.S. 660 (1962), that a state violates the Eighth Amendment by imposing cruel and unusual punishment when it imprisons one solely because of his status as a narcotics addict, but refused to apply that ruling when the state imposed the same punishment on a chronic alcoholic (Powell v. Texas, 392 U.S. 514 [1968]). It also held that a state denies due process when it confines to a state institution a mentally ill person who is not dangerous to himself or others without providing treatment to alleviate or cure his illness. (O'Connor v. Donaldson, 422 U.S. 563 [1975].) And in the ancient case of Buck v. Bell, 274 U.S. 200, 207 (1927), it held that a state did not deny due process or equal protection by sterilizing an institutionalized mentally retarded woman whose mother was also institutionalized and mentally retarded and who was the mother of an illegitimate, mentally retarded minor child because, as Justice Holmes put it in one of his epigrams, "Three generations of imbeciles is enough."

98. Gurmonkin v. Constanza, 556 F.2d 184 (3rd Cir. 1977). See Duran v. City of Tampa, 430 F. Supp. 75 (M.D. Fla. 1977), applying the same rule to one denied employment as a city policeman solely because of a childhood history of epilepsy.

99. Note 63, supra.

100. McMillan v. Board of Education, 430 F.2d 1145 (2d Cir. 1970); Pennsylvania Ass'n. of Retarded Children v. Pennsylvania, 343 F. Supp. 279 (E.D. Pa. 1972). See also Panitch v. Wisconsin, 444 F. Supp. 320 (E.D. Wis. 1977); Mills v. Board of Education, 348 F. Supp. 866 (D. D.C. 1972). Cf. McInnis v. Shapiro, 293 F. Supp. 327 (N.D. Ill. 1968), affirmed 394 U.S. 322 (1969).

101. Haderman v. Parkhurst State School and Hospital, 446 F. Supp. 1295, 1315 (E.D. Pa. 1978). Cf. Selph v. Los Angeles, 390 F. Supp. 58 (C.D. Cal. 1975), holding that a city was not required to incur the expense of locating voting

booths in buildings accessible to the handicapped where it provided them with absentee ballots.

102. One aspect of the matter is examined in Krass, *The Right to Public Education for Handicapped Children: A Primer for the New Advocate,* 1976 U. Ill. Law Forum 1016.

103. New York Times, July 30, 1978, p. 1.

104. Washington Post, October 17, 1977, p. 19.

TEN

THE SELF-REGULATED PROFESSIONS
AND THE PUBLIC INTEREST
Robert B. McKay

If the purpose of the William O. Douglas Inquiry is, as the name suggests, to ask questions more than to provide answers, my topic is ideally suited to the occasion. In this examination—or inquiry—into the self-regulated professions and the public interest it will be my objective to call attention to aspects of several of the most prominent and most important professions that I believe have escaped public attention; or at least the public has failed to ask appropriate questions about the control of these professions in relation to the interest of the public as a whole.

In the brief examination of law, medicine, accounting, journalism, and the military services that I propose, I shall not attempt to answer questions about the advantages and disadvantages of the relatively substantial autonomy accorded some professional groups as opposed to the more restricted freedom allowed others. The ultimate issue in each case should involve an assessment of the extent to which the public interest is served by allowing greater or lesser freedom for self-regulation on the part of each profession. The answer may well vary, as does present practice; the present aim is to look for common denominators by which judgments can be more readily made in each case in comparison with others, in the search for a proper balance between professional freedom and public control.

I do not suggest that these questions are new. If there is novelty in the present approach, it lies in the attempt to look for common ground among the professions rather than treating each in relative isolation. Too often in the case of individual professions the tendency has been to assume the right of self-regulation until something goes notoriously wrong. Until recent years, for example, all five of the professional groups here inquired into have been relatively free to set their own standards for admission into their professional ranks and relatively

Robert B. McKay is the director of the Program on Justice, Society and the Individual of the Aspen Institute for Humanistic Studies.

immune from external rules of discipline for conduct that might be regarded as unprofessional or even harmful to the public interest. For example:

• Lawyer members of law faculties have determined criteria for admission to law school; lawyers and judges have established the criteria for admission to the bar (sometimes with the aid of legislative bodies including more than a few lawyers); lawyers have written the rules of professional responsibility; and lawyers administer discipline for breaches of those standards. The circle of accountability and responsibility is tightly circumscribed, with lawyers screening every point of entrance and exit against intrusion by nonlawyers.

• Doctor members of medical faculties establish admission standards for entrance to medical schools; doctors prepare and administer the examinations for qualification to practice in general and in the specialties; doctors fix the standards of professional responsibility; and doctors administer the discipline.

• Although accountants may not control admission to schools of business and graduate schools of business administration, they certainly control access to their own departments; accountants prepare the examinations for certified public accountants, the almost indispensable qualification for admission into the status positions within the profession; and standards of conduct are established and enforced by the American Institute of Certified Public Accountants.

• The military establishment protects its independence in a somewhat different manner. Although nominations to the service academies are initially made through political channels, and reservists may come directly from hundreds of colleges and universities across the country, the honor code at the academies has been a powerful weapon for the imposition of common standards of discipline and morality. Moreover, performance ratings for promotion are based on standards devised by the military. Discipline, even for actions that would be subject to criminal prosecution outside the military, is largely confined to the sanctions specified in the Uniform Code of Military Justice, as implemented by the Manual for Courts-Martial. Although the manual is promulgated as a presidential order, it is in fact prepared by military personnel to meet the needs of the military.

• Journalists have in some ways been the most freewheeling and independent of all the professional groups here examined. In fact, some journalists deny that they are members of a profession since there is no formal credentialing process by which membership is definitively ascertained. There is little control, internal or external, over the standards by which admission to the journalistic enterprise is determined. Some enter from university schools of journalism, but many do not; and the likelihood of success is not clearly determined by the point of entry. However, once within the journalism fold the assertion of independence from external control is claimed for all under the mantle of First Amendment rights. Legislative regulation is resisted (except for shield laws reinforcing the right of nondisclosure); judicial authority is denied (not always successfully); and nongovernmental review of accuracy and fairness is sternly rejected.

*   *   *

To be a professional is to some undefined extent a preferred status in contemporary America. The triad of professions in the medieval university, law, medicine, and theology, have been vastly expanded in modern society. In this account we shall consider only five—law, medicine, accounting, journalism, and the military, although the number of occupational groups that are recognized as professions (or aspire to such recognition) is vast and expanding. In the field of health care alone, the more than 400,000 medical doctors are supplemented and surrounded by more than a million other health care specialists, dentists, nurses, and technicians with a variety of specialties, all asserting their right to professional status. The claim is by no means unreasonable; each specialty is capable of delivering particular health care services which cannot be as well performed by any other. The skills of the anaesthesiologist, the x-ray technician, and the pathologist cannot be readily undertaken by others who lack their training and certification.

The threshold questions remain unanswered: What is a profession? Who is a professional? The questions are not subject to confident response. The essential characteristics of a profession are nowhere defined in statute or judicial decision. The answer, then, must be sought in experience and concern for the public welfare. It is the initial purpose of this inquiry to search for characteristics common to those occupations generally acknowledged to be professions. The second and more important purpose of this inquiry is to examine the extent to which the professions, as now organized, serve the public interest.

This inquiry does not aspire to answer the hard questions. The more modest aim is to search for common ground among the five professional groups to be examined and to identify some of the issues which deserve further study. The need is for careful research to determine the ethical precepts that animate these professions; to review the standards of professional responsibility that guide the conduct of their members; and to determine whether the public interest is better served by leaving the professions to their own control or whether greater public intervention would be justified. The rather disparate professions selected for this preliminary inquiry may invite different answers, in kind or in degree. Yet the diversity among these professions is deliberate, since the intention is to look for points of similarity and for points of differentiation. Only thus, it is believed, will it be possible to identify the essential strands of "professionalism" and the justifications for, or the arguments against, self-regulation.

Even though public regard for the professions is low, as demonstrated in all recent public opinion polls, there is little reason to doubt that the professions of law, medicine, accounting, journalism, and even the military officer caste are high-status occupations. No matter how often lawyers are maligned for their litigiousness, their high fees, and their involvement in Watergate, the fact remains that law school applications continue to rise (as does the academic merit of the applicants); and individual citizens are quick to press their individual claims in court with the assistance of lawyers. Similarly, there is no shortage of applicants for medical school; and the proud refrain "my son the doctor" does not diminish as more and more frequently it becomes "my daughter the doctor." As auditors and accountants become increasingly indispensable for the doing of business, their claim to professional prestige (and ever higher fees) becomes more secure in the public mind. Individuals subjected to the probing inquiries of investigative reporters may object to the persistent intrusions into privacy, but the reading public demands more of the same and pays homage to those who score earliest and hit hardest. Whatever the revulsion many feel about military excesses in the name of national security, abroad or at home, the public as a whole respects the need for armed forces and pays on the whole considerable attention to the demands of the military for the costly support it has come to expect.

The professions must recall, however, that they have not always had secure status and relatively high prestige in the United States. In the Jacksonian period, for example, both law and medicine lost their monopoly over their respective fields of practice as statutory requirements for admission to those professions dwindled and often disappeared. Accounting, a relative newcomer to professional status, is a largely twentieth-century refinement of lesser callings. The succession from bookkeeping to accounting to certified public accountants to auditing is a latter-day bootstrap success story. Reporters and the military seem always to have been with us, but certainly their glory days have been in recent decades.

As the public looks more critically at those to whom it must turn for specialized services, it is by no means certain that the favored professions might not once again fall from grace. Although it is not likely that requirements for entry into such professions as medicine and law will again be removed, the late twentieth-century threat would be to take away the privilege of self-regulation and place the responsibility with legislatures and administrative agencies. That is what this inquiry is about. The purpose is to ask the questions that should be answered before decisions are made whether to reinforce the network of private regulation, whether to replace it with public control, or whether a mixed economy of private and public regulation is feasible and desirable.

The issue is not unique to these five professions. The professions selected for study are merely some of the most visible. Similar questions can be raised about other components of health care, from optometry to undertaking, about other professions from architecture to social work, and about many other occupational groups which have achieved or aspire to recognition as professions. The importance of the subject suggests the need for future research into the history of each profession, its present organization, requirements for entry, provisions for discipline and removal, and the effectiveness of its delivery of essential service to the public.

It would not be quite fair to charge the professions with failure to ask how well they serve the public interest. Every professional group asserts that obligation in its ethical prescriptions or its code of professional responsibility. But it would be fair to say that no profession invites external scrutiny of that question, and there is some reason to believe that some of the ethical requirements and prohibitions are not entirely free of self-interest. The time has come for that assessment, not only to meet the public demand for accountability, but as well to state the case for a continued right of self-regulation. But the case must be made; it can no longer be accepted as a given.

Before proceeding to the preliminary case studies which are a major purpose of this introductory inquiry, it is appropriate to identify the characteristics these five occupational groups have in common and on which they base their claim to be called professions. It must be remembered, however, that there is no absolute guide to nomenclature when we seek to identify an occupational group as a profession. The term is self-bestowed and can only be rejected by a public unwilling, for example, to say that a sanitarian is a professional or unprepared to concede that trucking or merchandising are other than trades. For better or for worse, there is no public body with the power to say that medicine is a profession and that the local grocer is a tradesperson. Accordingly, in the analysis that follows the reader must not expect that the five identified "professions" will neatly fit all the prescriptive standards. With that caveat here are the suggested characteristics.

1. *The professions are "learned."* The concept of special educational requirements was a prime characteristic of the original professions of

law, medicine, and theology, which have become known as learned. The same criterion applies to the present-day accountant who is distinguished by special training, usually acquired in a university. Similarly, U.S. military officers are almost invariably graduates of one of the service academies or recipients of specialized instruction in reserve officer training programs at the college level. Only the journalists are not required to have attained any particular level of education, although many are products of university-based schools of journalism; and one likes to believe that more than minimal literacy is required for success in the media.

The professions have sometimes sought shelter behind the concept of the learned profession as an insulation against government regulation. The legal profession so argued in claiming that its minimum fee schedules were immune from the inhibitions on price-fixing in the antitrust laws. Not so, said the Supreme Court of the United States in *Goldfarb v. Virginia,* 1975. In that case the bar association defended its anticompetitive fee schedules on the ground that "competition is inconsistent with the practice of a profession because enhancing profit is not the goal of professional activities; the goal is to provide services necessary to the community." But the Court noted that the fee schedules may not have been "wholly altrustic," since the challenged Minimum Fee Schedule Report began with this sentence: "The lawyers have slowly, but surely, been committing economic suicide as a profession." The Court therefore concluded,

> It is no disparagement of the practice of law as a profession to acknowledge that it has this business aspect. . . . In the modern world it cannot be denied that the activities of lawyers play an important part in commercial intercourse, and that anticompetitive activities by lawyers may exert a restraint on commerce.

The doctors have been similarly reminded by the Supreme Court that the medical profession is not immune from the strictures of the antitrust laws intended to apply to all commercial activities, including those of the learned professions along with trades, businesses, and other occupations (*United States v. Oregon State Medical Society,* 1952; *American Medical Association v. United States,* 1943).

2. *Access to membership in a profession is restricted.* A principal characteristic of a true profession is that entry is limited to those who satisfy the qualifications prescribed by present membership. In the case of medicine, law, and accounting the requirements are high, and many of those who aspire to join the ranks are denied admission for failure to gain entrance to, or inability to complete, the requisite course of

instruction at an institution of higher education, or failure to pass the credentialing examination. The military is somewhat more open, but is still a restricted society and one in which failure to be promoted at appropriate intervals blocks further advancement and may even require separation. Access to the various specialties in journalism (defined to include all the media news functions) is the most open among the professions here considered. But even journalism is not lacking in informal credentialing structures. Moreover, once accepted as a member of the profession, each journalist is subject to its code of ethics.

3. *The professions define and enforce applicable standards of ethical conduct.* Doctors are bound by the Hippocratic oath, administered upon receipt of the medical degree, and Principles of Medical Ethics, promulgated by the American Medical Association. Lawyers are bound by the American Bar Association Code of Professional Responsibility, as adopted by each state, sometimes with minor variations. Certified public accountants are bound by the standards promulgated by the American Institute of Certified Public Accountants. Journalists are bound by one of several codes (for editors and publishers as well as for journalists). And military officers are bound by various honor codes, beginning with training in the service academies, and later by the standards of conduct prescribed in the Uniform Code of Military Justice. Only the last-named of those is the product of governmental prescription and directly subject to judicial enforcement; but when enforcement is sought, it is ordinarily by court-martial or in other specialized courts of military justice.

The ethical standards drawn by each of these professional groups assert a formulation based on concern for the interest of those served, and no doubt that is accurate. However, since the codes have uniformly been formulated by members of the professions involved, the suspicion could be advanced that a tincture of self-interest might enter the deliberations from time to time, even if inadvertent.

One aspect of the codes deserves special mention. Ordinarily, there is a requirement of specified educational achievement as well as the credentialing provisions of the licensing requirements. Further, those who determine entry and set ethical standards for the professions also appoint the disciplinary boards to enforce those standards.

Other links among the five professional groups here identified arise out of the problems which they share. For example:

1. *Declining reputation.* Public disaffection with professions in general is certainly reflected in public disenchantment with the five professions here considered. It is scarcely necessary to recount the new lows to which these groups have sunk in public esteem. The significant fact is that dissatisfaction with the professions, exceeding that of a more complacent past, is now manifested in action as well as grumbling.

Complaints about medical incompetence have brought increasing numbers of malpractice actions and awards so high that insurers have sometimes backed away from a business whose risks they could no longer predict. In New York State, for example, it was necessary for the state to intervene to establish a state-controlled fund to which the doctors could pay their premiums.

Doctors often complain that the number and size of the malpractice awards are further evidence of lawyer-induced litigiousness, perhaps forgetting that the awards are made by jurors persuaded of medical negligence or worse. Meanwhile, actions against lawyers have also increased, as have those against accountants. The mystique of professionalism is no longer sufficient cover for incompetence or negligence or fraud. Consumers scrutinize professional services for defects much as they would any article of merchandise for which they hold a warranty of good performance.

Similarly, the courts are increasingly receptive to consumer challenges, not only as to individual complaints, but as well to the very premises on which the professions are based. For example, in 1973 the Supreme Court of the United States, in *United States v. Couch*, categorically told accountants that there is no accountant-client privilege. In 1975, as already noted, the Supreme Court told the lawyers that, however "learned" the legal profession, it could not set minimum fee schedules that amounted to price-fixing forbidden under the antitrust laws. Then in 1977 the Court ruled in *Bates v. State Bar of Arizona* that the provisions of the Code of Professional Responsibility forbidding all lawyer advertising conflict with the First Amendment. To its credit the American Bar Association responded in 1977 to permit newspaper and radio advertising that is not fraudulent or misleading and in 1978 extended the authorization to television as well. As a result of these decisions a new era of fee competition is predicted, with probable benefits for the consumer.

Clashes between journalists and the courts have been so frequent in recent years that they cannot all be recounted here. For the moment it is enough to say that the courts and the media have wrestled with questions of libel, so-called gag orders, shield laws and disclosure of sources, the right of reply to alleged media misstatements, and the search of newspaper premises for information implicating third parties in criminal activities.

Legislatures and administrative agencies have also responded to public dissatisfaction by increasing the burden on accountants to make more meaningful disclosures about the business affairs of their clients. The military has been put on notice that it can no longer conduct its affairs in secret under the mantle of national security. The paramilitary branches of government surveillance, the Federal Bureau of Investigation, the Central Intelligence Agency, and the National Security Agency, have all been subjected to a measure of executive and legislative oversight never before imposed.

2. *Challenges to competence.* Professional competence is being subjected to ever more rigorous scrutiny by the public, by the courts, and by legislative bodies. Perhaps as a result of sometimes less than sympathetic external examination, the professions are themselves tightening the standards by which judgment of competence is made and according to which discipline may be imposed.

The definitional question is by no means easy in an increasingly complex world. The ranks of generalists are rapidly thinning in medicine, law, accounting, and the military. Even journalists are often assigned specialized beats requiring more than casual understanding of science, economics, medicine, ecology, or judicial process. As knowledge becomes more and more compartmentalized and as information is increasingly computerized, the task of defining and monitoring competence of performance becomes almost impossibly difficult. As the call for mastery of the professed skills becomes more insistent, the challenge to each profession is to find better ways to insure adequate skills training and to define and enforce standards of excellence. If the professions are to continue their claim of a right to self-regulation, the public should not, and will not, settle for less.

3. *Confidentiality and openness.* Each of the professions here discussed asserts to some extent a need for confidentiality in some of its dealings. Law and medicine are assured a considerable degree of confidentiality in dealing with clients and patients by the evidentiary rules that define the attorney-client privilege and the doctor-patient privilege. While there is no formally recognized accountant's privilege, certainly the normal practice is to respect the confidences of a client and to disclose no more than is required by statute, by SEC ruling or, in the extreme case, by court order. Journalists, as is well known, will ordinarily refuse to reveal their sources, and that right of nondisclosure is reinforced by shield laws in about half the states as well as by judicial reluctance to interfere with the claimed First Amendment right to collect and report the news without governmental intervention. Only in the most unusual case, where the rights to a fair trial of a third party may be jeopardized by nondisclosure, are the courts likely to intervene with a demand for disclosure. The military assert the need for secrecy in planning for national defense and in the preparation for war. But the lines become blurred when the military demand the right to classify all research that might have military potential and to restrict the disclosure even of nonclassified data known to former employees of the CIA. It is

not yet clear just where the line between secrecy and openness should be drawn in the public interest. But at least the debate has been driven into the open, and the issues are now the subject of free discussion.

4. *Conflicts of interest.* The task of identifying conflicts of interest is one of the most difficult matters confronting each self-regulating profession. Under the strictures of the adversary system the ABA Code of Professional Responsibility takes elaborate precautions against a lawyer's representation of a client where the lawyer's own interests or that of his own clients or those of his partners might be adverse. But it is by no means clear that all the questions have been asked or that the best answers have been secured in every instance. The conflict-of-interest problems of accountants are not dissimilar when each large accounting firm represents a multitude of diverse clients who insist that their business affairs not be disclosed to actual or potential competitors. The conflict-of-interest problems of doctors, journalists, and the military are no less complex, only different to some extent in kind and in degree.

5. *Fees for services.* The fixing of fees that are fair both to the person rendering service and to the consumer is a problem that has always been troublesome and probably always will be. What was once a persistent concern has become an insistent aggravation; and the irritation has not been eased by the fact that charges for professional services, notably by doctors, lawyers, and accountants, have risen faster than the rate of inflation. The justifications for fee escalation are no doubt true. The demands for specialized service and for compliance with more complex bureaucratic regulations, as well as the cost of equipment and personnel, have all risen dramatically. But the patients and clients do not seem to understand. In truth, the professions have not been very good about explaining the basis for contemplated charges or how large the fees might be. Unless this can be worked out to provide greater satisfaction to the consumers of professional services, the demand for some sort of price control is likely to threaten the continued power of the professions to regulate their professional conduct.

*   *   *

The message of this exercise should by now be reasonably clear. The autonomy of the independent professions to continue on their preferred course of self-regulation is threatened by public dissatisfaction with the way in which the professions have exercised their self-asserted right of professional control. The professions cannot long defer their response, which might be made in one or more of the following ways:

1. The professions might respond to their consumer critics on a point-by-point basis, resolving each issue in a way that will meet the criticism or at least make comprehensible the reasons for the complained-about practice.

2. The professions might hope to satisfy their critics by including significant public representation on all bodies that set standards for access to the profession and on credentialing boards, disciplinary bodies, and rule-making agencies.

3. The professions could acknowledge that the task of serving the public to its satisfaction is beyond the capacity of a professional group in the private sector, and therefore accept regulation by the public sector.

The third alternative, to relinquish private control of the professions in favor of public regulation, is not likely to meet a favorable reaction from the professions. Nor do I think it should. An important strength of the American economy is that it remains largely free, despite continuing encroachments from the public sector. If the professions serve the public interest best by remaining largely free of external controls, and if their vigor is attributable to that freedom, the effort must be made to preserve that tradition. But the answer is not self-evident; the case for freedom from external regulation must be made. Each profession must assess the extent to which its regulatory structure serves the public interest in terms of accountability and responsibility. If convinced that it does meet that test, each profession must make its case to a skeptical public. Very likely that will require participation by nonprofessionals in the governance structure of each profession. That prospect need not be alarming or threatening to professional integrity—it is more likely that the experience will be profitable, perhaps even pleasurable.

* * *

What follows is in each instance only a preliminary sketch of the issues to be addressed. There is no attempt to be comprehensive. Careful analytic study of the principal self-regulating professions is recommended as a means of determining the extent to which their separate experiences can be useful across professional lines for better understanding of common problems.

Ethics and the Law

It is perhaps appropriate to begin this review of selected self-regulated professions with the law. Not only is it the most familiar to the author, but as well the law is the most introspective of the professions in terms of having developed a rather detailed code of ethical prescriptions. Lawyers, more than other professionals, have had occasion to examine questions of professional self-regulation because they not only have reviewed their own scheme but have also been called upon to examine and sometimes to challenge the sufficiency of other professional standards.

The legal profession and lawyers, individually and collectively, are subjected to searing criticism. It is nothing new. The Greeks had some uncomplimentary words for lawyers, as did Jesus, Shakespeare, Dickens, and many political leaders. President Jimmy Carter complained to the Los Angeles Bar Association in May 1978 that 90 percent of the lawyers serve 10 percent of the public. The president was not very specific about how to correct the imbalance, but his counsel, Robert Lipshutz, had an answer in August 1978 when he told the American Bar Association that private lawyers should undertake the representation of all indigents on a *pro bono* basis. He did not resolve the question of training corporate lawyers or tax lawyers in the skills required to handle the criminal defense, landlord-and-tenant, and social welfare problems of the poor. The important point is that these and other critics hit a responsive chord with the public whenever they complain about the unavailability of competent counsel at affordable fees, delay in court, and asserted breaches of ethical standards of conduct.

Public confidence in the legal profession is not strengthened when the Chief Justice of the United States complains that a substantial number of trial lawyers are not competent in the skills of advocacy. The Devitt Committee, appointed by the Judicial Conference of the United States to look into those charges, reported in September 1978 that there is sufficient merit in the Chief Justice's complaint to justify recommending a qualifying examination for any lawyer who wishes in the future to be allowed to practice in the federal courts.

Chief Justice Burger puts the blame to a large extent on the law schools for failing to train adequately in the advocacy skills. At the 1978 American Bar Association meeting in New York City the Chief Justice called for one year of internship training in the law schools. The ABA took the challenge seriously and immediately designated a committee on "The Competent Lawyer: The Role of the Law Schools."

The issue of competence of trial advocates is in any event only the tip of a more ominous iceberg. The only thing lawyers have to offer is their professional skill, loosely known as competence. But it is not easy to define competence, and in the increasingly specialized world of the law it is not easy to know what should be the content of legal education, what should be the reach of bar examinations, what should be the requirement, if any, for continuing legal education, and what requirements, if any, should be imposed for certification of competence in specialized fields of the law.

Meanwhile, patient research continues on a multiyear project to learn what skills lawyers in fact use, in the hope of better defining the elusive concept of competence. This massive study, sponsored by the Association of American Law Schools, the Law School Admission Council, the American Bar Foundation, and the Educational Testing

Service, has reviewed the performance criteria commonly used for admission to law school—college grade point average (GPA) and Law School Admission Test Scores (LSAT)—and found that in appropriate combination the GPA and LSAT are statistically significant predictors of law school performance and even of performance on bar examinations. What is not known, but is now being researched, is the relationship between those more or less mechanical criteria and performance in the real world of lawyering. Hence the inquiry into what lawyers in fact do, leading to the ultimate and hard question of how well the public is served in actual performance. At least the right questions are being asked. When answers are available, the information will be useful to legal educators, to bar examiners, to discipline committees, and to courts faced with the previously almost unanswerable question whether a lawyer has competently represented his or her clients, as required by the Code of Professional Responsibility.

Present Canon 6 of the code gives little guidance in its simple specification that "a lawyer should represent a client competently." Even the accompanying disciplinary rule is not notably helpful. DR 6-101 states that

A. A lawyer shall not:
   1. Handle a legal matter which he knows or should know that he is not competent to handle, without associating with him a lawyer who is competent to handle it.
   2. Handle a legal matter without preparation adequate in the circumstances.
   3. Neglect a legal matter entrusted to him.

DR 6-102 is scarcely more revealing.

A. A lawyer shall not attempt to exonerate himself from or limit his liability to his client for his personal malpractice.

That is all there is on the subject of competence. It is accordingly not surprising that discipline is seldom imposed for lack of competence except in the most egregious cases of incapacity or neglect.

The more traditional questions of ethical standards for lawyers are no more readily answered. In fact, the hard questions were not even much asked until well into the second half of the twentieth century. The 1908 Canons of Professional Ethics were concededly inadequate, but the current Code of Professional Responsibility was not approved by the ABA until 1969, to be effective in 1970. In less than a decade that too was found inadequate because it was neither comprehensive enough in its answers nor demanding enough in the accountability and responsibility required of lawyers. In 1977 a new Commission to Evaluate Professional Standards was designated by then ABA President William Spann, and in 1978 two nonlawyers were added to the commission to provide for the first time representation of the public viewpoint. The commission's assigned task is not simple. Consider some of the conceptual and practical problems.

First is the persisting uncertainty about the meaning of terms too loosely used. Professor Geoffrey Hazard, in his book *Ethics in the Practice of Law,* helps steer a course through that tangle:

> *Ethics* refers to imperatives regarding the welfare of others that are recognized as binding upon a person's conduct in some more immediate and binding sense than *law* and in some more general and impersonal sense than *morals.*

Functional analysis of the ethical obligations of lawyers, although somewhat obscured in the present Code of Professional Responsibility, confirms the statement of Dean Ray Patterson:

> The basic relationships of the lawyer are only three in number: with the client, with the tribunal, and with opposing parties. Ethical problems for the lawyer will arise with the client when he does not provide the client with good and faithful service, that is, fails in the duty of loyalty to the client; with the tribunal when he is not honest in his presentation to the tribunal, that is, fails in his duty of candor; and with the opposing party when he is overreaching in his tactics, that is, fails in his duty of fairness.

Manifestly, the three basic commands of loyalty to the client, candor to the tribunal, and fairness to third parties are not self-answering ethical prescriptions. For example, the obligation of client loyalty, a central tenet of the adversary system in the Anglo-American world, includes the following obligations, each with its own ambiguities: (1) competency, the uncertainties of which have already been noted; (2) communication, that is, advising the client about alternatives, informing the client about progress (or lack of progress) on the matter undertaken, and open discussion of fees for services; (3) conflicts of interest; and (4) confidentiality in all dealings with the client's disclosures to the lawyer.

The duty of candor to the tribunal and fairness to third parties raises again what Professor Monroe Freedman has called the three hardest questions:

> May a lawyer put a witness on the stand who he knows will commit perjury?

May a lawyer discredit a witness who he knows to be telling the truth? May a lawyer accept any case, regardless of how flimsy, and fight it to the last?

Professor Freedman suggests that in some circumstances all three questions can be answered in the affirmative under the present code, and that the result is justified by the obligation of client loyalty. Obviously, however, to answer these questions in the affirmative impinges on the obligation of candor to the court and fairness to third parties, and the public is unlikely to accept affirmative answers to those questions as ethical responses.

These are only some of the questions that lurk behind the present attempt to restructure the code. Answers must be found to satisfy the public without undue restriction upon the valued relationship between lawyers and their clients, who are after all members of the public with a special interest in the outcome of the issue.

The ultimate question remains. Should the legal profession be permitted to continue to regulate itself, beginning with admission to law school and continuing through the entire professional life cycle of the lawyer? The answer is yes if the profession can demonstrate that the public interest will best be served by leaving the matter to the legal profession. The answer will be no if the legal profession does not better respond to current challenges than it has in the past. Jethro Lieberman puts the issue bluntly in the title of his book, in which he asserts that there is an ethical *Crisis at the Bar.*

Ethics and Medicine

The ethical problems of doctors are no less acute and no more readily answered than those of lawyers. Yet broad distinctions can be drawn between the two.

First, despite all the uncertainties about the lawyer's ethical obligation, there is at least a substantial body of rules and a vast array of decided cases, recorded actions of discipline committees, and opinions of ethics committees. In short, there is no lack of the customary legal paraphernalia of precedent in writing and in experience. In the case of medicine the Principles of Medical Ethics of the American Medical Association contain less than a thousand words, including a Preamble and ten sections that can best be described as homilies. To get the flavor consider the Preamble and three representative sections:

> *Preamble.* These principles are intended to aid physicians individually and collectively in maintaining a high level of ethical conduct. They are not laws but standards by which a physician may determine the propriety

of his conduct in his relationship with colleagues, with members of allied professions, and with the public.

Section 1. The principal objective of the medical profession is to render service to humanity with full respect for the dignity of man. Physicians should merit the confidence of patients entrusted to their care, rendering to each a full measure of service and devotion.

Section 4. The medical profession should safeguard the public and itself against physicians deficient in moral character or professional competence. Physicians should observe all laws, uphold the dignity and honor of the profession and accept its self-imposed discipline. They should expose, without hesitation, illegal or unethical conduct of fellow members of the profession.

Section 9. A physician may not reveal the confidences entrusted to him in the course of medical attendance, or the deficiencies he may observe in the character of patients, unless he is required to do so by law or unless it becomes necessary in order to protect the welfare of the patient or of the community.

That is the entire guidance as to the protection of the public against medical incompetence, the protection of the patient against disclosure of confidences, and the obligation of "service to humanity with full respect for the dignity of man."

Manifestly, that is not all; and medical schools now take seriously their obligation to provide instruction in accountability and responsibility that goes beyond these hortatory guidelines. But much remains to be done if the public is to allow the medical profession to continue in large part to set its own standards for access to medical education, for credentialing, and for discipline.

Second, the public feels more deeply involved in the ethical questions involving the medical profession than in those relating to the legal profession. Lawyers can aspire to no higher tribute for their profession than that the public regard it as a service profession in which the service is rendered in a competent and efficient manner at reasonable cost. Doctors, on the other hand, have both the opportunity and the risk inherent in the fact that their patients regard them as members of a caring profession. To the extent that the medical profession can satisfy that high expectation, it will indeed deserve the special regard which the public has generally held for doctors. But when that expectation is dashed by performance perceived to be incompetent or "noncaring," the fall from the heights of affection can be precipitous.

The medical profession is comparable to the legal profession in one important respect. The training of doctors, like the training of lawyers, operates as a continuum. The formal training for medicine begins with medical school and continues through internship and residency training (in many cases) and lifetime continuing education. Accreditation and certification procedures function at each level. Accreditation is given to each program, school, and institution that meets prescribed standards. Certification and licensing are the credentialing procedures for individuals as they emerge from the various educational levels.

Each component in the medical educational continuum is accredited by a medical body external to the educational unit. All these accrediting organizations are coordinated and reviewed by the major policy body, the Coordinating Council on Medical Education (CCME), which receives its authority from five sponsoring bodies: the American Hospital Association, the American Medical Association, the Association of American Medical Colleges, the Council of Medical Specialty Societies, and the American Board of Medical Specialties.

Certification and licensing is the responsibility of different agencies at the various levels. The M.D. degree is conferred by individual schools of medicine, requirements for the license to practice are determined by the state board of medical examiners, and specialty certification is by specialty boards.

Although the procedures are more complex than in legal education (the stakes are perceived to be higher), the basic principle is the same. The process is largely in the hands of the medical profession itself (despite somewhat heavier involvement of HEW in the accreditation process). Accordingly, the questions of public accountability in medicine are not essentially different from those in law.

In large measure the ethical problems of the medical profession are also comparable to those of law. Doctors, who have traditionally stood at the pinnacle of public respect and admiration, stand now on a lower and more precarious pedestal. Problems of incompetence, allegedly excessive fees, conflict of interest, and confidentiality plague the profession. Moreover, and perhaps more serious, patients often perceive doctors in general, and sometimes even their own doctors, as uncaring. A few examples will suffice.

Matthew Lifflander, director of the Medical Practice Task Force set up by the New York State Assembly in 1977, estimates that the number of incompetent physicians is "conservatively 15 percent," and that "as many as 25 percent of physicians are incompetent to do some of the things they do."

On the question of internal discipline the Lifflander Task Force Report was strongly critical.

Our first look at the way medicine is practiced in New York reveals a see-no-evil-hear-no-evil-speak-no-evil attitude which pervades the profession with respect to reporting the incompetence or misconduct of physicians.

Dr. William E. Fuller Torney, a Washington physician and psychiatrist, writing in the *Washington Post* in July 1978, identified a number of respects in which he believes the medical profession has failed to deal effectively with unethical behavior, disability, and incompetence, including the following:

1. General practice licenses and specialty licenses are valid for what amounts to an unlimited period of time. Although some states require continuing medical education for license renewals, there is little or no assurance that the courses are actually taken seriously and no guarantee that any substantial learning takes place. "Predictably, continuing medical education works best for those who need it least, and incompetent physicians are unaffected."

2. Professional Standards Review Organizations (PSROs) were established by federal law in 1972, in the expectation that they might provide a way of identifying at least the most incompetent physicians and that ways could be found through these bodies to reduce the high cost of health care. Although the results are said to be disappointing, this is a significant beginning of what may be a new partnership between the private and public sectors to meet the demand for public surveillance of deficiencies perceived to exist in the private sector.

3. The policing of incompetence and unethical behavior, which could be undertaken either by licensing boards or by local medical societies, is said to be ineffective. There is no deeply ingrained sense of obligation on the part of physicians in general to report or otherwise police the activities of deficient colleagues.

Meanwhile, the medical profession is confronted with a host of new and challenging problems, each of which raises severe ethical problems that go to the heart of the relationship between doctor and patient and the obligation of the profession to society. Consider, for example, such issues as the following: (1) When does life begin, and when does it end? (2) What controls should be placed on experimentation with behavioral modification, fetal manipulation, and cloning? (3) Should doctors ever lie for the presumed benefit of their patients—to speed recovery or to conceal the approach of death?

The overriding issue, in medicine as in law, remains that of finding ways to restructure the accreditation, licensing, and certification process to insure that the public interest is protected by procedures devised and enforced by the profession.

Ethics and Accounting

If the lawyer is in popular parlance the hired gun of the client, perhaps the accountant is the hired computer. Both analogies are unfair, but each reveals something of the problem between members of the profession and the members of the public it serves. Lawyers should no more be available to do the bidding of clients, whether lawful or not, than should accountants be considered mere automatons who perform entirely mechanical functions.

There is one important ethical link between accountants and lawyers. In the modern world of complex government regulations it is almost accurate to say, as some have asserted, that no businessman or business organization can commit commercial fraud without the connivance, or at least the knowledge, of his accountant and lawyer. Ironically, if the skills of lawyers and accountants were less essential to the certification of regularity of procedures and reports, the two professions might have fewer ethical problems. The new professional responsibility problems faced by the two professions are, in a curious way, tributes to expertise.

Dean Norman Redlich correctly identified the central proposition in a 1974 address to the ABA National Institute on Responsibilities and Liabilities of Lawyers. Although his reference was to lawyers, the relevance to acountants is obvious:

> It is both our burden and our glory that we are expected to live by a high professional standard and earn a living at the same time. We do not have the luxury of the clergy who can live in the temple and condemn the market place. Nor do we have the more flexible standard of those who live solely in the market place. We have to carry the standards of the temple into the market place and practice our trade there. That is why a country which questions its moral behavior inevitably questions its lawyers.

And, it might be added, a country which questions its moral behavior also inevitably questions its accountants.

When compared with law and medicine, accounting is a relatively young profession, whose rapid rise to prominence is the creature of commercial necessity. In many respects accounting does not conform to the self-regulating pattern of law and medicine. The education route to accounting is not tightly prescribed, although increasing numbers of those who become certified public accountants are graduates of business schools with specialized instruction in accounting; indeed, they often take graduate business degrees as well. The principal requirement for entrance to the profession is, however, controlled by accountants. The examination and other procedures for licensing as a CPA are prepared by and monitored by accountants or persons designated by them. Moreover, the ethical standard-setting body for the profession, the American Institute of Certified Public Accountants, remains internal to the profession.

Since accounting as a profession is relatively young, there is not a long tradition of self-regulation and independence from government control. Thus, when there is public criticism of accounting practices, or when the courts find deficiencies in audit statements, Congress is likely to respond. The SEC has imposed increasingly rigorous disclosure obligations upon accountants and auditors as they approve their clients' reports to stockholders or offerings to the investing public.

Perhaps the most significant extension of government control appears in the Foreign Corrupt Practices Act of 1977. Although most of the public attention has been given to the penalties for bribes of foreign officials, the act is much broader in its regulation of business activities and thus in its impact on the accounting profession. The act provides for controls on the way in which a publicly held company keeps its records and is governed. Offenders may be subjected to fines or even jail sentences.

Whether in response to public criticism or moved by a genuine desire to improve the profession by internal reforms, the CPA profession has made substantial changes. Probably the most important was the creation of the Financial Accounting Standards Board (FASB), based on recommendations of the Wheat Commission. The Trueblood Committee further defined the "objectives of financial accounting." And the AICPA study group, chaired by former SEC Chairman Manuel Cohen, made recommendations to close the gap between what the public looks for in the work of auditors and what auditors can reasonably be expected to accomplish.

The crucial issue for the future of the profession is whether the FASB, in performing its standard-setting function, will satisfy the public and the SEC. If not, Congress could well step in with its own legislation authorizing a network of government-imposed regulations to govern accounting standards. Private industry is apparently willing to stand behind continued standard-setting in the private sector. In September 1978, Thomas A. Murphy, chief executive officer of General Motors and chairman of the Business Roundtable, spoke in favor of strengthening the role of the FASB.

The real danger—that we all must guard against—is the possibility of failure of the FASB which would inevitably result in standard setting in the public sector. . . .

One way to prevent such a "government takeover," in my opinion, is for all of us in business and in accounting to get involved with the system we have—to work to improve it, to advance it. . . . And, more importantly, once the issues are settled and the standards finally set—even if we don't agree with them—we should be guided by them and see that they are implemented.

Ethics and Journalism

Many journalists would object to the inclusion of journalism among the self-regulated professions. Journalism, the complainants would assert, is not a profession; and, even if it is conceded to be one, some would deny emphatically that it is self-regulating. Murray Rossant, a former newsman and now director of The Twentieth Century Fund, considers journalism a "craft, since it never had ethical standards." But surely that categorical denial of the ethical imperative is not acceptable to most journalists. More telling is the argument that journalism is not a profession since its practitioners are not licensed as are doctors, lawyers, and CPAs. That argument may prove too much. But whether trade, craft, or profession, journalism cannot avoid accountability to the public in terms of ethical responsibility. For present purposes it is enough that journalists acknowledge their obligation to comply with ethical standards designed to serve the public interest. Thus, the Statement of Principles of the American Society of Newspaper Editors, as revised in 1975, states firmly,

> The primary purpose of gathering and distributing news and opinion is to serve the general welfare by informing the public and enabling them to make judgments on the issues of the time.

Similarly, the 1973 Code of Ethics of Sigma Delta Chi defines the responsibility of journalists as follows:

> The public's right to know of events of public importance and interests is the overriding mission of the mass media. The purpose of distributing news and enlightened opinion is to serve the general welfare.

It is not unimportant to the point at issue that Sigma Delta Chi describes itself as The Society of *Professional* Journalists (emphasis added).

Even those who agree that journalism is a profession (or at least that journalists are professionals) may deny that it is self-regulated, pointing to the extensive controls exercised by the Federal Communications

Commission over radio and television and the regular battles over media independence in the courts. But that is exactly the point. The pencil press has argued with force, and considerable success, that the command of the First Amendment is that the press be left free of legislative, executive, or judicial control. But surely every qualified journalist would agree that the purpose of the apparently absolute prohibitions of the First Amendment is to benefit the public and not to afford special privilege to individual journalists or to the press as an institution. Justices John Paul Stevens, William J. Brennan, Jr., and Lewis F. Powell made the point succinctly in their dissent in *Houchins v. KQED, Inc.*, 1978:

> [First Amendment] protection is not for the private benefit of those who might qualify as representatives of the "press" but to insure that the citizens are fully informed regarding matters of public interest and importance.

Presumably, no member of the Court would disagree with that statement and its implication that the right of self-regulation of the press may be restricted only when the public interest requires limitation. Differences on the Court do not relate to the ordinary right of self-regulation but to where the public welfare line should be drawn in the exceptional case.

The electronic media are regulated more extensively by the government, on the theory that the channels of radio and television communication are limited, thus requiring some restrictions on access to the broadcast channels and to the fairness of the presentation. Although the soundness of that justification for federal regulation is contested by the media, there is little doubt that freedom remains the dominant principle. Accordingly, the need for media definition of ethical standards continues, as clearly recognized in the Code of Broadcast News Ethics. The Board of Directors of the Radio and Television News Directors Association has developed elaborate procedures for interpretation of the Code of Broadcast News Ethics and for the discipline of those who violate the ethical standards.

The thrust of the present argument is that journalism, if not a profession like other professions in all respects, at least acts like a profession in the essential point of recognizing its obligation to the public interest and the corresponding necessity of promulgating ethical standards to be enforced through its own institutions, rejecting external control.

It is not my present purpose to force journalism or journalists into an unwelcome professional mold. No more is intended than to suggest points of similarity between journalism and other professions, and thus to justify further inquiry into the central question whether the public interest is well served by the extent and manner of self-regulation. The media recognize the issue. That is, in fact, the question in the media cases that reach the Supreme Court. Whether the immediate issue involves the reach of libel laws, disclosure of sources, publication of classified material, gag orders, search of newspaper premises, or obscenity, the underlying question always involves the media assertion of freedom from regulation, even freedom from the restraint of other constitutional provisions, in order better to serve the public.

Whether the balance has been properly struck is not here the point. The ebb and flow of judicial rulings and of legislative benefits or burdens on the media is likely to depend on public perception of the extent to which the media do in fact serve the public interest as claimed. When the public is convinced that the media interposes First Amendment claims in preservation of self-interested objectives, state legislatures will refuse to enact shield laws, and the courts may be expected to decide more often in favor of fair trial than in favor of free press.

If First Amendment freedoms are to be kept strong in the hands of the media, and if self-regulation is to be preserved, it is important that the media distinguish carefully between those circumstances in which the public can be made to understand its interest in the free press issue and those instances in which the right is more dubious. To press too hard in the latter situation is to risk defeat on the larger issues. Faithful adherence to the cause of media freedom should not blind its supporters to the fact that the First Amendment is not self-defining. Answers to individual questions are not carved in stone. Legislators and judges will be more or less supportive depending on how they assess the balance between media regard for its self-interest and media concern for the public interest.

The ethical issues that confront journalism are in broad outline similar to those which every other profession must face, although understandably the particular applications differ considerably. For example:

1. Competence in journalistic skills is difficult to assess. Reporters have traditionally been generalists, expected to move from story to story and subject to subject without hestitation. But it is no longer sufficient to "get the facts." To inform the public often requires specialized knowledge that cannot be acquired on the way to an interview. In an earlier and simpler day it may have been sufficient to demand accuracy and fairness in media reporting. Now the reading and viewing public demand, and are entitled to receive, in-depth information and

interpretive reporting. The public has little choice but to rely upon the media for an independent, informed, and impartial scrutiny of the forces that move society.

2. Conflicts of interest are particularly troublesome in journalism. As the ASNE Statement of Principles observes, "Every effort must be made to assure that the news content is accurate, free from bias, and in context, and that all sides are presented fairly." Moreover, there must be "a clear distinction for the reader between news reports and opinion. Articles that contain opinion or personal interpretation should be clearly identified." Potential difficulties arise in a number of circumstances, of which the following are illustrative:

    a. Failure to distinguish between fact and opinion in news stories, the writings of columnists, and editorials.
    b. Ownership dictation about stories to be reported and stories to be omitted, as well as the "correct" approach to news.
    c. "Cooperation" between journalists and government officials who ask for private reports on the activities of public figures.
    d. "Checkbook journalism" in which reporters, columnists, or editorial writers fail to disclose their own financial interest in matters reported on.

3. Perhaps the most serious problems for the media arise out of the new zeal for investigative reporting, or what is sometimes called adversary journalism. The advantages to the public of aggressive investigation are well known, but the push for the story can lead to excesses. Reporters, for example, do not always identify themselves as such to individuals from whom they seek information. Enthusiasm sometimes overcomes good judgment about invasions of privacy and sometimes leads to actual illegality in theft of documents or trespass on private premises. The ASNE Statement of Principles is clear on the point. "Journalists should respect the rights of people involved in the news, observe the common standards of decency and stand accountable to the public for the fairness and accuracy of their news reports."

4. The most controversial ethical issue in journalism involves the relationship between the reporter and his or her source. Although no evidentiary privilege of nondisclosure protects the news source against reportorial disclosure, journalists insist with reason that sources must not be disclosed where confidentiality has been pledged. In no other way, it is asserted, can information be secured that is vital to the public. Leaks from public or private sources are justified by the need for blowing the whistle on corruption and other wrongdoing. The difficulty is that the unscrupulous reporter could falsify a story damaging to individuals or institutions and prevent correction by

insistence on nondisclosure of nonexistent sources. Similarly, fair trial rights, which are also protected by the Constitution, can sometimes be interfered with by unwillingness to disclose the source of adverse information reported to the public. Since the balance is ordinarily made in favor of nondisclosure, the ethical obligation on media reporters is especially important.

5. The growing concentration of control over the news media is a matter for increasing concern. Most communities are denied the pluralism of views ordinarily considered healthy to development of choice in a democratic society. The problem is revealed in the 1975 statement of Ben Bagdikian:

> Sixty years ago there were 689 cities with competing dailies; today there are fewer than 45. We have over 1500 cities with daily newspapers and in over 97 percent of them there is only one newspaper. Some chains are growing so fast that they have stopped swallowing individual papers and have begun swallowing themselves.

Chain control has gained further ground since 1975. For example, Gannett Company, already controlling seventy-nine papers, proposed in September 1978 to take over Combined Communications Corporation and its five VHF and two UHF television stations plus a number of radio stations and newspapers in Oakland, California, and Cincinnati, Ohio. If the diversity of viewpoint to which the public is entitled is to be preserved, the media must develop new and ingenious devices to ensure pluralism.

6. Finally, since the media are given such freedom to search out the news and report it fully, they bear special responsibility for accuracy and fairness. The Sigma Delta Chi Code of Ethics deals with the issue in its section on Fair Play, as follows:

> 4. It is the duty of news media to make prompt and complete correction of their errors.
> 5. Journalists should be accountable to the public for their reports and the public should be encouraged to voice its grievances against the media. Open dialogue with our readers, viewers, and listeners should be fostered.

The principle is clear, but implementation is difficult. Even the most responsible media are often reluctant to concede error, to provide effective opportunity for reply by those charged with wrongdoing, or to submit to external criticism. Only a few news organizations have established internal ombudsmen. Surprisingly, a number of the most respected media refuse to cooperate with the National News Council, a private voluntary organization dedicated to freedom of the media and to accuracy and fairness in reporting. (In the interest of the standard of disclosure here supported, I note that I am vice-chairman of the News Council.)

Journalism, like other professions, must be constantly on the alert to make sure that its actions serve the public interest. As in the case of other professions, to the extent that obligation is not satisfied, journalism will run the risk of public regulation or the private sanction of loss of credibility by the reading and viewing public.

Ethics and the Military

No professional group has been subjected to sharper criticism than the military. In many university circles the conventional wisdom includes derogation of the military, and many elected officials are similarly skeptical of the ethical standards and practices of the military.

The importance of this reaction is not easily exaggerated, because of the impact not only on those who select a military career, but also on issues of national security. If the public is to be a significant extent discontented with the individuals and the institution charged with defense of the nation, problems of recruitment and institutional morale are likely to become severe. In the present context public dissatisfaction translates quickly into increased regulation and official oversight of functions and activities once considered the sole preserve of the military.

In the United States the tradition of civilian control over the military has been a consistent theme of American political history, beginning with the debates in the Constitutional Convention. The Constitution imposes three principal restraints on the exercise of military authority—the power reserved to Congress to declare war, the two-year limitation on appropriations, and the specification of a civilian commander-in-chief. Yet the debate continues whether these and other restraints on the military are excessive or whether the civilian controls are inadequate to prevent military abuses.

The intensity of the debate reflects in part the larger struggle for control between Congress and the chief executive. Whatever the constitutional inhibitions imposed upon the president, earlier presidents were not prevented from leading the nation into full-scale wars in Korea and Vietnam. Thus, the 1973 War Powers Act was not so much intended by Congress as a restraint on the military as a rebuke to the president. More recent restrictions on the CIA and demands for increased congressional oversight of intelligence activities may similarly be viewed as a congressional effort to gain—or regain—legislative control over the military arm of government.

Although the issues posed in the struggle between openness and secrecy in the military are framed somewhat differently than in the other professions here considered, the basic question is not dissimilar. To what extent should the military be allowed to determine its rules and procedures without external control? Obviously, the military has already lost the contest to a considerable extent, no doubt as a manifestation of commonly held views that self-regulation by the military was not being exercised in the public interest.

The debate over the extent to which the public interest is advanced by military self-regulation is multifaceted. For example:

1. Are the honor codes at the service academies consistent with ethical standards which the American public is entitled to insist upon?
2. Is the American public prepared to accept the requirement of unthinking obedience to the command of military support to act in ways contrary to morality or even in violation of law?
3. Is it essential to military authority that the constitutional right of free speech be limited by adherence to the established position on controversial matters?
4. How much secrecy is essential in military research, development of war plans in time of peace, and military strategy in time of war?
5. To what extent should the military be allowed to conduct clandestine surveillance of citizens and noncitizens within the United States and abroad in time of peace and in time of war?

These are only some of the questions which must be addressed by the military if it is to maintain its present level of self-regulation, let alone to regain ground already lost to its critics. Arrogant assertion of the right to decide for itself, without public discussion of the issues, is almost certain to bring further restriction on the right of independent decision making.

Conclusion

The inquiry ends as it began—with unanswered questions. What are the common characteristics and the shared problems of the professions? To what extent, in a free society, should the professions be encouraged to develop their own rules for access, credentialing, definition of ethical standards, and discipline? With respect to the professions in general, and with respect to each profession, is the public interest better served by professional autonomy or by public control?

It is hard enough to frame the questions, which has been the initial purpose of this inquiry. The hope now is that this exercise will stimulate others to seek appropriate answers to these questions. It is important that the correct balance be struck between professional freedom and the public interest.

ELEVEN

ACCESS TO THE MEDIA:
LEGAL ISSUES IN THE ATTEMPT
TO SECURE DIVERSITY
OF IDEAS AND INFORMATION

L. A. Scot Powe, Jr.

We seek truth, and in that search a medley of voices is essential. That is why the First Amendment is our most precious inheritance.

— *William O. Douglas*

Freedom of the press is guaranteed only to those that own one.

— *A. J. Liebling*

They're both right, of course, and that's the rub. How, consistent with the First Amendment's command that government not abridge the freedom of the press, is it possible to reconcile the rights of the press to print or not, as it pleases, with the needs of the public for relevant ideas and information? This problem often goes under the shorthand name of "access," and it has many facets: local media monopolies, regional and national media oligopolies, suppression of information because of conflict of interest, the impulse to avoid controversy, and a tendency toward homogenized positions because the owners of the media have nearly identical sets of views. Not only does the "access" problem have many facets, it also has the disturbing quality of demonstrating that initially obvious solutions are not as appealing on analysis as they seem at the inception.

I

The predominant strand of First Amendment thought is that a marketplace of ideas is mandated and that an essential feature of the market is a medley of voices offering differing viewpoints. Justice Holmes wrote in his classic dissent in *Abrams v. United States,* 1919:

When men have realized that time has upset many fighting faiths, they may come to believe even more than they believe the very foundations of their own conduct that the ultimate good desired is better reached by the free trade in ideas—that the best test of truth is the power of thought to get itself accepted in the competition of the market, and that truth is the only

---

L. A. Scot Powe, Jr., is professor of law at the University of Texas.

ground upon which their wishes safely can be carried out. That at any rate
is the theory of our Constitution.

This basic insight, that ideas must have a free rein lest we perpetuate
fallacy, has been a fundamental premise in this century's First
Amendment adjudications.

Hannah Arendt aptly noted that "freedom of opinion is a farce unless
factual information is guaranteed." Thus if information or ideas are
suppressed—whether because they are offensive to those in control of the
media or because they are thought unworthy of serious consideration or
for any other reason—there is cause for concern. For years we have
known that the marketplace of goods and services is flawed in its
distribution patterns. If the marketplace of ideas is similarly flawed,
how can society guarantee that essential information will be available to
its citizens?

A survey of the media today provides a picture of newspaper chains
covering large areas, the elimination of competing newspapers in
almost all communities, and the cross-ownership of newspapers and
broadcast stations. The huge start-up costs of new outlets seems to make
it certain that a newspaper ownership will enjoy a natural monopoly in
its geographic market. The power to inform and shape public opinion is
held in fewer and fewer hands. Furthermore, the media are unwilling, as
always, to provide effective criticism of their own performance. The
market is indeed flawed.

The marketplace analogy invites the answer offered in the case of
comparable maldistribution of essential goods and services: governmental action to redress the blockages resulting from excessive
concentration. The marketplace concept is fundamental to those
seeking to ensure the individual's "access" to the mass media. However,
this is not the only value informing First Amendment thought. Another
significant value is associated with the writings of Alexander
Meiklejohn, the philosopher who perceptively argued three decades ago
that the First Amendment was concerned with the powers of citizens to
control their government. In opinions of Justice Douglas this position
often merged neatly with the marketplace theory. His dissent in *Dennis*
is illustrative.

Free speech has occupied an exalted position because of the high service it
has given our society. Its protection is essential to the very existence of a
democracy. The airing of ideas releases pressures which otherwise might
become destructive. When ideas compete in the market for acceptance, full
and free discussion exposes the false and they gain few adherents. Full and
free discussion even of ideas we hate encourages the testing of our own
prejudices and preconceptions. Full and free discussion keeps a society
from becoming stagnant and unprepared for the stresses and strains that

work to tear all civilizations apart.

Full and free discussion has indeed been the first article of our faith. We have founded our political system on it. It has been the safeguard of every religious, political, philosophical, economic, and racial group amongst us. We have counted on it to keep us from embracing what is cheap and false; we have trusted the common sense of our people to choose the doctrine true to our genius and to reject the rest. This has been the one single outstanding tenet that has made our institutions the symbol of freedom and equality. . . . We have wanted a land where our people can be exposed to all the diverse creeds and cultures of the world.

In this view of the marketplace, the need of the people to make informed political decisions restrains government interference. This view, which is almost unique to Justice Douglas, has received explicit recent notice in a major work by Professor Vincent Blasi, who persuasively argues that a central value of freedom of expression is that it functions to check the abuse of official power.* Professor Blasi's view is at once old and novel. It is old because a look at the writings during the formative period of our nation will demonstrate strong distrust of government and recognition of the need to keep it in check. It is novel because, despite its importance, until recently one rarely found it mentioned by the Supreme Court.

During this decade we have been provided with two especially strong statements of the checking value. In the last opinion Justice Black wrote before his death, dealing with the Nixon administration's efforts to enjoin publication of the Pentagon Papers, he concluded: "Only a free and unrestrained press can effectively expose deception in government." Two years later Justice Douglas quoted that statement in support of his own belief that the Bill of Rights was part of an integral scheme "to take government off the backs of the people."

This view, expressed by Black and Douglas after each had spent over thirty years delineating the rights of expression in a liberty-loving society, weighs heavily against actions designed to force owners of the media to open their newspapers or broadcast stations to those whose views they find either disagreeable or unimportant. Using government to force printing or broadcasting against the desire of the owner strips

---

*Another extremely prominent strain of First Amendment analysis is not implicated by the access problem. There is much in the writings of Brandeis and Douglas about the importance of freedom of speech as integral to the process by which persons consciously choose among alternatives, the process of realization of potential. This value of autonomy is not implicated by access for two reasons. First, it is hard to claim that the right to demand access to the mass media to present one's own ideas is integral to self-fulfillment. Second, when a corporation or a conglomerate is the owner of the media in question, one simply cannot believe that the speech uttered through the media has anything to do with the corporation's sense of self-fulfillment.

away the basic independence of the press. The checking function is based fundamentally on a fear of governmental abuses, and this mitigates powerfully against official actions which encroach on press autonomy.

As this brief discussion demonstrates, the values at the heart of the First Amendment do not necessarily point in the same direction. Sometimes, they do, as when the government is attempting to impose sanctions on a person for the content of his views. Then, marketplace and checking function values, as well as that of individual autonomy, dictate that governmental action be held unconstitutional. But when we turn to issues of "access" to the mass media the marketplace value and the checking function value seemingly point to different results. One emphasizes the need for corrective action, in the belief that the marketplace is basically incapable of taking the necessary remedial steps; the other counsels an attitude of laissez-faire, fearing that any governmental action will unnecessarily abridge media freedom.

II

Thus marketplace and checking value theories pose a dilemma when one deals with attempts to ensure necessary information for an informed citizenry. But posing a dilemma does not make the problem go away, and as a series of examples demonstrates, the problem is very real.

Item: "Anything that is good for Bluefield [West Virginia], the Shotts' newspaper, TV, and radio have backed 100 percent," one resident stated when critics suggested that the local media were serving the interests of the coal operators in failing to reflect problems of miners such as black-lung disease. "What isn't said in the newspaper and on TV is more important here than in most places because it is the only place it can be said," countered the local NAACP president. The publisher of the newspaper responded, "someone has to decide what's going in the paper, so we do." As to the conservative nature of the paper: "We get very few complaints about our politics. People around here just don't want to hear any other point of view." In any event it would be hard for them to do so. The Shotts own Bluefield's only newspaper, TV, FM radio station, and the more powerful of the two AM radio stations.

Item: In May 1978 "a whale swallowed a whale" when Gannett Co. announced plans to merge with Combined Communications Corporation. The new "whale" will have seventy-nine daily newspapers and a maximum twenty-one broadcast licenses. Over the years Gannett has moved from a strong position in upstate New York into the national market, with dailies in thirty states, mostly in medium-sized or smaller communities. The acquisition of Combined Communications was not its first multimedia bite; two years ago it bought another chain of thirteen dailies.

Item: In 1966 International Telephone and Telegraph and the American Broadcasting Company proposed to merge, and a pliant FCC approved. An antitrust threat from the Department of Justice blocked the merger, but the issue went beyond the possibility of a potential oligopoly in communications. In the light of what we now know about the actions of ITT and the CIA in regard to the Allende government in Chile, how would the news coverage of ABC have been affected?

Item: In February of 1976 Sears, Roebuck and Co. went on trial in Chicago before an administrative law judge of the Federal Trade Commission. The charge was that Sears has systematically engaged in bait-and-switch tactics. The hearings lasted eleven days and yet the largest newspaper in Chicago, the *Tribune* (circulation of almost three-quarters of a million), carried not a line about the case from the beginning until the end. A week after the trial the *Tribune* offered its readers a condensed four paragraph story from the *Wall Street Journal.* The *Tribune,* it is hardly surprising to note, receives $5 million a year in advertising from Sears.

Item: The three national television networks will not accept issue-oriented advertising. This policy, based on the claim that it guarantees the independence of their treatment of public policy questions, was used to block paid broadcasts arguing the case against the Vietnam war. The networks believe they must control the public-issue messages they air. The result, whether intentional or not, is that claims on behalf of toothpaste can be advertised ad nauseum, but significant positions on issues cannot be. An exception is made for legally qualified candidates for public office; section 315 of the Communications Act guarantees candidates the right of equal treatment by the broadcast media. If a station sells or gives time to one candidate it must also do the same for all others seeking the office. It is the most explicit guarantee of a form of "access" to the mass media. It also, and necessarily, provides that a broadcaster cannot censor a candidate—and we have had ample evidence of how offensive an uncensored candidate can be.

Item: Newspapers are not subject to section 315. When Pat Tornillo ran for the state legislature in Miami, the *Miami Herald* savaged him in a pair of well-written, if wholly one-sided, editorials. Tornillo wrote replies to the editorials, but the paper did not publish them—and the Supreme Court upheld the *Herald*'s right of refusal. Tornillo lost the election. If he had been a member of the Shott family in Bluefield, or a Gannett, or the president of a conglomerate that includes broadcasting properties, he might have fared better; at least his replies would have been published. If, as Liebling said, freedom of the press is guaranteed only to those that own one, it follows that it is a privilege of the rich; and, if media giants can swallow one another at will as they accumulate millions of spare dollars, ideas and information can and will be suppressed at the whim and will of their proprietors.

All of these items illustrate the issues that arise from the problem of "access" in a large, industrialized, interrelated, and increasingly complex society. How can we ensure that citizens will have available the information needed if they are to make relevant judgments about the community, nation, and world in which they live? By guaranteeing each individual the "right" to give voice to his or her views in the mass media? By guaranteeing that all significant new ideas will be fairly discussed in the mass media? By guaranteeing that monopolies and oligopolies will be controlled under rules relating to the "fairness" of their content, or by applying antitrust doctrines? Finally, can the problems of "access" be cured by recourse to the legal system?

III

It is hardly surprising that the Supreme Court cases dealing with "access" do not provide a neat, coherent whole. There are three key decisions dealing directly with the issue.

During the Progressive Era, Florida passed a law that required a newspaper to provide equal reply space free of charge whenever it "in its columns assails the personal character of any candidate for nomination or for election . . . or charges said candidate with malfeasance in office or otherwise attacks his official record." This was the basis of Pat Tornillo's action against the *Miami Herald* cited above. The Supreme Court in *Miami Herald v. Tornillo,* 1974, dealt at length with the argument for a right of access. However, despite the Court's seeming recognition that concentration of media outlets and uniformity and conformity of media views had indeed marked a significant change from the time of the ratification of the First Amendment, it was unanimous in striking down the statute as an abridgment of freedom of the press. The Court found that the First Amendment carried the implication that government could not compel editors to publish that which " 'reason' tells them should not be published." The opinion ended with the blunt conclusion that "it has yet to be demonstrated how governmental regulation of this crucial [editorial] process can be exercised consistent with First Amendment guarantees of a free press as they have evolved to this time."

However comforting the opinion in *Tornillo* is to editors, it gives pause to students of the Supreme Court by its failure to as much as mention an almost completely contrary opinion written only five years earlier. In *Red Lion Broadcasting v. FCC,* 1969, the Court sustained rules of the Federal Communications Commission that allowed an individual whose honesty, character, or integrity had been attacked in a broadcast free time to respond. In the course of the decision the Court found that promotion of diversity in broadcasting was an acceptable goal. The government may, consistent with the First Amendment, ensure that the public "receives suitable access to social, political, esthetic, moral, and other ideas and experiences." The Court focused on the receiving rather than the transmitting of ideas and concluded that the rights of viewers and listeners rather than the rights of broadcasters were at stake.

Word for word the analysis in *Red Lion* is inconsistent with the contrary conclusion of *Tornillo*. The only possible justification for the result is that one case dealt with broadcasting while the other dealt with print, and there was a belief on the Court that broadcast frequencies were scarce and limited resources while print facilities were not. Whatever the validity of this conclusion—and many scholars have severely questioned it—it provides no real excuse for the Court's not explaining in *Tornillo* why it held that the right of publishers rather than that of readers was at stake. *Red Lion* rested on a marketplace notion and required access; *Tornillo* can be seen—and justified—as resting on the checking value and the necessity of an independent press.

Between *Red Lion* and *Tornillo* the Court decided *CBS v. Democratic National Committee*, 1973. *CBS v. DNC* was a companion case to the attempt by antiwar businessmen to puchase air time to present their particular views on the war. Although building on *Red Lion*, the Court rejected the claim that either the First Amendment or the public interest standard of the Communications Act supported a right to paid access to network air time, the opinion seemingly rested on the belief that the public's interest in a diversity of views might well be harmed by such paid access. It made a link with the later analysis of *Tornillo* in its conclusion that "for better or worse, editing is what editors are for; and editing is selection and choice of materials."

These three cases are basically all we have from the Supreme Court on individual access to the mass media. They hold that it is unconstitutional for the government to provide for access to the print media, but that the government may, but need not, allow access to the broadcast media. They are consistent only if one accepts a distinction between print and broadcasting media. All the cases to some extent considered the values of diversity implicit in Holmes' marketplace metaphor. None rested on the other First Amendment values. Professor Blasi suggests that the Court in *Tornillo* "perceived the print media as having historically enjoyed an adversary relationship with government which could only be compromised, symbolically as well as materially, if officials could dictate what the content of a particular publication must be." I would go further and argue that *Tornillo* was not only correctly decided, but that the Court's position should govern all attempts to force access, whether paid or free, to print or the broadcast media.

Access theories rest more comfortably on the notion of diversity than on any other First Amendment values. The diversity value when applied in the access context takes some sort of governmental involvement to determine what facts or ideas need access. Here I think it wise to ask how the government will fairly determine what ideas or facts the public does not know or knows insufficiently. Implicit in this process is the conclusion that someone has knowledge of what the public *ought* to know. This would require governmental supervision of the media to ascertain what views are presented, or are presented insufficiently, and governmental action to correct any resulting imbalance in the marketplace of ideas. Rather than adopt this approach, I would rest on the simple historical fear of governmental encroachment embodied in the First Amendment. The government is vastly larger today, and is no less capable of invading the prerogatives of the press, than it was two centuries ago. Indeed a case could be made that it is both more capable and more likely to do so today. No first step toward making such intervention easier should be taken.

Yet this does not mean that nothing can be done about the various problems I mentioned at the outset. Two other cases, each dealing with concentration in the media, are illustrative.

In *Associated Press v. United States,* 1946, the Supreme Court was presented with the argument that the print media were immune from the antitrust laws because of the First Amendment. The Court resoundingly rejected that argument, noting that the First Amendment, far from providing an argument against applying the antitrust laws to the media, instead provides a powerful argument in favor of their application. Relying on the marketplace theory, Justice Black wrote:

> That Amendment rests on the assumption that the widest possible dissemination of information from diverse and antagonistic sources is essential to the welfare of the public, that a free press is a condition of a free society. Surely a command that the government itself shall not impede the free flow of ideas does not afford nongovernmental combinations a refuge if they impose restraints upon that constitutionally guaranteed freedom. Freedom to publish means freedom for all and not for some. Freedom to publish is guaranteed by the Constitution, but freedom to combine to keep others from publishing is not. Freedom of the press from governmental interference under the First Amendment does not sanction repression of that freedom by private interests.

The Court has never backed away from Justice Black's conclusion as to the validity of governmental actions designed to allow a better functioning of the marketplace by opening up the instrumentalities of speech under general laws not aimed at the content of speech. Such action is held to be consistent with the purpose of the First Amendment;

just as the government may attempt to eliminate monopolies in the market for goods and services, it may do the same with respect to the marketplace of ideas.

Similar conclusions have been reached with respect to broadcasting. In a recent action the FCC dealt with the issue of newspaper-broadcast co-ownership in the same communities. There were a number of proposals: ban them all and require divestiture; ban them all prospectively; ban only the worst; do nothing. The FCC chose to enact a prospective ban and also to order divestiture in sixteen cases of egregious existing monopolies. Bluefield, West Virginia, was one of the sixteen. The FCC reasoned that benefits from diversification were speculative and so it was unwilling to risk the possible interruption of service in areas of cross-ownership except in the cases of actual monopoly.

On review, the District of Columbia Circuit Court of Appeals held that the prospective ban did not go far enough and that the FCC should have realized that the First Amendment, and the public interest standard of the Communications Act, required the total elimination of cross-owned media in the same community to meet the goal of maximum diversification of media viewpoints—the goal the FCC recognized with its prospective ban. The Court suggested that "limiting divestiture to small markets of 'absolute monopoly' squanders the opportunity where divestiture might do the most good . . . in large markets."

The Supreme Court, in *FCC v. National Citizens' Committee for Broadcasting*, 1978, reversed, reinstating the FCC order in full. The Court also recognized that diversification would further First Amendment goals, but deferred to the FCC's supposed expertise in weighing other intangible factors, and concluded that strong local service might suffer if co-owned outlets were divested. The link between the First Amendment and the public interest standard established in *CBS v. DNC* was ignored and the *NCCB* opinion reads as if the Court simply did not take the case or the problem seriously. Nevertheless, the Court made clear that if the FCC had chosen to order total diversification, that, too, would have been sustained: "Here the regulations are not content-related; moreover, their purpose and effect is to promote free speech, not to restrict it."

These, then, are the five most significant cases dealing with access to the media either directly or through removing bottlenecks in the free flow of additional information. Where do they leave us? First, they show a strong tendency to emphasize the marketplace of ideas as a prime value of the First Amendment. Nevertheless, it is not the sole value, and both *Tornillo* and *CBS v. DNC* have recognized an alternative value of governmental noninterference and the need for an independent press.

Indeed they support the view that governmental interference might seriously distort the marketplace in favor of views acceptable to the government. Second, they have demonstrated that governmental action that is content-related—that is, action triggered initially because of the content of the message presented—is unconstitutional with respect to the print media. With respect to broadcasting the issue is more complex, and government may take some limited content-related actions if they are designed to promote a diversity of views. Third, other governmental actions, not content-related, are not unconstitutional, and indeed these governmental policies designed to encourage diversity of viewpoints are not only valid, but entirely consistent with the Court's delineation of First Amendment objectives.

IV

Within this judicially circumscribed framework, what are the policy alternatives available to deal with the various facets of the "access" problem? Consistent with the First Amendment, what would a sound public policy be with respect to mass communications? The easy answer is that the governmental objective should be to encourage as much diversity of ideas and information in the media as possible. The harder question is how to do this. My own view about a wise public policy is that the government should refrain from attempts to impose individual speakers and their views on the media, but should pursue an active policy to deconcentrate control of the media and facilitate the development of communications technologies. I grant that this solution is not ideal and I acknowledge that it does not wholly avoid the dilemma posed by the opening quotations from Justice Douglas and A. J. Liebling. I am not even sure it is the best available solution in this complex area; it is simply that I can see none better.

Although *Tornillo* dealt with free rather than paid access to a newspaper its language appears so broad as to foreclose the issue of paid access, and *CBS v. DNC* is at least supportive of this conclusion. Even if the issue is open, a requirement to provide access to all who can pay ought not be enacted. I admit that a good case can be made that once space is already committed to some form of commercial advertising it hardly seems a great interference to require a preference for political or issue-oriented ads over those detailing the price of an electric can opener. There are, after all, rather obvious diversity gains in preferring the former over the latter. Yet what of editorial autonomy? There is something jarring about the thought of a Roman Catholic journal being *forced* to carry ads for an abortion clinic or a Jewish journal being made to print ads defending the PLO position in the Middle East.

Although government interference with editorial autonomy is

minimized in the situation of paid advertisements, forcing an editor to run an ad that he finds offensive is to take away the presumption that editors should be allowed to determine what is appropriate for publication. Whether editors err or not, theirs is a repository of judgment preferable to that of a governmental agency, no matter how limited the powers or well-meaning the individuals staffing it. Newspapers may be timid, and may avoid issues, but it is not because of fear of governmental second-guessing.

The tradition of newspaper freedom is best kept by not calling it into question. As an illustration, until the Pentagon Papers case there was no consideration of the circumstances under which a newspaper could be enjoined from publishing information. There is now. That case ended a tradition. Now many judges and lawyers reduce the issue to one of tailoring injunctions to appropriate circumstances rather than facing the question of whether injunctions may be issued under any circumstances. When we begin to trench on some of the rights of editors we implicitly call all the rights into question. The risks to press autonomy from that questioning seem to me to justify the bright-line rule of no interference.

There has been no similar tradition of freedom with respect to the electronic media. It has been subject to certain access requirements, such as the Fairness Doctrine, Personal Attack Rules, and Equal Opportunities Provision. Because the Supreme Court has sustained a different constitutional status for the electronic media it is easy to conclude that these rules are valid under the Court's current doctrines. The creation of an inferior constitutional status for the primary means of mass communications in the United States is, I think, largely a product of the difficulty the Court traditionally has in applying the Bill of Rights to new and unforeseen technological developments. Nevertheless, since the Court has done so, and done so recently, the constitutional argument for equal status must await a different, younger, and more adaptable generation of judges.

For present purposes the question is whether the benefits from these various doctrines outweigh their burdens. Paramount among the issues raised is that these doctrines hold the power of broadcasting in check and serve to ensure a timidity in the presentation of public issues. Yet *timidity* may stem from reasons wholly unrelated to government regulation: maximum audiences not changing channels breed higher profits. Nevertheless the effect of governmental regulation cannot be ignored. NBC's fine documentary, *Pensions: The Broken Promise,* won both a Peabody Award and three years of litigation. Special interest groups have learned well how to use the threats of license challenges to attack programming of which they disapprove. And at least once, as

Fred Friendly has detailed, the Democratic National Committee understood FCC rules so well that in the early 1960s it intentionally attempted to "chill" right-wing radio commentaries by monitoring their programs and threatening legal actions.

That the access doctrines do "chill" discussion is probably unprovable, since proving that something would happen "but for" something else is always a fruitless task. I do not doubt that the various access doctrines have at least in part operated to place certain information on the air that otherwise might not have been aired (or would not have been aired on the particular station). But they have also been used to justify the silencing of the Reverend Carl McIntyre in Philadelphia because his programming was not balanced, even though any listener who wished to hear views contrary to McIntyre's was both free and able to do so. We also know that until the fraudulent distinction the FCC promulgated to allow the televising of the presidential and vice presidential debates in 1976, the Equal Opportunities Provision operated to deny free time to major candidates because similar time would have to be given to minor candidates. The electoral process is hardly aided by that result. Nevertheless the fear behind the Equal Opportunities Provision, that a broadcast station might be "given" over to a candidate or that a candidate might not even be able to buy time for ads, does seem to be genuine.

It is difficult to mediate and balance in the area. Much must be taken on faith and different people of good will have different faiths. Mine, as should be clear, fears governmental involvement with the content of speech, assumes that doctrines created for the best of reasons will at some point be abused or misused by governmental officials, and believes that abuses by private power centers are more likely to prove transitory than those of the government. I would, however, do all I could to encourage volunteerism. I would free broadcasting of the FCC and access requirements, but hope the idea of "free speech messages," whereby a station gives over a certain amount of time to air opinions and statements by members of the local community, would be widely implemented. Stations should be encouraged as a matter of sound journalism to do this, just as newspapers now wisely seem to be giving added space for letters to the editors and "Op-Ed" opinions that sometimes tell more about a community than anything else in the newspaper. Methods of *voluntarily* opening up some pages of a newspaper and broadcast time are consistent with both the marketplace and diversity ideals of Justice Holmes as well as the checking view of Justice Douglas. But a word of caution. It is always too tempting to see a desirable idea and then wish to enforce it. My position here is that "free speech messages" are a sound journalistic idea; it is not that some branch of government should determine that they be imposed.

V

That diversity may not be directly created by the government picking and choosing voices does not leave the government without options. Diversity can be assisted by deconcentration and that in turn may be achieved by facilitating development of new technologies and the entry of new groups to the media as well as by acting to reduce actual concentration of control. Probably the single most useful policy the government could adopt would be to direct its efforts to the facilitation of new entry into the communications industry. Additionally, although the effort may well be greater and the benefits more speculative, certain concrete steps could be taken to attempt to split up existing media combinations.

It is fashionable to talk of the values of antitrust law whether they be increased competition, efficiency, or the prevention of large-scale accumulations of private power. Unfortunately, the values are more apparent than any successes in achieving them. Throughout the twentieth century the goal of an effective antitrust policy has at best been just that, a goal; at worst it has been an illusion. Whether it can or would be more effective in the communications field is a genuine question and one that only a genuine effort of deconcentration will answer.

The principal issues involved go the necessary size of communications corporations. The president of CBS, John D. Backe, has argued that the three commercial networks embody important values of scale. I am less interested in how size relates to new entertainment programs and competition for viewers and advertising than I am in how size relates to news and information. On this point Backe argues that "only big communications companies with extensive resources can properly report on, and investigate, and stand up to the powers of big government, big business and big labor." One might usefully counterpoise Eric Sevareid's statement of twenty years ago: "The bigger our information media, the less courage and freedom of expression they allow. Bigness means weakness." I suspect the answer lies somewhere nicely between Backe and Sevareid. Resources are useful in providing the time and energy to delve and discover. They are also useful when one enters any kind of litigation. But the "big communications companies" have a tremendous stake in society, and assuming an adversarial role with the other dominant interests may be a great deal less likely than finding a place for themselves as a part of the same governing establishment.

The example of the attempted suppression of the *Glomar Explorer* story two years ago richly demonstrates the way large media corpora-

tions may be persuaded to merge their own interests with that of
government. The CIA used all its efforts to keep the story of the attempt
to raise a sunken Soviet submarine out of the press; but for columnist
Jack Anderson's intransigence it might have succeeded. Virtually all the
key pillars of the press establishment complied with the CIA request to
withhold the story: the *New York Times*, the *Washington Post*, the
Washington Star, the *Los Angeles Times*, *Time*, *Newsweek*, *Parade*,
NBC, and ABC. (CBS apparently never had the story.) And who was the
story kept from? And why? What harm has occurred because of its
publication?

Size and money can provide options that may lead to superb
journalism. But one does not have to be a giant to be large enough to be
resourceful; and there appears to be precious little evidence that
allowing media corporations to grow and grow returns to the public
benefits of journalistic excellence. It must be conceded, however, that
many local papers are improved after being swallowed by national
chains. Tom Wicker has stated that the first law of journalism is that a
newspaper inevitably reflects the character of its community. This I
suspect is far more true when the ownership is local. Thus I would
expect Wicker's youthful experience at the *Sandhill Citizen*, where a
question asked each Thursday was "Did Tom write anything
controversial this week?," is far more likely when ownership is
integrated with the community than when the editor only has to answer
finally to a distant owner. Local ownership holds out the possibility of
caring more for the community, of better understanding its problems
and its roots. But it can have drawbacks. Twenty years ago Robert M.
Hutchins concluded that "if the soliloquy [of the publisher] is that of
one of the richest men in town, it is more than likely that it will sound
the same political note as other soliloquies in other towns, rendered by
other rich men. . . ." He might have added that it will also sound similar
notes to other rich people in its own town.

Even if chain ownership improves the quality of the average local
paper, there are costs. Provincialism at least produces a variety of local
journalistic styles and prejudices; chain operation tends to impose a
single journalistic ethic across broad geographical lines.

The quality issue probably cannot be resolved, but it does suggest that
other considerations are probably of more significance in the equation.
Principal among those considerations is a diversity of outlets. A feasible
goal is the immediate divestiture of co-owned local media outlets. It may
be difficult to determine the appropriate number of broadcast stations or
newspapers for one owner to control, but it should be easy to recommend
that the outlets of communication within the same area should be
owned and operated by different people. This cannot, of course,

guarantee diversity given either typical patterns of ownership or the existence of widely shaped values and assumptions. But it can make diversity more likely. Different owners may have different ideas or they may be forced to look for new and novel ways to compete with the other owners. Diversity is no panacea. It cannot ensure good coverage; it does not ensure that all ideas will see the light of day. But it makes this more likely than concentration—and that, of course is the alternative.

The FCC effectively has forbidden future newspaper-broadcast combinations as well as future radio-television combinations in the same community. Over a long enough period of time, assuming some sales, the FCC's rules could result in the end of local combinations. But as John Maynard Keynes noted, in the long run, we're all dead. Either Congress or the FCC has power to implement divestiture and both should be encouraged to do so.

Currently, a licensee is allowed to control seven television stations (of which as many as five may be VHF), seven AM, and seven FM stations. It seems clear that the allowable number of jointly owned television stations, and probably of AM stations, is too high. Any number selected is arbitrary, but the current limit, set during the infancy of broadcasting and designed to encourage whoever was willing to enter the field to do so, is a relic of an era decades in the past. The formula would appear to be too generous by over a half. Furthermore, qualitative limitations of holdings in major media markets are in order. Again, these actions could be taken by either Congress or the FCC.

More difficult to deal with is the increasing growth of media chains. Over three decades ago, under the chairmanship of Robert M. Hutchins, the Commission on Freedom of the Press noted with some satisfaction that the number of papers controlled by newspaper chains was declining. The trend the commission noted has not been totally reversed; during the past five years chains have been acquiring individual papers at an average of one each week. We have no history of dealing with this phenomenon and the antitrust laws are not designed (or at least not interpreted) to cope with it. Yet at some point a halt must be called, and if the antitrust laws are inadequate, they should be rethought and, if necessary, strengthened.

These problems are no longer beyond the horizon. Of the 1,759 daily newspapers in the United States only 691 have avoided chain ownership. Currently chains control 67 percent of the circulation in the United States and a look to the future suggests the growth will continue. Given inheritance taxes and the truly staggering prices newspapers are bringing on the market—the 18,000-circulation Santa Fe New Mexican sold for almost $12 million—many independents must ultimately succumb. One estimate has it that only 100 dailies are in a position secure enough to hold off chain acquisition. It would be a serious mistake, both from the point of view of the First Amendment and an informed citizenry, to wait until a few media oligopolies have a viselike grip on the news channels. The time to act is before the problem reaches an absolutely critical stage.

Relatedly there is the problem of conglomerate ownership of the media. Once again the current state of antitrust law is of no assistance. When one looks at conglomerate media takeovers there is special reason for concern. To take an egregious example, I cannot conceive of any appropriate ends in an ITT takeover of a television network. Bigness and far-flung interests create the all too powerful urge for private censorship lest the media end of the conglomerate interfere with profits in other sectors of the company. What will be the environmental reporting of the Cox Newspaper chain when other parts of Cox Enterprises are constructing a $350 million oil refinery?

Much more tentatively I would suggest that thought be given to the possibility that corporations having major interests outside the communications industry be prohibited from controlling media outlets. The positive side of this proposal would be its ability to handle in a neutral fashion the potential conflict of interest problems of conglomerate media ownership. This would also make more effective my other proposals because in context the size of these corporate units could then be limited by national and local monopoly considerations. Nevertheless this proposal needs vastly more thought than I am able to provide here and on reflection might itself violate the First Amendment either by limiting entry to "the press" or by running afoul of the Supreme Court's recent decision in *First National Bank of Boston v. Bellotti*, 1978. That case upheld a corporate right of free speech and struck down a state statute prohibiting corporate spending on referendum proposals. The implications of the decision may well be that no efforts to restrict corporate media ownership are possible, although I do not believe that *Bellotti* itself reaches so far. At this point I simply wish to flag both *Bellotti* and limitations on corporate entry as problems that deserve consideration.

VI

Thus far I see two principal objections to what I have said. The first is that my views on deconcentration, while seemingly within *AP v. US* and *FCC v. NCCB*, are inconsistent with my emphasis on the checking value. This argument proceeds simply. Why, it would be asked, should I be any more willing to trust the government in its choice of deconcentration remedies than I am in its efforts to use the more limited remedy of placing individual views in the mass media? After all, I have suggested that people should naturally assume that governmental actions against the media may well be motivated by disapproval of what the media are saying—and indeed the three networks made precisely that allegation as a defense to the antitrust suits filed against them during the last years of the Nixon administration. I have several responses. First, to accept this argument is to hold *FCC v. NCCB* wrong not only on the sixteen cases of divestiture, but also on the prospective ban on cross-ownerships. Quite simply it means that society is virtually helpless to counter the growth of media giants. I find this too stark a conclusion to accept. Second, I believe that the contours of governmental efforts to deconcentrate can be objectively stated in advance of any actions. This would assist in demonstrating the bona fides of subsequent actions. Finally, I would advocate the recognition and generous use of a defense of harassment to assure further that the deconcentration efforts were based on objective criteria rather than on the content of the media.

The second objection to what I have said is the not implausible rejoinder that I have it all wrong. One might as well attempt to stop the tides as deconcentrate the mass media in the United States. Thus, only individualized access, a remedy I have rejected as unconstitutional, holds any promise of adding voices to the nation's dialogue. This might well be further underscored by noting who is in a position to purchase a newly "deconcentrated" media outlet. When newspapers sell for between thirty and sixty times earnings and a major urban television station will go for close to nine figures, using traditional First Amendment concepts (as I have) has the unfortunate look of an eighteenth-century solution to a twentieth-century problem. And to some extent I must agree.

We should all be concerned with how the First Amendment—which may well have had as its primary value the idea of individual autonomy for both editor and speaker—can be applied as we ready ourselves for the twenty-first century where the communications industry is controlled by corporate giants. I think it quite plausible that the First Amendment may seem increasingly absurd as applied in press situations when more and more the issue looks like special privileges for billion dollar corporations. The hostility displayed by Chief Justice Burger toward the national news media may well become far more pervasive if the perception grows that these corporate giants are no different from other corporate giants.

Only a fool would assume that the growth of the media corporations can continue unabated without arousing a strong counterurge to "do something"—something that would break through the traditional restrictions of the First Amendment. It is a difficult urge to repress, and the fact that I am attempting to do so does not mean that others will.

What, if anything, can be offered to those who would accuse my solutions of being myopic at best and nonexistent at worst? The answer may well be technology. There is the possibility that one way or another newer technologies may provide a methodology for vastly increased exchanges of ideas and information. Quite possibly the best hope for freedom of the press is that they can.

The government should foster diversity in communications either by facilitating the creation of new channels of communication through policies encouraging development or by subsidizing, directly and indirectly, certain forms of communications where necessary. The policy issues here are of a simpler order. It is almost impossible to be against policies that will reduce barriers to entry for new communications technologies. One can make a better argument against the provision of governmental subsidies, either because it is perceived that government should not in general provide subsidies to parts of the American economy or because a government subsidy in the press area is peculiarly inappropriate. The former concern is beyond the scope of this chapter as it has nothing to do with First Amendment problems. The latter is troublesome. Justice Jackson in one of his numerous quotable phrases stated that "it is hardly lack of due process for the government to regulate that which it subsidizes." In the area of speech and the press the concern is obvious—encroachment.

Nor is the concern illusory. The grant of the right to free use of the public air has carried the burden of the access rules and other regulatory quid pro quos. Public broadcasting was held on an exceptionally short leash during the Nixon years. The temptation to encroach on First Amendment rights will always be present when the government is involved in the process of expression and the temptation may be almost irresistible when government is providing the funds. As both the commercial and public broadcasting histories suggest, various elements of government would like to see the media neatly in check for various reasons, and any form of subsidy invites continuation and extension of that problem. This may be enough for some to say that no subsidies to the media are tolerable given the risk of encroachment. I can understand that, although I think that some governmental subsidies are capable of significantly expanding the ranges of choice available to all of us. The second class mailing privilege for magazines and newspapers is my best example.

In evaluating a specific subsidy in order to ascertain whether the likelihood of abuses is high or low, there are indicia of potential encroachment. Any subsidy that requires periodic determinations of performance—PBS is a classic example—should be suspect. When government ties subsidies to performance, the urge to monitor, to evaluate, and to move the rate of subsidy up or down on the basis of performance (i.e., content) is too great. Relatedly, requirements of reporting, beyond capital expenditures, operating time, and the like, should be carefully analyzed. A subsidy in the field of expression should be as far removed from governmental scrutiny as possible. The objective would be to have an immediately and ministerially ascertainable formula which would be open to all without the necessity of governmental monitoring of content. Tax credits or accelerated depreciation on construction would fall within the category.

Currently, technological communications improvement is almost synonymous with cable communications. Cable, with its multichannel capacities, offers the promise of a great variety of programs and information entering each wired home. Unfortunately that promise has been offered for the past fifteen years, and remains largely unrealized. The reasons are not wholly unidimensional, but a not insignificant part of the blame for cable's retarded growth lies with the Federal Communications Commission. The FCC has been an unwilling parent that raised an unwanted child in such a way that it would not interfere with the favorite child—over-the-air broadcasting. The wonder is that cable actually has managed to penetrate ten million of the seventy million television homes in the face of FCC efforts to hinder its development.

There does remain the problem of economics. Cable systems are typically small and many owners appear to see little farther than the next dollar. Thoughts of laying excess channel capacity for future and different growth are often beyond their vision or desires. And yet without additional channel capacity for future growth, cable's future may be limited to replicating its present. Recently a circuit court has held that the FCC overstepped its jurisdiction in ordering cable systems to have access channels available to the public. That decision seems almost inescapably correct under the Communications Act, and *Tornillo* carries with it the strong implication the decision may have been constitutionally compelled as well. Yet it would be a most unfortunate development to see cable systems with only twelve channels when twenty to forty channel systems are clear possibilities. Some form of subsidy either direct or indirect (such as accelerated depreciation or tax credits) should be provided for cable systems that build excess capacity channels and then dedicate a certain number of those channels to public use.

Just as cable is currently challenging the existing technology, we can be certain that further technological development—whether it be satellites, fiber optics, or something else—will provide substantial advances over cable. The unfortunate lessons of cable's retarded growth should provide a clear message about regulatory policy. There is an inherent desire to protect the large economic investments in the existing technology, and this can only be fulfilled at the expense of newer and improved systems. This must be resisted. The First Amendment should be seen as having technological implications which guide public policy towards facilitating, rather than hindering, newer and improved technologies of communication.

Second-class mailing privileges were designed to encourage "the dissemination of news and current literature of educational value" in the words of a sixty-five-year-old Congressional Report. And they have done so. But during this decade, following the Postal Reorganization Act of 1970, second-class rates have jumped significantly. Larger publishing companies may well be able to handle the increases and consider shifting to private distribution systems, but smaller publishing companies may not have the option available for their journals. For them, postal rates increases may well be a death sentence, although the evidence is not without ambiguity. We should nevertheless not experiment with their existence. Too many magazines have died during the past two decades and sound policy should be to add new voices while retaining the old. One way this can be done is to learn from the past. Second-class mailing privileges have been a significant historical success in achieving their intended goals. It is the type of program that merits continuance.

VII

To the obvious question, "But is it all worth it?," I think there is only one answer: "Yes." The values at the core of the First Amendment are central to a functioning democracy. Freedom of speech and freedom of the press function to enlighten and enliven, and as Justice Douglas noted, to "bring anxiety or even fear to the bureaucracies, departments, or officials of government." It is true that we cannot guarantee that all or even most of the hoped-for benefits of the First Amendment will accrue to the public. We cannot, even if we mistakenly think we know how, legislate goodness. But we can create an environment where freedom of the press and speech *may* flourish. The faith of our founding fathers in freedom of expression is "our most precious inheritance." Writing for the Court in *DeJonge v. Oregon*, 1936, Chief Justice Hughes concluded that freedom of expression provides an environment where "government may be responsive to the will of the people, and that changes, if desired, may be obtained by peaceful means. Therein lies the security of the Republic, the very foundation of constitutional government." He was right.

The Center for the Study of Democratic Institutions/
The Fund for the Republic, Inc.

Robert M. Hutchins (1899-1977)

Officers:

The Center:

2056 Eucalyptus Hill Road, Santa Barbara, California 93108
Mailing Address: Box 4068, Santa Barbara, California 93103
New York Office: Suite 1015, 527 Madison Avenue, New York,
New York 10022